Evidence of Being

Evidence of Being

The Black Gay Cultural Renaissance
and the Politics of Violence

DARIUS BOST

The University of Chicago Press
Chicago and London

The University of Chicago Press, Chicago 60637
The University of Chicago Press, Ltd., London
Published 2019
Printed in the United States of America

28 27 26 25 24 23 22 21 20 19   1 2 3 4 5

ISBN-13: 978-0-226-58979-4 (cloth)
ISBN-13: 978-0-226-58982-4 (paper)
ISBN-13: 978-0-226-58996-1 (e-book)
DOI: https://doi.org/10.7208/chicago/9780226589961.001.0001

Library of Congress Cataloging-in-Publication Data

Names: Bost, Darius, author.
Title: Evidence of being : the black gay cultural renaissance and the politics of
    violence / Darius Bost.
Description: Chicago ; London : The University of Chicago Press, 2018. |
    Includes bibliographical references and index.
Identifiers: LCCN 2018017662 | ISBN 9780226589794 (cloth : alk. paper) |
    ISBN 9780226589824 (pbk. : alk. paper) | ISBN 9780226589961 (e-book)
Subjects: LCSH: African American gay men—Washington (D.C.). | African
    American gay men—New York (State)—New York. | Hemphill, Essex. | Dixon,
    Melvin, 1950–1992. | American literature—African American authors.
Classification: LCC HQ76.27.A37 B688 2018 | DDC 306.76/6208996073—
    dc23
LC record available at https://lccn.loc.gov/2018017662

♾ This paper meets the requirements of ANSI/NISO Z39.48–1992
(Permanence of Paper).

CONTENTS

Introduction

On Black Gay Being

I may not be there for the development of gay literary history, but I'll be somewhere listening for my name. . . . You, then, are charged by the possibility of your good health, by the broadness of your vision, to remember us.

—Melvin Dixon

We Were (Never) Here

In 1992 in Boston, black gay writer Melvin Dixon—thin, balding, and dressed in a voluminous African robe—stepped to the podium at the third annual OutWrite conference for gay and lesbian writers. He was about to give what would be his last public speech before his death from AIDS. Described by journalist Brian Rafferty as a "queer black femme shaman," Dixon was well aware of how his black, gay, and disabled body might influence the reception of his speech.[1] He was, after all, addressing a primarily white gay and lesbian audience, and testifying to the tangible and intangible ways that AIDS had affected his life and his social world: "I come to you bearing witness to a broken heart; I come to you bearing witness to a broken body—but a witness to an unbroken spirit. Perhaps it is only to you that such witness can be brought and its jagged edges softened a bit and made meaningful." Dixon's concern regarding how his audience would receive his speech must be contextualized within the early AIDS discourses, which stigmatized nonnormative expressions of gender and sexuality, blackness, and poverty, and deflected attention away from the state's failure to address a devastating health crisis in its marginalized communities. Because he spoke at a lesbian- and gay-themed conference, the "you" of this line suggests that the audience's shared experiences as sexual minorities in the age of AIDS might positively influence their reception of his speech. But Dixon's use of the term *perhaps* suggests a reservation owing to his racial difference. He was surely aware of how longer histories of race and sexuality have often marked black bodies in general, and black gay male bodies in particular, as beyond the pale of public sympathy.

Despite the risk of failure, Dixon spoke out about his experiences because of the very real threat of historical erasure. In his speech, he gave the example of his friend and former student Greg, a black gay man who had recently died of AIDS. Dixon noted that Greg's siblings refused to be named in his obituary, which was published in a prominent newspaper, because of the shame attached to being connected with someone who had died of the disease. At his funeral, his family refused to acknowledge his sexuality and the cause of his death. To redress these silences, his lover and friends held a second memorial service. Afterward, while eating a meal with Dixon and others, Greg's lover realized that he had left extra copies of the funeral program in the rental car he had just returned. He went back to the rental agency but arrived too late to retrieve them: they had already been "shredded, burned, and the refuse carted away."[2] Dixon recalled this experience as analogous to the disposability of gay lives in general and black gay men's lives in particular: "I was reminded of how vulnerable we are as gay men, as black gay men, to the disposal and erasure of our lives."[3]

This erasure was happening in both heterosexual black communities and white gay communities. In the context of a white-dominated gay publishing industry that mostly refused to publish the literary works of gay men of color, Dixon feared that the disposability of black gay lives extended to black gay expressive cultures.

> As white gays become more prominent—and acceptable to mainstream society—they project a racially exclusive image of gay reality. Few men of color will ever be found on the covers of the *Advocate* or *New York Native*. As white gays deny multiculturalism among gays, so too do black communities deny multisexualism among its members. Against this double cremation, we must leave the legacy of our writing and our perspectives on gay and straight experiences. . . . Our voice is our weapon.[4]

For Dixon, writing and publishing would ensure black gay survival against "double cremation." He commented that although Greg's body and funeral programs were gone, the work he had produced as a journalist still existed. Yet Dixon was not so naïve as to believe that immortality was inherent in art. Rather, he asserted, "we must . . . guard against the erasure of our experiences and our lives."[5] He tasked this imagined "we" with more than a narrow model of inclusion in mainstream gay and black historical narratives. His use of the term *double cremation* suggests that he was more concerned about the structural forces that threatened to render black gay personhood as an impossible mode of being. *Double cremation* signals how the obliterating forces of antiblackness and antiqueerness doubly mark the black gay body for social and corporeal death. The black gay body must be doubly cremated, not only to maintain the norms of race and sexuality, but also to maintain the fiction that these categories are bounded and discrete, not overlapping and intersecting. But Dixon's plea for black gay men to "leave the legacy of . . . our perspectives on gay and straight experiences" and his claim that "our voice is our weapon" suggest that black gay cultural production offers a way of asserting black gay personhood amid this "double cremation." His call for black gay men to "guard against the erasure of our experiences and our lives" anticipates what Christina Sharpe has termed "wake work." She defines this term as a conscious inhabiting of the imminence and immanence of (social) death that marks the quotidian experiences of black lives in an antiblack world.[6] To guard against "double cremation" of black gay lives, such "wake work" must extend to the antigay forces that collude with antiblackness to foster the erasure of the black gay body from black and gay memory.[7]

Melvin Dixon's final speech exemplifies the contradictory effects of antiblack and antigay violence on black gay men. He detailed how the historical trauma of AIDS had influenced his physical health and social life: "I've lost Richard. I've lost vision in one eye, I've lost the contact of people I thought were friends, and I've lost the future tense from my vocabulary. I've lost my libido, and I've lost more weight and appetite than Nutri-system would want to claim." Aware of the devastating impact of AIDS on gay literary communities and of his own impending demise, Dixon directly addressed the project of gay literary historiography: "I may not be there for the development of gay literary history, but I'll be somewhere listening for my name. . . . You, then, are charged by the possibility of your good health, by the broadness of your vision, to remember us."[8]

The "I" in Dixon's speech that has "lost" almost everything—the unbecoming "I" reduced to deteriorating black flesh—marks the unattainability of black gay personhood in an antiblack and antigay world. But the "I" that has lost almost everything is not the same "I" that will be "somewhere listening" for his name. Dixon's vow "I'll be somewhere listening for my name" serves as the title of and a constant refrain in his speech. This refrain is drawn from the sorrow songs of slaves, who used them as an expression of collective trauma and as a catalyst for fugitivity in their attempts to escape slavery.[9] It is this fugitive "I"—the "I" that resides at the parting of voice and flesh, the collective "I" that compels historical remembrance from some radical elsewhere, the "I" that imagines the possibility of black gay being amid the violent forces that usher black gay bodies toward premature death—that orients this study of black gay cultural movements.

Evidence of Being explores how black gay men have created selves and communities amid the ubiquitous forces of antigay and antiblack violence that targeted them.[10] It also examines how structural violence—racism, capitalism, homophobia, and AIDS—and responses to it shaped black gay identity and community formation as well as black gay aesthetics and cultural production. It does so by exploring the renaissance of black gay cultural production in the 1970s, 1980s, and 1990s, focusing in particular on cultural formations in Washington, DC, and New York City. Though the forces of antiblack and antigay violence converged at the site of the black gay body during this historical moment to mark black gay personhood as a site of double cremation, this convergence of antiblack and antigay violence also created the conditions of possibility for a black gay cultural renaissance.

More specifically, *Evidence of Being* illuminates how black trauma (rooted in slavery and its afterlife) and queer trauma (rooted in homophobia, transphobia, and AIDS) converged during this historical moment to doubly mark the black gay body as a site of social and corporeal death. Many prominent black gay writers of this period succumbed to AIDS, which has contributed to readings of black gay social life in the early era of AIDS as wholly determined by (social) death. While acknowledging that the black gay body was a site of loss during this period, I turn to black gay literature and culture as evidence for reimagining black gay personhood as a site of possibility, imbued with the potential of creating a more livable black gay social life. Following Dixon's fugitive "I" that enunciates the historical and future possibilities of black gay being through writing and publishing, I focus on black gay literature and culture produced from the late seventies to the midnineties. This body of literature insists on the fact of black gay social life amid widespread violence, and serves as an archive of black gay men's collective, political longings for futures beyond the forces of antiblackness and antiqueerness. Pushing against antisocial and pessimistic strains of black cultural theory and queer theory, *Evidence of Being* locates black/queer optimism in the black gay literary and cultural imagination.[11]

A Black Gay Cultural Renaissance

In a 1983 article published in *Blacklight* magazine, activist and publisher Sidney Brinkley tracks the development of self-identified black gay politics in the United States to local coalition building in Washington, DC, and Baltimore in 1978: "Though black gays had been involved in DC politics for years, it wasn't until the formation of the DC-Baltimore Black Gays, and its local outlet, the DC Coalition of Black Gays in 1978 that a group named as one of its objectives, 'To pursue political power . . . as Black lesbians and Black gay men.'"[12] By 1979, the DC Coalition of Black Gays became a local branch of the National Coalition of Black Lesbians and Gays, with other local chapters forming in Philadelphia, Detroit, and Chicago.

Broader economic, social, political, and cultural shifts also created the conditions for this movement's formation. Black gay movements emerged in the context of shifts in mainstream US politics, including the rise of the Christian Right, the New Right, and conservative backlash against civil rights gains made in the 1960s and 1970s. These movements developed as well in relation to dominant political and cultural forces in black America, including Black Power, the black arts movement, and the Nation of Islam, all of which held complex ideologies about lesbians, gays, and gender-nonconforming people. Labor migrations for work (especially in the public sector) and sexual migrations for leisure drew many black gay men to urban centers in the 1970s.[13] Washington, DC, for example, had been home to private black gay male social clubs like the Rounders, Best of Washington, and Washington Capitalites; black gay bars and nightclubs like Nob Hill, Brass Rail, the Clubhouse, and Bachelor's Mill; and gay-friendly black cultural arts hubs like dc space and Enik Alley Coffeehouse. However, many black gay men had been born and/or raised in these urban centers. Black gay bars, social clubs, and cultural arts hubs provided spaces for these men to convene without losing ties to the black community. For example, the Oscar Wilde Bookshop and the Lesbian and Gay Community Services Center, both located in the Greenwich Village neighborhood of New York City—the city's best-known gay district—offered meeting spaces for black gay men who lived in predominantly black enclaves in Harlem and Brooklyn.

Various other factors influenced the formation of this movement. Racist and homophobic representations of black gay men appeared in black and gay media, including racist personal and housing ads in gay-themed media, and pathological constructions of gender and sexual difference in black popular media.[14] Black gay men faced cultural and political exclusion in white gay communities. Examples include being barred from entering white gay-owned bars and nightclubs through discriminatory identification policies, and invisibility in predominantly white gay social movements against homophobic street violence.[15] Moreover, black gay men experienced homophobia within black communities—which they often depended on for economic survival and cultural belonging—and sometimes had to negotiate their nonnormative gender and sexual identities through the politics of discretion.[16] Black gay writers expressed frustration with stereotypical depictions of black gay men in white gay literature and culture, and confronted distorted images of themselves in African American literature and culture, if they were imagined at all.[17] Early lesbian and gay scholarship very rarely included people of color as subjects of inquiry, and dominant paradigms in African American studies such as Afrocentrism and black liberationist thought depicted gender and sexual nonconformity as either an interruption to black freedom struggles or as a convenient scapegoat for the damaging psychological effects of racism.[18]

Scholars often cite and anthologize the work of a few prominent figures of this period—Essex Hemphill and Joseph Beam, for instance—but very little sustained critical attention has been paid to their individual works, and even fewer efforts have been made to contextualize the emergence of the cultural movement in which they took part. Black gay artists and activists used a range of cultural forms and practices to articulate more complex narratives of their racial, gender, and sexual selfhood, and to build political and personal connections among black gay men. By naming this proliferation of black gay cultural production a renaissance, I hope to demonstrate the significance of collectivity to black gay aesthetics, cultural production, and politics, and to black gay men's everyday struggles against the various formations of violence targeting them. As Dagmawi Woubshet argues, "This wave of art represented a self-conscious renaissance that reaffirmed the existence of black gay men as individuals and as a collective group."[19] Martin Duberman notes that the proliferation of artists' collectives and publications in the 1980s "helped to spawn the widely shared sense that an outburst of creative energy was in play strong enough to warrant being called a second Harlem Renaissance."[20]

Some of these efforts were aimed at local community development; others sought to develop a sense of a national network of black gay artists. As a DC-based black gay activist, Brinkley led student movements to institutionalize the first lesbian and gay organization on the historically black campus of Howard University, and published *Blacklight*, the black lesbian- and gay-themed magazine, from 1979 to 1985. The magazine became an invaluable cultural and political resource to Washington, DC's black same-sex-desiring communities, who often negotiated their sexual desires through the politics of discretion. In 1980, Harlem-born Isaac Jackson founded the Blackheart Collective, a group of fellow New York City–based black gay artists who channeled their creative energies into producing a black gay-themed literary journal. Jackson had met New York City migrant Fred Carl, who comanaged the Oscar Wilde Bookshop, and architecture student Tony Crusor, and together they posted a flyer in the shop calling for the formation of a black gay artists' collective.[21] Blackheart published three journal issues: *Yemonja* (1982), *Blackheart 2: The Prison Issue* (1984), and *The Telling of Us* (1985). The group's decision to title its first journal *Yemonja*, after a Yoruba water deity who embraces all genders and sexualities, and to focus its second journal on black/gay prison writing demonstrates how it sought to queer dominant black intellectual traditions like Afrocentrism, and to extend the gay liberation movement's concern with prisoner rights and prison reform to a broader race- and class-based critique of carceral state power.

Because of the ravages of HIV/AIDS on black gay communities, the Black-heart Collective disbanded in 1985, and another black gay writing group formed in its wake. In 1986, former Blackheart member Daniel Garrett called for the formation of the Other Countries Collective, a writers' work-shop based at the Lesbian and Gay Community Services Center in New York City. Its mission was to develop, disseminate, and preserve the diverse cultural expressions of black gay men. The group produced two journals in the early years of the AIDS epidemic, *Other Countries: Black Gay Voices* (1988) and the book-length *Sojourner: Black Gay Voices in the Age of AIDS* (1993). While the first journal displayed the group's commitment to developing a black gay aesthetic tradition worthy of preservation, the latter journal emerged from the political urgency of AIDS, documenting and memorial-izing the losses accrued from the epidemic both within the collective itself and in the broader black gay community.

One of Other Countries' most prominent members was Haitian-born poet, performer, playwright, dancer, and activist Assotto Saint (born Yves François Lubin). Saint's most significant contribution to the black gay cul-tural renaissance was the development of Galiens Press in New York City in the late 1980s, through which he self-published two collections of poetry, *Stations* (1989) and *Wishes for Wings* (1994), and two anthologies of black gay poetry, *The Road Before Us: 100 Black Gay Poets* (1991) and *Here to Dare: 10 Black Gay Poets* (1992). Saint would gain further prominence after his protest at his friend and literary contemporary Donald Woods's funeral. Woods was a well-regarded poet, performer, and arts administrator in New

York City, and a member of the Blackheart and the Other Countries Collectives. In his 1992 obituary in the *New York Times*, Woods's family listed the cause of his death as cardiac arrest, and at the funeral denied his contributions to the black gay community. Pained by the erasure of these aspects of Woods's life, Saint rushed to the front of the church during the funeral and proclaimed that Woods was gay and died of AIDS.[22]

Silence surrounding one's status, though this time self-imposed, plagued the life of another important figure in the black gay cultural renaissance. Philadelphia-based black gay writer and activist Joseph Beam became a leader of the movement after editing and publishing the groundbreaking literary collection *In the Life: A Black Gay Anthology* (1986). Upon its release, *In the Life* was the best-selling gay men's book in the country, and it received mostly favorable reviews in the gay press. Despite Beam's claim that the book was meant to end the silence surrounding black gay men's lives, he told no one about his seropositive status. His decomposing body was found in his Philadelphia apartment in 1988, two years after the release of *In the Life*.

Before his death, Beam had begun work on a second anthology of black gay men's writing. With the help of Beam's mother, his close friend and literary interlocutor Essex Hemphill completed the editorial work on a new black gay anthology, *Brother to Brother: New Writings by Black Gay Men* (1991). Its publication demonstrated and consolidated the development of a rich black gay literary and intellectual tradition throughout the 1980s.[23] Hemphill had published several poetry chapbooks in that decade; and in 1983, with musicians Wayson Jones and Larry Duckette, he formed the black gay performance group Cinque in Washington, DC. He gained international prominence after his poetry and his artistic collaborations with Cinque were featured in gay black British filmmaker Isaac Julien's award-winning *Looking for Langston* (1989)—a meditation on black queer male sexuality during the Harlem Renaissance—and Marlon Riggs's *Tongues Untied* (1989), an experimental documentary about black gay life that right-wing politicians condemned after its 1991 airing on public television as part of PBS's *POV* series.

Hemphill's AIDS-related death in 1995 marked the end of the black gay cultural renaissance. But as I discuss in my analysis of the diaries of creative writer, translator, and scholar Melvin Dixon, who also wrote and published throughout these years, black gay artists employed writing as a mode of "textual survival," of archiving the self for future generations, and as a way of imagining futures beyond the antiblack and antigay forces that marked them for death.[24] The publication of the black gay-themed poetry collection *Change of Territory* (1983) marked Dixon as a leader of the burgeoning black gay arts movement. A contributor to *In the Life* and *Brother to Brother* and a poetry editor of *Other Countries*, he accelerated his literary output after being diagnosed as having AIDS. Before his death from the disease in 1992, he had published two award-winning novels, *Trouble the Water* (1989) and *Vanishing Rooms* (1990); a book of literary criticism, *Ride Out the Wilderness: Geography and Identity in Afro-American Literature* (1987); and translated from French to English *The Collected Poems of Leopold Senghor* (1990), the longtime Senegalese president.

The force of structural violence in black gay men's lives created the conditions for the outpouring of their cultural production in this period. Simon Dickel notes that these artists referenced literary figures of earlier periods, such as James Baldwin and the black queer literati of the Harlem Renaissance, in order to validate their identities amid the forces of racism and homophobia, discursive constructions of gayness as whiteness, and the threat of AIDS.[25] José Muñoz believes that "beyond and beside the simple fact of 'identities,'" the movement coalesced around "(re)telling of elided histories that need[ed] to be both excavated and (re)imagined . . . states that blindly neglect[ed] the suffering bodies of men caught within a plague, the explosion of 'hate crime' violence that target[ed] black and gay bodies, and a reactionary media power structure that would just as soon dismiss queer existence as offer it the most fleeting reaction."[26] This book explores how these geographically disparate movement activities were linked by black gay men's shared relationship to epistemological, state-based, antiblack, and antigay forms of violence, and by a creative practice that rendered black gay interior and social life visible and valid.

Making Selves amid Damage

Black gay men's political investments in collectivity and creative practice were informed by the emergence and visibility of black lesbian feminist culture and politics during the 1970s and early 1980s.[27] The highly visible cultural work of black lesbian feminists in New York City—many of whom were associated with Kitchen Table: Women of Color Press—shaped the scope and aims of black gay activism. Moreover, the creative work of lesbian feminists of color Barbara Smith, Audre Lorde, Michelle Cliff, June Jordan, Cherríe Moraga, and Gloria Anzaldúa exemplified how literary and cultural forms could challenge structural violence, and demonstrated how everyday experience and interior life could serve as sites and sources of political struggle.[28] The Combahee River Collective, a Boston-area black feminist organization, modeled the modes of community building and care that black gay men would take up. The collective's intersectional politics—as witnessed in the Combahee River Collective Statement and in its analysis of black women's vulnerability to violence—offered a framework for articulating black gay identity and developing an integrated analysis in the face of interlocking systems of racial, heterosexual, and class oppression.[29]

Influenced by and in solidarity with black lesbian feminism, black gay men politicized their identities through the arts in the late 1970s, 1980s, and 1990s because doing so was an accessible and timely mode of expressing self- and communal formation in a heightened moment of antigay and antiblack violence. Christina B. Hanhardt discusses how in the late 1970s increasingly liberal white gay antiviolence activists presumed that the spate of attacks against gay men in the Chelsea neighborhood of New York City was perpetrated by neighboring poor youth of color. Hanhardt's research suggests that the discourses of deviance attached to black and brown bodies marked them as perpetrators of homophobic violence, thereby rendering them as impossible victims of such violence.[30] Given black gay men's increased vulnerability to violence and erasure as its victims in this period, black gay artistic production provided a space to articulate their political subjectivities amid dissembling discourses of deviance.

Responding to white gay activists' failures to advance an intersectional analysis, Isaac Jackson believed that black gay men must create their own movement to integrate their blackness and their gayness.

> The white gay male movement is not equipped to help me integrate my gay-ness and my blackness. It has no intention of listening to what we have to say, let alone the voices of our black sisters. . . . We have to change all of this. In so doing, we must form an autonomous black gay movement. . . . [W]e have to reach out to the brothers who are isolated from each other, caught in a damaging web of self-images that are the negative creations of white men.[31]

But this "damaging web of self-images" did not come only from white men. In *Brother to Brother*, Ron Simmons, Charles I. Nero, and Marlon Riggs chart out the pervasive distortion of the image of black gender and sexually variant subjects in black political, popular, and literary cultures. While these scholars find it important to contest the narrow conceptualization of black gender and sexual diversity within these fields, their work foregrounds the primary task of black gay movement building as self-definition rooted in positive constructions of black gay identity.[32] Simmons calls for the development of "a new epistemology, a new way of knowing" that focuses on "develop[ing] an affirming and liberating philosophical understanding of homosexuality that will self-actualize black gay genius."[33] Black gay movement intellectuals like Jackson and Simmons advocated for a cultural movement that would promote forms of black gay collective self-making amid prevailing and pervasive discourses of damage.

Evidence of Being focuses on how black gay men's literary and cultural narratives were essential to fulfilling this aspect of the movement. It emphasizes how black gay men used literature and culture in the production of selves and community by drawing from Muñoz's arguments about these fields as "contested field[s] of self-production." Muñoz argues for literary and cultural production as a "technology of the self," and asserts that this fictional self is a "disidentificatory self whose relation to the social is not overdetermined by universalizing rhetorics of selfhood."[34] These "universalizing rhetorics of selfhood" abound in fields of knowledge that might otherwise provide a theoretical framework for exploring the complex relationship between black gay personhood and damage. While the psychoanalytically informed fields of queer theory and trauma studies have depended on ahistorical notions of the psyche and universalized notions of human subjectivity, antiracist discourses—from liberal social psychology to black liberation psychiatry—have diagnosed black gender and sexual variance as a psychopathological symptom of racism.

Black queer studies scholars such as E. Patrick Johnson and Marlon Ross have challenged the foundational assumptions of queer theory, unearthing how theorizations of queer subjectivity as a fluid and antiessential formation have depended on either the disavowal or the fixity of racialized bodies.[35] Trauma studies scholars Maurice Stevens and John Rich have examined how processes of racialization have constituted black bodies as "phobic objects," thereby marking them as the constitutive outside of traumatized subjectivity.[36] Historians Daryl Scott and Kevin Mumford have outlined how postwar liberal social scientists mapped the damages of US racism onto the psyches of black people; Mumford looks in particular at how social psychologists and policy makers that informed senator Daniel Patrick Moynihan's infamous report *The Negro Family: The Case for National Action* deemed male effeminacy and homosexuality as psychopathological symptoms of racism.[37] Black liberation psychologists and psychiatrists such as Julia and Nathan Hare, Frances Cress Welsing, and Alvin Pouissant rejected liberal racial damage discourse and embraced more positive constructions of black self-image, but did so at the expense of black male gender and sexually variant subjects—they labeled gender nonconformity and homosexuality as pathological symptoms of the psychic damage accrued from racism.[38] This theoretical double bind has constituted black gay personhood as an impossible *object* of inquiry.

Evidence of Being moves beyond this intellectual impasse by demonstrating how black gay men used literary and cultural forms for collective self-creation, outside narrow, deterministic readings of racial, gender, and sexual identity formation. It explores how this archive of black gay literary and cultural production challenges the liberal, antihomophobic, and antiracist knowledge forms that have historically marked black gay personhood as an impossible mode of being. The book also demonstrates how black gay artists and activists have used narrative and poetic forms to contest these pathologizing discourses of black gay personhood, even as they drew from these discourses in their negotiations of the psychic and social damages accrued from living and dying as racial and sexual minorities in the 1970s, 1980s, and 1990s.

In attending to black gay men's subjective and social lives, I insist on black gay being, even in the face of structural violence and death. For the purposes of this study, "being" is closely aligned with Frantz Fanon's theorization of "the fact of blackness," or "the lived experience of being black," which he advanced in his seminal study *Black Skin, White Masks*.[39] To account for the cultural particularity of black gay lives, I have coined the phrase "black gay being" to describe the lived experience of being black and gay. "Black gay being" asserts the fact of black gay social life lived amid the multiple formations of violence that target black gay men. The term pushes against the "double cremation" of black gay personhood as a form of structural violence necessary to the racial projects of white supremacy, black racial normativity, and heteronormativity.[40]

Building on debates in black studies about whether everyday acts of defiance and creation of communal bonds count as acts of political resistance, "being" documents the complex forms of collective self-making and world-making made possible through living life in the space of multiple marginalizations.[41] "Being" (as opposed to "doing" and as a form of "doing") also attends to the micropolitical and intersubjective processes that are missed when the imperative is "do something."[42] By subordinating the processes of individual and collective self-making and self-preservation to dominant frameworks of political resistance and rebellion, scholars miss the immaterial and unquantifiable forms of violence accrued from social and psychological damage, and the individual and collective efforts to alleviate this damage.[43] In sum, the concept of black gay being attends not only to the forms of structural violence that usher black bodies to corporeal death but also to the foundational violence that renders the ontological status of black gay men as imperiled.

Queering Social Death

In his 1993 poem "Vital Signs," black gay writer and activist Essex Hemphill situates his vulnerability to HIV amid the structural conditions of black gay social life.

> Some of the T cells I am without are not here through my own fault. I didn't lose all of them foolishly, and I didn't lose all of them erotically. Some of the missing T cells were lost to racism, a well-known transmittable disease. Some were lost to poverty because there was no money to do something about the plumbing before the pipes burst and the room flooded. Homophobia killed quite a few, but so did my rage and my pointed furies, so did the wars at home and the wars within, so did the drugs I took to keep calm, cool, collected. . . . Actually, there are T cells scattered all about me at doorways where I was denied entrance because I was a faggot or a nigga or too poor or too black.[44]

The social ills of racism, capitalism, and homophobia had existed long before the recognition of AIDS in the United States in 1981. For Hemphill, these ills produced the conditions for his susceptibility to the virus and for the worsening of his illness. If "race" and "class" and "sexuality" are fundamental to how someone can lay claim to life and personhood, then racialized, classed, and sexual discourses and practices fundamentally shaped who was understood as a *person* with AIDS, who was deemed worthy of recognition and sympathy, and who was provided with state resources. Hemphill's prose counters narrowly conceptualized scientific responses to the virus, which privileged epidemiological approaches that focused on sexual behavior and ignored the social determinants of health.[45]

Following Hemphill, *Evidence of Being* intervenes in current methodological approaches to the study of the literatures and cultures of the AIDS epidemic by centering the experiences of black gay men, whose multiple forms of exclusion—from white gay communities, heterosexual black communities, and the nation-state—require a broad analytical framework that views the death of a generation of black gay writers from AIDS as "stemming from a constellation of life experiences as well as a discrete happening."[46] My focus on violence as a broad framework, which includes AIDS, builds on the work of queer scholars of color who have also demonstrated how racial and national exclusion intensified the experience of AIDS in communities of color while ensuring the erasure of their suffering from history and memory.[47]

Extending these concerns to black gay men necessitates an engagement with the legacy of antiblackness that has marked black people as "socially dead," thereby rendering their suffering as normative and unremarkable. Orlando Patterson first introduced the term *social death* in his influential 1982 study *Slavery and Social Death*. For Patterson, the social death of slavery comprises three basic elements: (1) total powerlessness, (2) natal alienation or "the loss of ties of birth in both ascending and descending generations," and (3) generalized dishonor, this last element being a direct effect of the previous two.[48] While Patterson offers a model of what social death in slavery looked like in the past, Saidiya Hartman describes how it persists in the present. She foregrounds the "incomplete project of freedom" and the "afterlife of slavery," which is witnessed in the "skewed life chances, limited access to health and education, premature death, incarceration, and impoverishment" of contemporary black people.[49] Hartman's claims echo and extend those of Hemphill by locating the social inequalities that render black bodies more vulnerable to AIDS, and the failed claims to personhood that prohibit black bodies from being recognized as subjects of AIDS, as indexical of the ongoing effects of slavery on the lives of contemporary black people. However, AIDS-infected black gay bodies often signify as absence and negation in dominant scholarly and popular chronologies of antiblack violence—slavery, lynching, mass incarceration, and police brutality. As such, a framework is necessary for thinking about how black gay men's marginalization within black communities intensifies their precarity.

In her groundbreaking study of AIDS and black politics, Cathy Cohen demonstrates that AIDS became a "cross-cutting issue" because its impact was rooted in differences, cleavages, and fault lines of the black community. She argues that as the devastation of AIDS became more visible, black leaders pursued a more aggressive campaign of denial and distance, employing what she terms "secondary marginalization" to mark black people with AIDS as outside the larger black community. The crisis of AIDS exacerbated distinctions within the black community between a "good and moral" middle class and those deemed unworthy or tainted by outside evils. Words like "junkie, faggot, punk, and prostitute" were used as codes to designate expendable black bodies.[50] Cohen shows that African Americans' quest for moral citizenship depended on the denial of suffering from other members of the community who were deemed disposable. She describes how the historical emergence of something that might be called a black subject is premised on constituting gender and sexual others as its constitutive outside.

Moreover, Robert Reid-Pharr, extending Fanon's theories to black male homosexuality, argues that "the Black," who had been conceptualized in slave culture as an inchoate, irrational nonsubject, has in the late twentieth century produced its own normativity and bid for inclusion in the liberal nation-state by violently Othering the black male homosexual: "To strike the homosexual, the scapegoat, the sign of chaos and crisis, is to return the community to normality, to create boundaries around Blackness, rights that indeed white men are obliged to recognize."[51] In the post–civil rights era, African American claims to rights and inclusion in the nation-state have depended on marking gender-nonconforming and nonheterosexual formations as the black nation's constitutive outside.

Cohen and Reid-Pharr point out why the black gay body continues to signify as absence and negation in histories and theories of antiblack violence. In the context of slavery's afterlife, asserting the presence of black gay bodies signals how contemporary theories of antiblackness replicate the historical processes of secondary marginalization experienced by blackness's others. Just as importantly, these disposable bodies point out the structural antagonisms existing within blackness itself, antagonisms premised on an array of social, cultural, and political shifts that have occurred from slavery to the present. What Cohen terms "secondary marginalization" might be better understood, in the context of slavery's afterlife, as an internal structural antagonism. By refusing to acknowledge histories of black struggles for humanity, contemporary conflicts within black communities, and black subjectification as citizen-subjects, however partial and differentiated, studies that examine slavery's impact on the present inadvertently mark black LGBTQ social life as "the inexistent existence."[52] Moving beyond this impasse requires us to locate slavery's afterlife in the present through a dynamic process that reads the ruptures of black diasporic trauma alongside the cultural, social, and political shifts that conditioned the emergence of a black gay cultural renaissance.

Violence in the Black/Queer Archive

Evidence of Being traces the signs of black gay social life amid the structural violence of antiblackness and antiqueerness through an exploration of historical archives. I read black gay literature and culture, oral history narratives, interviews, magazines, newspapers, and archival materials as "sites of memory" that give partial access to black gay experience in the 1970s, 1980s, and 1990s.[53] These sites of memory—poetry, performance, essays, speeches, gossip columns, diaries, and anthologies—allow me to consider the formal and aesthetic choices made by each author in my interpretations of their historical significance. For example, in chapter 2, I read Essex Hemphill's literary constructions of loneliness as indexing a structure of feeling for black gay men in the 1980s. Though loneliness signals the isolation, alienation, and pathologization black gay men felt during this period, loneliness is also a feeling of bodily desire, signaling these men's longings for better life, health, and sociality during this period.

To locate my archives within the ruptures of black diasporic trauma, I turn to scholarship on the archives of slavery, as the researchers in this field have performed the greatest amount of work in conveying how the legacy of antiblack violence shapes the project of archival recovery. I focus on whether a more complex interpretation of black gay personhood and a more optimistic black queer politic can be recovered from the ashes of black gay history if that history has been subject to double cremation. In her groundbreaking meditation on the absent narratives of female slaves in the archives, Saidiya Hartman asks, "What are the kinds of stories to be told by those and about those who live in such an intimate relationship with death?" She is concerned with how the absented voice of Venus, a black female slave, "haunts the present."[54] Hartman suggests that scholars practice "narrative constraint" in their interpretations of slavery's archive, and notes that the "intent of this practice is not to give voice to the slave, but rather to imagine what cannot be verified, a realm of experience which is situated between two zones of death—social and corporeal—and to reckon with the precarious lives which are visible only in the moment of their disappearance."[55] Hartman is troubled by the contradictions embedded in interpreting the archives of slavery wherein it is impossible to discern black agency from the forces of black subjection.

I turn to Hartman because her orientation away from historical recovery and toward narrative restraint is governed by her interest in "illuminat[ing] the intimacy of our experience with the lives of the dead, to write our now as it is interrupted by this past."[56] I seek to (re)locate the death of a generation of black gay writers within the longer history of antiblackness that animates slavery's afterlife, even as I disidentify with contemporary theories of antiblackness that would erase gay male cultural particularity, and black gay collective visions of futurity. Though I refuse to move away from the "terror of [my] evidence"—an archive of the black gay bodies ushered to premature death—I read the literature and culture that black gay men produced in the 1970s, 1980s, and 1990s as an alternative site of memory that gestures toward black gay being and becoming.[57]

Queer theorists also have challenged traditional historical methods for interpreting the LGBT past, criticizing in particular those that utilize the past for validating present-day identity formations. Heather Love argues that the problem of queer historiography lies not with attempts to recognize and situate ourselves in history for our own present identity formations, but rather in the consistent search for valorization in the affirmative aspects of the past instead of the identity-shattering aspects of the past.[58] Heeding Love's concerns, my emphasis on black gay being does not ignore the historical realities of loss and death during this period, and my archive does not necessarily lead to either consoling or shattering forms of recognition. These black gay archives of violence reflect the contradictions of black gay being in the 1970s, 1980s, and 1990s. The death from AIDS of a generation of black gay writers reminds us of the fact of their blackness and queerness in an antiblack and antiqueer world. But the renaissance of black gay literary and cultural production in this same period gestures toward "the power to imagine beyond current fact, to envision that which is not, but must be."[59]

However, the proliferation of black gay cultural work amid multiple formations of violence that sought to "doubly cremate" black gay men's historical existence does not negate the inextricable connection between black gay life and social death. Black gay writing acts as what Tina Campt calls "the future real conditional" or "that which will have had to happen" in order for a more livable black gay social life to be both imagined and imaginable.[60] The archive of black gay writing at the center of this study poses a challenge to black/queer studies that center social death as their sole interpretive framework. I privilege the archival recovery of authors and texts marginalized in black studies and queer studies that allows for readings of loss and abjection alongside political longing and subjective possibilities. Rather than approach black gay history through a narrow model of inclusion, I stress the significance of archival recovery as a hermeneutic for engaging theoretical questions that emerge from black cultural studies, queer studies, and black queer studies. To identify the contradictory effects of violence in the archive, I examine various forms of black gay expressive culture that record traces of black gay historical trauma as well as black gay men's collective and political longings. I argue that the gendered and sexualized formations of antiblack violence that wiped out a generation of black gay cultural activists in the early era of AIDS also forged the imaginative possibilities for black gay world-making.

From Loss to Longing

The "Plum Nelly" special issue of the black diasporic literary and cultural studies journal *Callaloo*, one of the earliest collections of essays in the emerging field of black queer studies, was dedicated to the memory of Melvin

Dixon and Audre Lorde.[61] That these black queer writers died of AIDS and cancer demonstrates that the black body, which has been *the* formative site for black cultural interventions into queer studies, is also a site of illness and death. The "Plum Nelly" special issue featured a sampling of Dixon's poetry, an interview with him, a published version of his speech at the Out-Write conference, and a critical essay about his acclaimed novel, *Vanishing Rooms*. This extensive memorial demonstrates that the cultural and material losses of AIDS were central to the formation of black queer studies. Central-izing the AIDS dead in black queer theory affirms Karla Holloway's claim that "African Americans' particular vulnerability to untimely death in the United States intimately affects how black culture represents itself and is represented."[62]

The ongoing trauma of the AIDS epidemic in black gay communities and its effects on black gay representation are evidenced in a recent Centers for Disease Control and Prevention report stating that half of all black gay men will become HIV positive in their lifetimes. In a February 2016 article published in the LGBT newspaper *Georgia Voice*, black gay journalist Darian Aaron notes that this statistic generated controversy and outright rejection among black gay men. Johnnie Kornegay, director of digital strategy and stakeholder engagement at the Counter Narrative Project, an activist group committed to foregrounding the narratives of black gay men as a vehicle for social change, understands this statistic as a "call to action": "Stigma, spiritual violence, racism, criminalization, homophobia, economic distress, lack of access to healthcare and lack of comprehensive sex education all contribute to the vulnerability of HIV acquisition for black gay men. These things can't be solved in any traditional way. Undoing hundreds of years of structural disenfranchisement can't be solved with pills or ads to 'get tested.'"[63] This quote links black gay men's contemporary struggles against AIDS to Hemphill's claims regarding how histories of racism, capitalism, and homophobia produced the conditions for his susceptibility to the virus and for the worsening of his illness. Black gay men's call to action is signifi-cant, because it lays bare the structural forces that continue to define black gay life through narratives of illness and (social) death.

Love argues that "rather than disavowing the history of marginalization and abjection that marks queer historical experience . . . we embrace it, ex-ploring the ways it continues to structure queer experience in the present."[64] She calls for critics to "reckon adequately with their difficult histories," fear-ing that the rush to transform the past toward "futural imaginings" ignores important historical realities and the persistence of the past in the present.[65] While I agree with Love's claim that centering loss in our approaches to the queer archive might hold open a space for those to whom narratives of stigma, shame, and deviance continue to cling, I am concerned about the ethical stakes of embracing loss and abjection for black gay men in particular. The rejection many black gay men faced by the state and society, white gay communities, and black straight communities during the 1970s, 1980s, and 1990s attests to their historical and political abjection, as "the black male homosexual" was figured as a living "sign of chaos and crisis" in this period. If Hartman is correct in her premise that our approach to the archives of the dead should be "to write our now as it is interrupted by this past," then we should be concerned about how our approaches to this very near history "interrupt" our historical present. Since society continues to see black gay men as living "sign[s] of chaos and crisis," as the statistic mentioned above confirms, they continue to understand their own bodies and desires as a burden to black and queer freedom, as that which must be must be erased from historical existence and memory.[66] Embracing loss and abjection in black/queer studies colludes with the epistemological and structural violence that doubly marks the black gay body for social and corporeal death.

While I align myself with scholars who have demonstrated the centrality of loss to black, queer, and black queer politics, this book also reexamines the stakes of privileging loss in our critical interpretations of black/queer archives. If our critical stance toward black/queer archives is that of the bereaved and our imagined black/queer subject is always dead or death-bound, what does this mean for our future horizon? If black queerness is always imagined as dead or death-bound, we risk losing any consolation for our racial and sexual grief. If we privilege the losses accrued from racism, capitalism, homophobia, and AIDS as the dominant critical approach to our interpretations of black gay literatures of the 1970s, 1980s and 1990s, we might not see how black queerness emerges, even in this archive, as a structure of longing that exceeds the black gay body's undoing.

While acknowledging that the black gay body was a site of loss during the 1970s, 1980s, and 1990s, *Evidence of Being* turns to black gay literature and culture as evidence for reimagining the period as more than a site of grief. Drawing from the work of Vincent Brown, who asks us to see social death as "productive peril," and José Muñoz, who theorizes queerness as a structure of "utopian longing," I show how black gay men living in these decades employed literary and cultural forms to both assert the fact of black gay social life in a moment of widespread violence and reorient black queer politics beyond the constrained space and time of biological life and social death.[67] My focus on black/queer optimism allows me to interpret 1970s,

1980s, and 1990s black gay literature and culture as embodying a set of re-fusals and openings, to "broaden our repertoire of what is thinkable" about black gay social life in the late twentieth century.[68] While the body of black gay literature and culture discussed here refuses to disavow the patholo-gies attached to blackness and queerness, it yearns for modes of being out-side the constrained space and time of biological life and social death that black gay men embody. I consider emotions like grief, loneliness, fear, and uncertainty as indexing the violence, alienation, and isolation that attend processes of racialization and sexualization, but also read these as political feelings that index black gay men's collective longings for futures beyond the forces of antiblackness and antiqueerness.

Evidence of Being focuses on two cities, Washington, DC, and New York City, to offer a broader comparative perspective on urban black gay sub-cultural life. Scholars have devoted very little attention to Washington, DC, as a key site in the emergence of LGBT culture and politics in general, and black LGBT culture and politics in particular. In the section on this city, I also track a historical shift in the development of black gay politics, from a focus on making black bodies intelligible as sexual minorities to the state and to white gay and lesbian communities (chapter 1) to one affirming the sexual heterogeneity of black communities, and struggling alongside the broader black community against the devastating impact of neoliberal capitalism and AIDS (chapter 2). And while New York has been understood as one of the centers of the LGBT social movement and cultural activities, scholars have been less attentive to the contributions of racial minorities. In the sec-tion on New York, I confront the whiteness of AIDS histories by questioning the dominant political forms and spaces associated with histories of AIDS activism (chapter 3), and by challenging theoretical frameworks that have defined the literatures and cultures of AIDS (chapter 4). Moreover, I con-centrate on these two cities in particular because of the interaction between the individuals and the collectives featured in this study. Essex Hemphill led workshops and performed with the Other Countries Collective. Melvin Dixon served as poetry editor of the Other Countries Collective, and con-tributed to *In the Life* and *Brother to Brother*. Other Countries performed in black gay bars and performance venues in Washington, DC. Sidney Brink-ley's *Blacklight* magazine circulated in New York City, and would have been read by New York's black gay community. I claim these disparate cultural activities as a renaissance partly because of the mutual influence of these individuals and groups. But I also attend to the local specificities that shaped each individual's or group's efforts.

Because I have chosen to focus on movement activities in these two cities, this book does not offer a comprehensive overview of the black gay cultural renaissance. Many prominent figures and collectives engaged in movement activities in other major metropolitan areas across the globe—such as filmmaker Marlon Riggs, writer Gary Fisher, performance group Pomo Afro Homos, and singer Blackberri in San Francisco; filmmaker Isaac Julien and photographers Ajamu X and Rotimi Fani-Kayode in London; and novelists Steven Corbin and Larry Duplechan in Los Angeles—are not included in this study. However, I have supplemented this study with biographies of major figures and groups as well as descriptions of major publications of the black gay cultural renaissance (see the appendix).

Because the renaissance took place all over the world, I am careful to read the historical actors in my study as African diasporic subjects, thereby acknowledging the various migrants integral to US black gay movements in the 1970s, 1980s, and 1990s (many of whom were Caribbean immigrants or the descendants of Caribbean immigrants), the transnational circulation of black gay publications, the transnational alliances evident in black gay movement politics, and the global impact of HIV/AIDS. In *Globalizing AIDS*, Cindy Patton argues that even though efforts to address AIDS were often local and particular at the height of the epidemic, people living with and fighting against AIDS experienced the national and international dimensions of it through the global flow of information.[69] While I focus on how black gay men engaged in forms of collective self-transformation amid the global transformations of the 1970s, 1980s, and 1990s, I also acknowledge that global flows of capital, bodies, cultures, and ideas shaped black gay culture and politics at the local level.

By claiming the disparate cultural and political activities of black gay men from the late 1970s to the mid-1990s as a renaissance, I push against the interpretation of this period as solely about trauma and loss. I concentrate instead on how black gay men attempted to forge a tradition amid widespread violence, trauma, and loss as a way to make a future possible. John Drabinski argues that the relations and traditions shared between black people forge the notion of a possible future, and further notes that "this future is never anything like forgetful or utopian in the sense of a dreamscape disburdened of the past. In fact, quite the contrary, it is rooted in a tradition that expresses, 'the long and painful experience of a people.'"[70] My historicist perspective seeks to locate a black gay cultural tradition through which a black/queer future becomes possible. Thus, this book combines literary and cultural analysis with methods drawn from history to contextualize the work of individual black gay writers and activists amid black gay collective attempts at aesthetic development and preservation, community building and political mobilization, and collective self-transformation in the early era of AIDS. My focus on black gay cultural movements during the 1970s, 1980s, and 1990s places theories of social death in conversation with cultural and historical analyses of black gay social life. I locate black gay being at this theoretical, cultural, and historical conjuncture. In the discussions, debates, confrontations, and moments of embracing others, taking care of the sick, and mourning the dead, black gay men contested the structural forces that converged to mark their bodies as expendable and disposable. Though structural violence ushered a generation of these men to premature death, *Evidence of Being* demonstrates that the renaissance of black gay cultural production in the 1970s, 1980s, and 1990s embodies their collective political longings for richer subjective and social lives.

I open my study with an analysis of *Blacklight*, a DC-based black lesbian- and gay-themed magazine that circulated from 1979 to 1985. By beginning my study in the late 1970s, I challenge the normative periodization of the black gay cultural renaissance, usually thought to have begun after the appearance of AIDS.[71] Chapter 1 examines the magazine's representations of a string of unsolved murders targeting same-sex-desiring and gender-nonconforming black bodies in Washington, DC, in the late 1970s and early 1980s. My analysis of *Blacklight* demonstrates how the emerging black gay press became a central mode of racial and sexual knowledge production for black same-sex-desiring Washingtonians, despite the fact that most of these men were not "out" during this period. I then explore these serial murders as an alternative historical site for examining the problem of value as a raced, classed, gendered, sexualized, and spatialized term. Despite the responses to the murders by a few "out" black gay political activists, the victims' lives and deaths remained stigmatized because of their engagement in forms of sexuality and sociality that challenged the respectability politics of a largely middle-class black gay community in Washington, DC. That community's failure to mobilize around these "trick murders" exposes the entanglements of grief with the violence of value. Through close readings of a poem and performance piece that responded to these murders, I show that while acknowledging the fatal risks of being "in the life," black gay literature and culture embodied the possibilities of black gay personhood by offering traces of queer optimism and gesturing toward a time and space where black/queer personhood would not be conditioned by value.

Chapter 2 explores diverse constructions of loneliness in the work of Essex Hemphill, especially in his elegies to his contemporary Joseph Beam, a black gay writer and activist who kept his AIDS diagnosis a secret and died alone while fighting to end the cultural silence around black gay men's lives.

I theorize loneliness as a traumatic structure of feeling and as an expression of black gay men's collective political desires in the 1980s and 1990s. By positing loneliness in relation to black gay men's collective and political longings for richer subjective and social lives, I read Hemphill's work as an alternative to recent antisocial and pessimistic strains of black and queer theory. While constructions of loneliness in Hemphill's work archive the feelings of isolation and alienation that sometimes attend the experience of social death, I argue that loneliness is also a form of bodily desire and expresses a yearning for an attachment to the social. By positing loneliness as black gay longing, I demonstrate that the queerness of blackness is located both in histories of racial and sexual violence that continue to fix blackness as a site of injury, abjection, and pathology, and in black literary and cultural imaginings of futures beyond the forces of antiblackness and antiqueerness.

Chapter 3 focuses on the history and cultural production of the Other Countries Collective, an NYC-based writers' group. Drawing from queer theories of "melancholic mourning" that see melancholia as aesthetically, culturally, and politically productive for sexual minority subjects, I argue that the devastating impact of AIDS in black gay communities in New York City in the late 1980s and early 1990s produced a historically and culturally specific form of mourning that was animated by a desire for collectivity and self-determination. Through analysis of oral history narratives and archival materials, I provide an overview of the history of Other Countries, focusing on its major components—writers' workshops, poetry performances, and literary publications. I closely read elegiac poems and prose from the collective's second publication, *Sojourner* (1993), to outline how black gay aesthetic forms are mutually imbricated in historically and culturally specific practices of mourning. I draw from interviews with surviving members of the group to discuss how mourning has been a central aspect of black gay activism against AIDS. Finally, I read the interviews of survivors and their remembrance of the sorrowful history of the early era of AIDS as a form of black/queer optimism. By contesting the erasure of the ongoing epidemic from public discourse and refusing to consign to the past the associations between blackness, queerness, and death, their collective memories disrupt contemporary forms of black/gay liberalism, thereby producing a more radical present.

Chapter 4 examines the diaries of Melvin Dixon, which he kept from 1965 until 1991. Together, they comprise one of the most extensive accounts of black gay social life in the post-Stonewall era. I consider these diaries not as a biographical supplement to Dixon's published literary works but as integral to his literary oeuvre. I challenge dominant theorizations of the AIDS diary by positioning Dixon's struggles against the disease within a transatlantic history of antigay and antiblack violence that was indexed in his diaries since the 1970s. Centering uncertainty and self-doubt as affects produced by the traumas of black/gay diasporic subjectivity, I show how the diary operated for Dixon as a mode of self-making in the context of the persisting negativities of post-Stonewall life. Building on my theorization of the text as an alternative site for theorizing black gay personhood, I suggest that the very form of the diary—its episodic structure, dated entries, and open-endedness—allows us to imagine possibilities of black gay being neither bound by the finite temporality of Dixon's life nor yoked to the present of the diary's witnesses.

The epilogue revisits some of the book's major arguments by analyzing a photograph taken by black gay activist Joseph Beam alongside a poem that Other Countries cofounder Daniel Garrett wrote in response to the photograph. The photograph shows various figures of the movement in joyous embrace, and the poem is an ode to the power of art and community, however ephemeral, as a mechanism for black gay survival. Both the photograph and the poem offer alternative sites for remembering 1980s and 1990s black gay life in their depiction of this pleasurable moment of black gay sociality. My analysis considers the ethical stakes of bearing witness to the 1980s and 1990s as a renaissance of black gay culture rather than focusing solely on the communal trauma and loss associated with the early era of the AIDS epidemic.

ONE

The Contradictions of Grief

Violence and Value in Blacklight *Magazine*

In September 1981, the *Washington Post* reported on a series of murders of eight gay men who frequented "a popular downtown gay strip on New York Avenue between 12ᵗʰ and 13ᵗʰ streets" and "had been found stabbed, beaten, or shot to death in their homes, apartments, or cars within the last year, according to D.C. police." The writer of the story seemed unfamiliar with gay men's ongoing struggles against violence, and cited "claims" by gay activists that eight gay men also had been killed over an eleven-month period ending in August 1978. The article marked a turning point in the state's attention to murders targeting gay men. Though the murders had been treated as ordinary homicides and distributed individually among detectives, in 1981 the police formed a special task force of homicide detectives to investigate the murders as "gay-related." In a story about this task force, the *Post* interviewed black gay activist Ray Melrose, who led the DC Coalition of Black Gays, a local black lesbian and gay activist group which had set up a committee to investigate the murders. Melrose estimated that the murder toll was closer to twelve than the eight the police had reported. He also expressed concern that the killings were representative of homophobic violence against the city's increasingly visible gay community, especially its black members, noting that eight of the murder victims were black. In the same article, the *Post* interviewed Andy Hirsch, vice president of the Gay Activist Alliance, about whether he believed that blacks had been targeted. He replied, "A number of the victims have been whites. I have no reason to believe that there is a racial motive here."[1]

Hirsch's failure to consider a "racial motive" aligns with Lindon Barrett's claim that violence is a precondition of value. In Barrett's formulation, "violence is an impeachment of the Other, the willful expenditure of the Other in an imposing production of the Self."[2] In this case, any "racial motive" must be willfully expended from consideration for these "homosexual murders" to accrue political value to the (white) gay community. However, Melrose's inquiry into the racialized nature of this violence demonstrates how "the perspective of the Other . . . reveals relativities of value as ratios of violence."[3] In this chapter, I draw from Barrett's work to demonstrate how claims to liberal gay personhood, mediated through struggles against violence, have depended on the excision of blackness as a term of political value. But this devaluation of blackness under a white gay gaze produces "other" modes of valuation. Black cultural and political responses to these murders have produced an alternative conception of black life and death beyond normative economies of value.

The mainstream press coverage of these murders can be attributed to the victims' status as middle-class men. But their identification as closeted gay men who risked their lives in pursuit of illegal, transactional sex acts with trade—a term referring to straight-identified men who have sex with gay men for money or pleasure—also positions them as outside the norms of gender and sexuality, especially within the context of the increasing homo-normativity of gay rights. These murders serve as significant sites of black/ queer memory because they demonstrate how the formation of black gay social life was shaped by state-based violence, even before the appearance of AIDS.[4] Moreover, the murders of black/gay men in the late seventies and early eighties operate as sites where race, class, gender, sexuality, and vio-lence converged to mark black bodies for death, even as the shame and stigma attached to sexual practices and cross-class desires marked these deaths as ungrievable. Through close readings of black gay media, poetry, and performance, I demonstrate how black gay men used culture to con-test systems of valuation that marked these lives as ungrievable, and to re-imagine black gay personhood beyond normative economies of value.

This chapter first examines the discourse surrounding the murders in the local black lesbian- and gay-themed periodical *Blacklight*, revealing how the threat of murder became central to the formation of black gay conscious-ness in late 1970s and early 1980s Washington, DC. *Blacklight's* reporting demonstrates how the emerging black gay press became a central mode of racial and sexual knowledge production for black same-sex-desiring men, despite the fact that during this period most of these men were not "out." I then explore these serial murders as an alternative historical site for ex-amining the notion of value as raced, classed, gendered, sexualized, and spatialized. Despite the responses to the murders by a few "out" black gay political activists, these victims' lives and deaths remained stigmatized be-cause of their engagement in forms of sexuality and sociality that challenged the respectability politics of a largely middle-class black gay community in Washington, DC. That community's failure to mobilize around these "trick murders" exposes the violence of value—how value is distributed unevenly even when conferred outside the white gaze. Through close readings of a poem and a performance piece in response to these murders, I show that while acknowledging the fatal risks of being "in the life," black gay literature and culture embody the possibilities of black gay personhood by archiving a sense of queer optimism and gesturing toward a space where black/gay personhood is not conditioned by value.

Blacklight and Black Gay Political Responses to Violence

In his history of the significance of communication networks to gay and lesbian identity and community formation, Martin Meeker argues that most homosexuals first became "connected to" knowledge that same-sex attraction meant something, that it had social ramifications, and that it had a name before they "came out" to the gay world or to the larger public as homosexual.[5] As an important site of racial, sexual, and cultural knowledge production, *Blacklight* offered this connection to same-sex-desiring men in Washington, DC, in the late 1970s and early 1980s; most of these men were not "out," despite the growing local political visibility and state protections offered to lesbians and gays. In 1979 in "Blacklight Fills a Real Need," Dick Munn of the DC paper *Washington Blade* interviewed *Blacklight* founder and publisher Sidney Brinkley about his new publication. Brinkley commented on how racial difference shaped the emergence of the black gay cultural scene away from the public culture of bars and nightclubs, stating that "the majority of Black social life doesn't even touch on the bars." He implied that much of DC's black gay collective activity took place in more informal venues, such as the black male social club meetings and private parties held at peoples' homes.[6] Since at least the mid-twentieth century, male social clubs such as the Rounders, Best of Washington, and Washington Capitalites created a space for many same-sex-desiring black men to act on their sexual desires through their politics of sexual discretion. Brinkley hoped to reach members of these social clubs and the guests of their events through *Blacklight* by tailoring the magazine to the needs and desires of an insular black gay community. He ensured the discretion of his subscribers by guaranteeing privacy in mailings, stating, "Some of us are unable to be as free or as open with our gayness as we would like to be. For that reason BL will arrive each month completely enclosed to assure privacy."[7]

Blacklight became an especially important site of knowledge production in the context of the street violence affecting gay men in the late seventies and eighties. In a June 1981 article it published, Brinkley discussed the series of murders targeting gay men in Washington, DC: "We are all familiar with the murders that have taken place in Atlanta. But closer to home, right here in Washington, D.C. there have been a number of murders of another type. Gay murders." In this article, he mentioned the "Atlanta child murders," mass killings that targeted twenty-eight youth, primarily poor and African American and male, in Atlanta from 1979 to 1981. The killings received very little media coverage until *20/20* and *Nightline* broke the story on ABC in late October 1980.[8] Media coverage revealed that the police did not follow every lead in their investigation. This neglect caused many African Americans to question the role that race and class played in state valuation of black life.

By referencing the Atlanta child murders, Brinkley suggests that the devaluation of raced and classed bodies combines with the stigma attached to same-sex desire to structure the lack of media coverage of the murders of black gay men in DC: "The straight media often times do not report it as such but we know. We know because many of the victims have been friends and family." He reported that six murders had been committed from January through August of 1981—roughly one per month, and noted that "once a month in some part of the city a familiar ritual takes place: Friends gather, shed tears and talk of how nice the person was. Then it's business as usual, until next time."

Brinkley believed that there would always be a "next time," because "too many Gay men are into hustlers or rough trade." He then posed the question of what the black gay community could do to end these attacks. "The answer is *we* can't. The solution lies solely with future victims. Until they evaluate their self-concept and their concept of manhood . . . there is very little we can do. If you know someone who likes his trade rough, have him think about this: The next one he picks up . . . may kill him." Though his initial reproach seems to place responsibility on the "future victims," Brinkley ended his editorial by emphasizing how an ethics of care fueled black gay activists to continue their efforts to end the murder: "We still try because we care."[9] Kwame Holmes notes that in the repeated emphasis on "we," Brinkley "speaks to a broader, if unnamed, community who not only knew the sexual identity of the victims but also knew of the economies of desire that attract black gay men to their victimizers."[10]

Blacklight's attempt to raise awareness about the murders within this imagined black gay community emerged in another unlikely site: the monthly gossip column, which first appeared in the September 1981 issue.[11] "Under Grace's Hat" was written by a socialite who wrote under the pseudonym Grace and attended and described the events of black gay social life, including birthday parties and social club gatherings, with her own unique style and flair. Grace gossiped about recent divorces, the quality of the events she attended, and those who left and returned to the DC black gay scene. Her column assumed the readers' knowledge of these people, places, and events, illustrating how her readership, though described by Brinkley as "a series of circles that may touch, but rarely overlap," was in fact significantly interconnected. Beyond her witty reviews of the social events of the season, Grace also informed her readers about important political matters in this community. In her signature high-camp aesthetic, displayed in her third-person narration, she provided an insider's perspective on the series of unsolved murders of black gay men: "On the subject of Gay murders, GRACE is very happy to hear that a task force between the LAMBDAs and the COALITION OF BLACK GAYS is assisting the police in solving the murders. It is also interesting to note that the police department is taking a more serious look at this problem."[12] By stating that the police were now "taking a more serious look," Grace hinted that they had not been investigating in earnest.[13]

At that time, DC had some of the nation's strongest human rights laws protecting on the basis of sexual orientation; these stemmed from the infiltration of lesbians and gay men into local government and the strong presence of national LGBT organizations in the nation's capital. Despite these protections, Robert Lomax, a high-ranking federal government official and president of the Best of Washington, believed that the overwhelming majority of the city's black gays would remain closeted for quite some time. In an October 1983 article published in the *Washington Blade*, Lomax opined that laws protecting gay rights could do little to alleviate the cultural stigma for black gay Washingtonians: "Most of them come from a religious background that is not compatible with the Gay lifestyle. The law does not protect them from their families, their colleagues, and their peers."[14] Therefore, gossip became a mode wherein black same-sex-desiring men could engage with urgent issues affecting their community while retaining the anonymity necessary for negotiating their complex political worlds.

Grace advised that individuals could take action to prevent becoming victims of violent crime: "However, Grace feels that there are some things we can do individually to lessen the chances of this happening to us. For example, it was reported that in one of the recent murders one of the children picked up not one but two pieces of trade. Now in 1981 you cannot take two pieces to your house and not know either of them, no matter how good they look."[15] Grace was most likely referring to the August 1981 murder of a black male high school teacher, who was shot to death in his home roughly four hours after being seen with two black men near the Brass Rail bar in DC's "hustler district."[16]

By including herself through the use of the pronouns *we* and *us*, Grace refuses to exempt herself from such "risky" sexual practices. However, she does construct a kind of hierarchy that would label taking home two pieces of trade as excessive and irresponsible, given the visible and frequent physical violence committed against gay men since at least 1978. Her caution exemplifies how cultural anxieties about the threat of violence shaped black gay collective subject formation in the late seventies and early eighties. Though class and degrees of outness were key sites of difference within DC's black community, influencing which spaces and bodies someone engaged for erotic fulfillment, the persistent threat of violence shaped collective consciousness across difference.

Grace ended her brief discussion of gay murders by suggesting that the gay social clubs intervene in these issues, writing, "It might be good if some of the Gay social clubs would sponsor survival techniques for the 80's. That would be a real service to the community especially since many of them charge 15 and 20 dollars per affair. This way some of the profits could be returned to the community."[17] While both Brinkley's and Grace's use of the collective "we" stresses the communal concern about the murders, Grace's critique of the social clubs exposes the limits of the black gay community's efforts to combat these murders through "internal transformation or private, interpersonal conversation."[18] While a workshop on survival techniques could take place outside the public sphere, the refusal of black gay social clubs to take a more central role in activist efforts against these murders seems to turn on class divisions *within* the community. In "Cliques," an editorial published in the December 1980 issue of *Blacklight*, an anonymous writer pointed out that many black gay men "did not possess the physical, social, or economic attributes that would permit them to exist on their own among Washington's black gay community, for the name of the game is acceptance." Those who did not possess those qualities were left to mingle among their own "peer" group or made to participate in more public forms of sociality, such as bars or cruising for sex in public spaces.[19]

Entry into black gay social clubs and members-only nightclubs was distributed along class lines, and the silence of black gay social club leaders and members regarding these murders suggests that the politics of respectability that governed membership also governed their responses. To pick up trade was to put oneself at risk by moving beyond the middle-class social and sexual networks that black gay social clubs provided, assuming that one had been provided access in the first place. Moreover, entering into the city's red-light district meant that one was cruising for sex beyond the private or semipublic spaces that "cliques" and social clubs had sanctioned and deemed "safe." While Brinkley's and Grace's columns attempted to reach an "imagined community" of black same-sex-desiring men in Washington, DC, social divisions within the community prohibited a greater outcry concerning these less-than-respectable deaths.

Serial Murder and the Value of Black/Gay Life

In a January 1979 article, the *Washington Blade* reported on the stabbing death of a top official of the US Department of Health, Education, and Welfare, the ninth in a series of "gay-related murders." The victim had been stabbed twenty-seven times in his apartment and links had been drawn to an eighteen-year-old hustler, though there was no clear "gay-identification" of the deceased.[20] Although the victim's racial and sexual identity went unreported in the media, rethinking his death as racialized and sexualized violence creates an opportunity to speculate about how black same-sex-desiring men experienced increased vulnerability to violence in the early years of black lesbian and gay political mobilization. The double vulnerability marking black gay men's federal employment in the 1970s and early 1980s provides a context for the ninth victim's "hidden" identity.

The public sector became a major site of employment for black people in the post–civil rights era, providing refuge when other realms of the political economy excluded them. The obtainment of these positions can be credited with the consolidation of an emerging black middle class.[21] However, such gains were partly offset by a "Lavender Scare" initiated by a congressional subcommittee during the Truman administration. The subcommittee argued that homosexuals were a threat to national security, because their sexual secrets might render them more vulnerable to treason in the Cold War era.[22] Such claims facilitated the elimination of gays and lesbians from employment in the federal government starting in the 1950s and continuing into the mid-1970s. The Lavender Scare also fostered a culture of discretion among same-sex-desiring black Washingtonians that would continue into the late seventies and early eighties. As black gay activist Courtney Williams explains in his oral history interview at the DC Rainbow History Project, being gay "was a nighttime and pastime thing."[23] And although many black lesbians and gay men had relocated to Washington, DC, for economic and cultural opportunities, the majority of the black gay community was from DC. The District of Columbia might have provided a place for

LGBT politics to flourish given its progressive human rights laws, prominent LGBT organizations, and election of LGBT officials to the municipal government, but DC's notoriety as a progressive town also created the conditions of constraint for black gay communities.

These structural failures led to multiple forms of cultural difference and rendered black gay men as a population more vulnerable to death. However, claiming these men as "unjustly" targeted participates in a neoliberal system of valuation that would attribute social value to the "john," as a life worth grieving, at the expense of the "hustler." This binaristic value construction of victims versus perpetrators is evidenced in an August 1981 *Blacklight* editorial written by Sidney Brinkley, which warned that the murders would continue, because "too many Gay men are into hustlers or rough trade." Brinkley labeled "hustlers and rough trade" as "usually dirty, foul-mouthed, under-educated, sexually repressed, emotionally immature and angry." He further espoused that "too many gay men equate these 'qualities' with being a 'real man' and eagerly pay for a few minutes of one-sided sex. Sometimes they pay with their lives."[24] Kwame Holmes notes that by labeling hustlers in this way, Brinkley "reproduces rhetoric popular within urban antiviolence activisms that linked the maladjustments of urban poverty to racialized violence."[25]

Attributing value to the gay male victims not only depends on a pathological and binaristic construction of the hustler as "perpetrator." It also occludes the vulnerabilities of other populations who live under the sign "hustler." This becomes apparent in the January 1982 murder of Ronald Gibson, who was found shot to death "in an area frequented by drag queens who solicit sex for money." According to homicide detective Lloyd Davis, Gibson, also known as "Star," was wearing a dress and high heels at the time of their death.[26] Laying claim to the value of black gay men murdered by hustlers inadvertently participates in the processes of Othering that mark as normative the violence done to drag queen prostitutes like Ronald Gibson/Star. In turn, this devaluation of their death reflects broader social divisions in the emerging black gay cultural landscape in Washington, DC. The previously mentioned "Cliques" article discusses the history of black gay community formation in DC, from private social clubs in the mid- to late 1960s to more public forms of sociality emerging in the mid-1970s and early 1980s, with black gay "cliques" springing up around places like churches, apartment complexes, and neighborhoods. The author notes that even when black gay men had only a few public places to go in the mid-twentieth century, class divisions in DC structured black gay nightlife. Uptown bars like Nob Hill were frequented by middle-class men to the exclusion of patrons of Cozy Corner, a downtown bar "whose clientele consisted of drag queens and others who were considered 'low lifes.'"[27] Transgression of these social and spatial boundaries marked bodies as more vulnerable to violence, and coincided with conservative logics of risk that would attribute blame to victims for their transgression of community-sanctioned bodily, social, and spatial norms. For example, Gibson's/Star's life and death become devalued, not only because they were found wearing women's clothing at the time of their death, but also because their body was found in "an area frequented by drag queens who solicit sex for money," indexing their nonnormative networks and spaces of sociality. Gibson's transgression of bodily, social, *and* spatial norms rendered their life and death as ungrievable.

Scholars such as Lindon Barrett, Lisa Cacho, and Terrion Williamson have discussed in different racial, gendered, sexualized, and geographic contexts how violence is a precondition of value.[28] Extending these concerns about the violence of value to black queer and gender-variant communities allows us to examine how we grieve for the lives of same-sex-desiring and gender-nonconforming black bodies without participating in the structure that would render one as valuable while rendering the Other as expendable. Which populations are deserving of life and which populations are deserving of death? Grace Kyungwon Hong puts it this way: "Insofar as our ability to live protected lives depends on their [vulnerable populations'] inability to do so, a politics that registers vulnerability to death simply as something to be eradicated and sees these deathly subjects as those we have yet to bring into the protection of life merely advances the protection of life that legislates their deaths."[29] Rather than replicate the conditions that create these death-worlds by making life the only site of meaning or possibility, Hong suggests that we might focus on the kinds of "knowledges, modes of being, affects, memories, temporalities, embodiments" that these death-bound populations produce.[30]

Following Hong, I will examine two poems as forms of knowledge produced in and through the deaths of black male johns and black drag-queen prostitutes. These poems produce queer forms of value that index ontological and political possibilities for black queer and gender-variant bodies. Each poem relies on a particular aesthetic strategy—transfiguration or juxtaposition—to lay bare the violence of value, even as these aesthetic strategies gesture toward the imaginative possibilities of (collective) black being that lie outside value. Essex Hemphill's poem "Homocide: For Ronald Gibson" was first published in *Blacklight* magazine in 1983 in response to Gibson's murder. In the poem, Hemphill merges the harsh realities of the drag queen prostitute with the fantasy world of the fairy tale. But rather than a happy ending, Hemphill ends on a note of grief, espousing a form of black/queer optimism that does not disregard the dangers of being "in the life," yet finds in the fairy tale genre ways of expressing an interest in optimism. I will also discuss a poem by the black gay performance group Cinque, of which Hemphill was a member. Cinque's signature piece, "The Brass Rail," is a call-and-response poem that alludes to Brass Rail bar, located in the "hustler section" of DC where many of the men murdered were last seen alive. Through close textual analysis of the poem, and by attending to the intricacies of Cinque's performance, I demonstrate how the poem enacts what L. H. Stallings terms a "communal erotics" that refuses the hierarchies of value that are unevenly distributed across racial, class, gender, sexual, and spatial boundaries.

The Materials of Grief

Black gay poet and activist Essex Hemphill became a central figure in politicizing homophobic violence as a condition of black gay personhood. In an interview with the *Washington Blade*, Hemphill proclaims that murder was at the forefront of his consciousness: "I'm very concerned with murder, particularly in the Gay community. I say in the Gay community because that is how I'm living—and to think I have to continue to run up against the possibility of being murdered or having a bad experience, that preoccupies me."[31] He envisioned his poetic voice as being rooted in a collective black gay imagination, so he strayed from "personal" poems that centered healing of individual trauma. As he explains, "If a poem is too personal, if it's something I need to write only to work it out for myself, then that will disqualify it."[32] Hemphill wrote about murder in much of his poetry, stressing how the threat of violence figured in the black gay imagination. Perhaps his best-known poem about murder is "Homocide: For Ronald Gibson," first published in a 1983 issue of *Blacklight*. In it, he takes as his epigraph the *Washington Blade* crime report on the murder of Ronald Gibson/Star. In the interview mentioned above, Hemphill claims he wrote about Gibson because "it was the loss of a human being. It was destruction."[33]

In the poem, Hemphill revises the cold (and perhaps misgendering) prose of the crime report into poetic form. He fuses the classical Cinderella fairy tale made popular by Charles Perrault in the seventeenth century and Walt Disney in the early twentieth with contemporary references. The drag queen prostitute becomes the Cinderella figure who waits on their "prince to come" in a "silver, six-cylinder chariot." They wear "a wig" and their "sister's high-heeled shoes"—not to go to the Prince's ball, but to "walk the water-front/curbsides" as a prostitute. The speaker of the poem "demand[s] pay/ for [their] kisses" while they "wait for [their] prince to come."[34] In examining the unique narrative modes developed by countercultural fairy tale writers, Jack Zipes argues that by experimenting with the "transfiguration of the classical fairy tale," the author seeks to "break, shift, debunk, or rearrange the traditional motifs to liberate the reader from the contrived and programmed mode of literary reception." He continues, "Transfiguration does not obliterate the recognizable features or values of the classical fairy tale but cancels their negativity by showing how a different aesthetic and social setting relativizes all values."[35] Hemphill invites readers to identify with Gibson/Star through shared desires for a dark prince to come and sweep them off their feet. However, Hemphill's transfiguration does not cancel the negativities of black social life, nor does it relativize all values. By juxtaposing the Cinderella tale to the contemporary cultural landscape of black drag-queen prostitutes in Washington, DC, he shows how racial, gender, sexual, and class norms undergird the Cinderella fairy tale's logics. As given by a poor, black, gender-nonconforming person, Gibson's/Star's narrative exposes the need to make one's living as preceding and subtending the quest for romance. And it further reveals this quest for romance as a means of social and economic mobility through the heterosexual marriage plot. Because of their gender nonconformity, Gibson/Star is excluded from the heteropatriarchal political economy of marriage and family, and street prostitution becomes their means of survival while they "wait" for [their] prince to come." Yet Star's race, gender, and class location mean that they lack the protections of domesticity and privacy that even Cinderella is afforded. Gibson's/Star's socioeconomic location, and their engagement in the pleasures and dangers of being "in the life," ultimately usher them toward premature death.

The poem opens and closes with emotions of grief.

> Grief is not apparel.
> Not like a dress, a wig
> or my sister's high-heeled shoes.
>
> (1–3)
>
> . . . .
>
> But grief is darker.
> It is a white dress
> that covers my body.
> It is a wig

that does not rest gently
on my head.

(31–35)

That grief is and is not apparel alludes to the contradictions of mediating antiblack or antiqueer violent crimes through LGBT and mainstream media. While the quest for media visibility is significant for creating the multiple publics around these issues, the focus on the victims' brutal deaths and "risky" sexual activities can serve to efface their complex subjectivity and thus their value as lost lives worthy of public grief. This is further supported by the fact that the metaphor of grief revolves around articles of consumption. Readers might simply consume these stories through existing narratives of individual pathology, and miss the structural issues undergirding the tragedies. These materials—the dress, wig, and shoes—are also essential to the construction of racialized genders and sexualities, especially for the racialized poor who depend on sex work for their everyday survival. Given that the subject of the poem is a black drag-queen prostitute, narratives of black cultural pathology—particularly narratives of black gender and sexual deviance—signal why the wig does not rest easy on her/his head.[36] By stating that grief *is and is not* apparel, Hemphill captures how multiply determined subjects—subjects produced within the contradictions of state and capital—provide a more complex framework for theorizing violence. The contradictions indicated in his metaphor of grief imply that Gibson's/Star's murder problematizes any easy categorization of the identities of those subject to antiqueer or antiblack violence. Rather, race, class, gender, and sexuality converge in the production of urban violence.

Eric Stanley argues that the logic of the racialized gaze is useful to our understandings of antiqueer violence, because it begs the question of how only certain bodies become intelligible as queer, and how the gaze functions to correctly levy violence against queers.

> After all, the racialized phenomenology of blackness under colonization that Fanon illustrates may be productive to read against and with a continuum of antiqueer violence . . . I ask why antiqueer violence, more often than not, is correctly levied against queers. In other words, the productive discourse that wishes to suggest that queer bodies are no different might miss moments of signification where queer bodies do in fact signify differently.[37]

Stanley demonstrates how the race analogy in LGBT politics might be productive in our understanding of antiqueer violence. Those opposed to the

race analogy often assert that nonheterosexual bodies are not visible as minorities. But Stanley believes that this argument misses how certain bodies
do signify gender and sexual difference. Hemphill's poem reveals the racialized logics that undergird acts of antiqueer violence through his image of
grief as apparel. Through the logics of the racialized gaze, Gibson's/Star's
apparel signifies difference, and marks exclusion from normative categories
of race, class, gender, and sexuality. Star's failure to signify "realness" within
a racialized and gendered field of vision marks their apparel as a site of social
and corporeal death, multiply marking Gibson's/Star's body as disposable
under the structures of antiblackness and antiqueerness.[38]

However, Hemphill's subversion of the Cinderella fairy tale gestures
toward an alternative imagining of Star's/Ronald Gibson's life. He ends the
poem with the lines "But grief is darker. / It is a white dress / that covers my
body. / It is a wig / that does not rest gently / on my head." Discussing Lynn
Nottage's extravagant attention to intimate apparel in stage directions and
dress in her play *Intimate Apparel*, L. H. Stallings argues that lingerie does not
simply accessorize the body, but also "provides a way to become a thing that
feels": "In the same way that [Ntozake] Shange utilized dance and poetry
to convey sensory experiences that were different from the visual in theater,
Nottage relies upon clothing, apparel, and fabric to do the same."[39] Stallings focuses on hapticality as a mode of producing pleasure in excess of the
death-dealing visual epistemes that constitute black women's vulnerabilities
in an antiblack and sexist world. Drawing from the work of Fred Moten
and Stefano Harney, Stallings notes, "The play's representation of sex work
begins and ends with hapticality and the undercommons's deregulation,
consciously and unconsciously, of that feeling."[40] Similarly, "Homocide:
For Ronald Gibson" begins and ends with the apparel to reimagine Ronald
Gibson as "Star," as a "thing that feels." Star's thingness signals how the
antiblack and gender-normative visual economy renders Gibson/Star more
vulnerable to death, and renders that death as ungrievable. But transfiguring
Star as the protagonist of a fairy tale centralizes expressions of desire, indexing how the erotic operates as a mode of expressing individual and collective
longings for alternative modes of black being. Hemphill subverts the fairy
tale narrative that relies on a male savior by privileging self-affirmation:
"While I wait, I'm the only man who loves me." Here the apparel becomes
resignified as a site of self-making, and as a site of pleasure that comes with
gender subversion and fulfilling the desires of the men that Star meets. By
centering Star/Gibson as the protagonist of the Cinderella tale, Hemphill
does not avoid the fatal risk of being "in the life," but the possibility of a
happy ending embedded in the fairy tale genre evinces an interest of opti-

mism.[41] Michael Snediker argues that "queer optimism . . . is not promissory. It doesn't ask that some future time make good on its own hopes. Rather, queer optimism asks that optimism embedded in its own present, be *interesting*."[42] Transfiguring Gibson/Star as a "thing that feels" acknowledges the forces of antiblackness and antiqueerness that doubly mark their body as disposable flesh, but Hemphill's deployment of the fairy tale genre indexes a trace of queer optimism in the black gay cultural imagination.

The Brass Rail

In 1983, musicians Larry Duckette and Wayson Jones joined Essex Hemphill to form the performance group Cinque (fig. 1). The group's name derives from Joseph Cinqué (Sengbe Pieh), the enslaved African who led a revolt of fellow slaves on the Spanish slave ship *La Amistad*. Cinque went through many permutations, and at one time included black gay artist Christopher Prince, black lesbian filmmaker and poet Michelle Parkerson, and Annette "Chi" Hughes, cofounder of the black lesbian activist group Sapphire Sapphos. The group performed in various clubs, theaters, bars, cafés, and outdoor venues in Washington, DC, Philadelphia, New York City, and Los Angeles. It held its first performance at dc space, a private, underground performance venue that featured musicians such as Cassandra Wilson, Sun Ra, and Laurie Anderson; various bands performing jazz, pop, and reggae; and nightly dinner theatre that subsidized these performances. Cinque also performed at the Enik Alley Coffeehouse, a salon hosted by Ray Melrose, which served as the cultural hub for the renaissance of black lesbian and gay arts in DC in the 1980s.[43] The group mostly staged multimedia performances that included a mix of visual elements (projected slides and minimal sets), poetry, music, and choreography. But it was its intricate vocal arrangements of poetry, mainly the work of Wayson Jones, that became the signature feature of the group's performances.

When I asked Jones to describe Cinque's performance style, he immediately referenced the group's signature piece, "The Brass Rail."[44] The piece was so memorable to black lesbian, gay, and bisexual communities that it was mentioned in several memorial tributes to Essex Hemphill on the important and long-running Gay, Lesbian, and Bisexual People of Color email listserv.[45] The Brass Rail was one of Washington, DC's oldest gay bars, serving clientele in that city's red-light district since the 1960s. In his essay "Without Comment," Hemphill described it as "the raunchy Black gay club" that "was bulging out of its jockstrap. Drag queens ruled, B-boys chased giddy government workers, fast-talking hustlers worked the floor, while

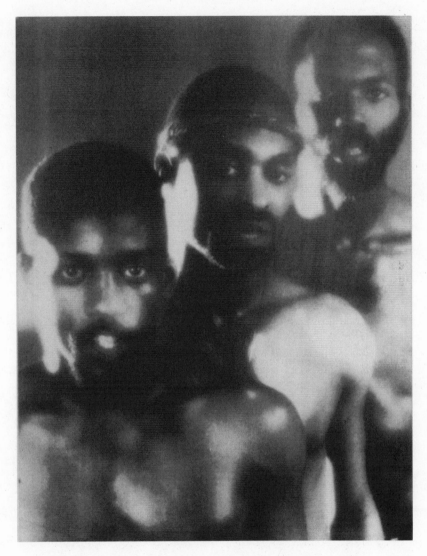

Figure 1. Cinque: Essex Hemphill, Larry Duckette, and Wayson Jones.
Photo courtesy of Sharon Farmer. © Sharon Farmer/SFphotoworks@att.net.

sugar daddies panted for attention in the shadows, offering free drinks and money to any friendly trade."[46] Many black gay middle-class men considered Brass Rail "dangerous" and "raunchy" because of its location and because it was frequented by hustlers and drag queens. In my interview with Jones, he described the bar as having "the best house music in the city." Though Jones was well aware that black gay middle-class men labeled Brass

Rail a "low-class environment," he and his friends attended "fairly often." Jones had grown up in a military family in the DC suburbs, and because the bar was hidden away among the industrial spaces of the red-light district, frequenting it brought a "sense of excitement" and an "outlaw feeling."[47]

Jones remembered the poem "The Brass Rail" as a response to the "string of trick murders" of gay men who would pick up a hustler in or around the bar, and "would be found [dead] the next day or week." He recalled that the poem was not so much about the murders as about their "milieu."[48] I have reproduced the entire poem here, because it is unpublished, and because it is necessary for the reader to see how the words are dispersed and stylized on the page.

CALL I saw you last night
RESPONSE Many occupants are never found.
CALL in the basement
RESPONSE Many canoes overturn.
CALL of the Brass Rail.
RESPONSE Your dark diva's face, a lake
CALL Lushing and laughing.
RESPONSE screaming behind your eyes.
CALL Dancing with the boys on the edge of funk.
RESPONSE Twilight.
CALL The boys dance, darling,
RESPONSE My tongue
CALL touching you indiscreetly.
RESPONSE walks along your thighs like a hermit.
CALL Your body a green light
RESPONSE I have been naked with you.
CALL urging them
RESPONSE Dear Diva, Darling:
CALL You were in the mirrors, the light. Their arms.
RESPONSE The boys whispered about you
CALL   singapore slings toasted you.
RESPONSE under the music pumping from the jukebox.
CALL They were promises chilled by ice cubes.
RESPONSE They were promises chilled by ice cubes.
CALL The boys whispered about you.
RESPONSE The sloe gin fizzes
CALL under the music pumping from the jukebox.
RESPONSE   singapore slings toasted you.

CALL You were in the mirrors, the light. Their arms.
RESPONSE Your body a green light
CALL Dear Diva, Darling:
RESPONSE The boys danced, darling
CALL I have been naked with you.
RESPONSE touching you indiscreetly.
CALL My tongue has walked along your thighs
RESPONSE Dancing on the edge of funk.
CALL I have found the scent. Twilight.
RESPONSE Your voice falling from the air.
CALL I hear the sea screaming behind your eyes.
RESPONSE Lushing and laughing.
CALL Your dark diva's face,
RESPONSE I saw you last night
CALL a lake.
RESPONSE in the basement
CALL Many canoes overturn.
RESPONSE of the Brass Rail
CALL Many occupants are never found.

As Cinque's signature piece, "The Brass Rail" exemplified the group's in-novative vocal arrangements, which it called "choral poetry." Cinque em-phasized the spoken voice as an instrument, and used pitch, inflection, and synchrony of vocal sound and movement to emphasize the musicality of the poem. According to Jones, the poem is arranged for two voices. One voice starts at the beginning of the poem and the other voice starts at its end, the latter reading backwards, creating a sonic aesthetic of juxtaposition. As the voices reach the middle of the poem, they cross each other, and overlap at the line "They were promises chilled by ice cubes."[49] Tempo and volume were significant to the performance; after the voices overlap, the tempo of the poem accelerates, the calls and responses interrupt each other, and the voices reach a crescendo. As the poem continues, the tempo slows and the calls and responses finally resume their distinctiveness at the last line, "Many occupants are never found."[50]

The poem also employs the call-and-response style of communication rooted in black religious traditions. Geneva Smitherman defines *call and response* as "spontaneous verbal and non-verbal interaction between speaker and listener in which all the speaker's statements (calls) are punctuated by expressions (responses) from the listener."[51] Drawing from Smitherman's work, Jan Cohen-Cruz translates "call and response" into "engaged performance," or performance that "foregrounds the many opportunities for interactivity between a theatre artist and the people involved in the situation in question."[52] Cohen-Cruz further notes the political and spiritual implications of "engaged performance."

> The "call-and-response" dynamic of engaged arts brings a community together for both political and spiritual reasons. Political because it provides a way for a group of any status to participate in a public discourse about issues that affect their lives; spiritual because a purpose is embedded in the process and goal of such work that goes beyond material results and day-to-day existence. Both the political and the spiritual provide models of how we live together, suggesting something bigger than our individual selves.[53]

Through engaged performance, Cinque situates the threat of death within the context of the "communal erotics" of the club space to move "beyond material results and day-to-day existence" toward "something bigger than [their] individual selves."

The poem begins with the lines "I saw you last night / in the basement / of the Brass Rail. / Lushing and laughing. / Dancing with the boys on the edge of funk." The speaker of the poem, who is always multiple—both omniscient narrator and a part of the desiring crowd—positions the hustler within the erratic movement of bodies in the Brass Rail bar, constructing an orgiastic site of the senses where sight, touch, taste, sound, and smell all commingle to produce a feeling of erotic ecstasy.

CALL: I have been naked with you. / My tongue has walked along your thighs / I have found the scent. Twilight.
RESPONSE: The boys danced, darling / touching you indiscreetly. / Dancing on the edge of funk.

In her examination of sexuality as a site of memory, L. H. Stallings explores how the multisensory spaces of "communal erotics" can be transformative to black political struggles: "The communal erotic gaze . . . enact[s] an interior ocularity that reorganizes the senses to detect sacred energies of others in relation to self so as to produce a new metaphysics of political struggle, rather than a movement that will simply mediate sex through a public sphere created and maintained by the authors of sex as knowledge, terror, violence."[54] She examines how the West's privileging of visual economies has foreclosed possibilities for black women to remember sexuality as a site of memory, and how spaces of communal eroticism and ecstasy might provide "interclass and androgynous contact very different from uplift work of past generations."[55] While male privilege has provided black gay men with many more spaces for public sexual leisure, the threat of violence during the late 1970s and early 1980s in Washington, DC—in the form of racialized bar discrimination, street violence targeting gay men and drag queens, and the racial, gendered, and sexual exclusions of the political economy—facilitated discreet sexual publics divided along the lines of race, class, and gender. With its mix of drag queens, B-boys, government workers, hustlers, and sugar daddies, the Brass Rail bar provided one such space of "interclass and androgynous contact" that might facilitate "life opportunities."[56] But the poem suggests that someone can enter this space only at the risk of his life. The threat of violence and death always lurks just behind the eyes of the hustler, as alluded to in the lines "sea screaming behind your eyes," wherein "Many canoes overturn. / Many occupants are never found." In the poem, the threat of violence haunts "the communal erotic gaze" that might "produce a new metaphysics of political struggle."

How do we hold on to the Brass Rail as an important site of sexual memory for black gay men while remembering the deaths of those murdered by "tricks" that they met there? To answer this question, we must avoid assigning value to the lives of these men through the same racial, gender, class, sexual, and spatial logics that disciplined their subjectivities while they were alive.[57] These same logics govern the spatialized arrangement of Washington, DC, marking the hustler district as a zone of death, and community-sanctioned spaces (home, class-based cliques, and work) as spaces of safety. The fact that many of the men invited hustlers into their homes, that some were found dead at work, or that the social vulnerabilities and class politics of "cliques" prevented them from lodging a public outcry after these men's deaths troubles the distinctions between the spaces of safety and the zones of death. These normative logics coincide with an uneven distribution of value accorded to bodies and spaces at the expense of "other" bodies and spaces. And while public memorial practices remain significant as alternative sites for meaning-making for the loved ones and communities of the devalued dead, the work of public memory can disrupt normative systems of value only temporarily, if they disrupt them at all. By reimagining "The Brass Rail" as a site of ecstasy and fear, of communal eroticism and the shared threat of terror, of life opportunity and the threat of death, across boundaries of class, race, gender—Cinque gestures toward "a space that is wholly beyond the rubrics of exchange that would consign [black queer and gender-variant bodies] either to the realm of the valued or to the realm of the devalued."[58]

But as engaged performance, Cinque forges communal politics that make intelligible the forces devaluing black queer and gender-variant lives. As choral poetry, its sonic arrangements and improvisation of the call-and-response form trouble the fixity of signs like race, gender, class, and sexuality that ascribe value to bodies and spaces. As Lindon Barrett argues, "The sign is iteration; iteration is closure; closure is power; and the singing voice, for the diasporic African, undoes all three in which iteration, closure, and power belie her or his presence." For Barrett, the singing voice disrupts existing sign systems because it emphasizes the "infinitude of 'unmeaning' that presupposes and inaugurates signification."[59] For the devalued dead, or rather the dead who create the conditions of value for the living, the singing voice reveals the socioeconomic and cultural conditions that mark their devaluation. The performers' voices overlap at the line "They were promises chilled by ice cubes," a reference to the various alcoholic drinks like the "sloe gin fizzes" and "Singapore slings" that appear in the poem. The image of the alcoholic beverage becomes a dense transfer point—both of power that indexes alcohol as stimulant for erotic ecstasy and of the desiring subject's impending demise signaled by "promises chilled by ice cubes." The clash of voices is resolved in the final line, "Many occupants are never found." This resolution gestures toward the subjective possibilities that inhere in the space of absence—on the outside of value—while expressing the collective sense of grief that attends processes of racialization and sexualization. The musicality of Cinque's performance, and its failure to adhere to the generic boundaries of call and response, mark its members' refusal to lay claim to the systems of valuation that deem their dead as devalued in the first place. But the performers' synchronicity and resolution sound communal politics that make those systems of (de)valuation intelligible to the audiences they are engaging.[60]

Black gay cultural discourse in the late 1970s and early 1980s begs a rethinking of grief as affective politics that must be understood in relation to social modes of (de)valuation. Even though black cultural discourse offers an alternative mode of valuing black bodies under white supremacist regimes that do not recognize black suffering, these other modes of value are also distributed unevenly according to racial, class, gender, sexual, and spatial hierarchies. Black gay literature and culture confront the violence of value by gesturing toward the possibilities of black gay being that lie outside value and by expressing an interest in optimism, a time and space in which black gay being is not structured by the violent forces of antiblackness and antiqueerness. But while gesturing toward these possibilities of being, black gay literature refuses to distance itself from blackness and queerness, or from the death-dealing visual epistemes that circumscribe them. Instead, black gay literature and culture gesture toward new possibilities of being while exposing the contradictions of grief—how grief becomes a mode of valuation that inadvertently devalues "Others," thereby rendering "other" lives as disposable and other deaths as ungrievable. Through its aesthetic strategies of transfiguration and juxtaposition, black gay literature reveals the entanglements of grief with the violence of value, even as its poetics of grief point to an elsewhere in which black gay personhood is not conditioned by value.

TWO

Loneliness

Black Gay Longing in the Work of Essex Hemphill

> *Do you think I could walk pleasantly*
> *and well suited toward annihilation?*
> with a scrotal sack full of primordial loneliness
> swinging between my legs
> like solid bells?
>
> —Essex Hemphill, "Heavy Breathing"

Essex Hemphill, a black gay poet, essayist, and performer, was one of the most prominent of the black gay intellectuals of the 1980s and early 1990s. His work addresses the psychological, social, and political struggles of urban black communities, and often maps the psychological, social, and political location of black gay men onto the black urban landscape. In "Heavy Breathing," first published in 1988 in the journal *89 Cents*, Hemphill takes the reader on a bus ride through the black Washington, DC, of the 1980s.[1] The speaker of the poem rides the "X2, the bus I call a slave ship," with the "majority of its riders Black." He defines the X2 as a "risky ride," with its "cargo of block boys, urban pirates." The imagery of the city bus as "a slave ship" and the riders as "cargo" conjures the historical trauma of the Middle Passage, suggesting continuity between the social death of antebellum slavery and the urban poverty and decay produced by neoliberal capitalism. The speaker goes on to describe the spectacular forms of violence that emerged in DC, as the line "the funerals of my brothers" partly alludes to how the widespread distribution and consumption of crack greatly impacted crime in cities like DC, whose homicide rate grew so high that the city eventually became known as the murder capital.[2] But the speaker attends these funerals only "at the end of heavy breathing," signaling the climax of public sexual encounters with other men. It is in this same black urban environment that he negotiates the dangers and pleasures of same-sex desire. Read within this context, the speaker's "brothers" are also his same-sex-desiring brothers, and the "funerals" are also for those who have succumbed to homophobic violence and AIDS.

A range of black cultural studies scholars, most notably Frank Wilderson and Jared Sexton, have also theorized continuity between antebellum slavery and contemporary blackness.[3] Drawing from Orlando Patterson's conceptualization of antebellum slavery as "social death" and Saidiya Hartman's conception of "slavery's afterlife," these theorists point out the specificity and ubiquity of antiblackness obscured by hegemonic discourses of multiculturalism and colorblindness in the late twentieth and twenty-first centuries.[4] Furthermore, Sexton defines the lived experience of blackness as a "social life of social death," and expresses a political refusal to distance himself from blackness "in a valorization of minor differences that bring one closer to health, life, or sociality."[5] But these theories have yet to fully account for gender and sexual difference, for the queer "brothers" of Hemphill's poem who also negotiate their lives under the sign of blackness. In Wilderson's formulation, queerness, as a "human" ontological category, depends on the non-ontology of blackness for its coherence; consequently, the gratuitous violence done to black queer and transgender people is subsumed under the structures of antiblackness. But Afro-pessimist theories fail to address how nonnormative black genders and sexualities visually signify their difference, and how these so-called minor differences oftentimes bring black gender and sexual minorities *closer to* illness, death, and social exclusion under regimes of antiblackness.

In Hemphill's poem, the line "the funerals of my brothers" brings forth the ghostly presence of 1980s and 1990s black gay intellectuals within contemporary theorizations of blackness fixed as pathology, and as embodied subjectivity marked by (social) death. In addition to the racial retrenchment affecting urban black communities during the Reagan era, black gay artists, intellectuals, and activists in the eighties and nineties also experienced amplified cultural stigma attached to homosexuality during the AIDS epidemic. Many of them carried in their bodies the literal pathology of AIDS, and a consciousness shaped as much by everyday black life as it was by black (social) death. Though the literary communities that they formed could neither prevent their deaths nor alleviate the debilitating psychic and social effects of state violence and cultural stigma during that time, their works live on as underexamined bodies of social thought and cultural criticism. Taking Hemphill as a representative of this movement, I suggest that the urgency of the cultural work produced by black gay intellectuals in the age of AIDS, the race against time to produce art and theory, merits putting this work in conversation with recent theories of racial blackness lived in/as social death. This chapter will trace constructions of loneliness in Hemphill's work as a traumatic feeling associated with the lived experience of black gay historical trauma in the 1980s and 1990s, and also as evidence of black gay men's collective political longings for better health, life, and sociality for future generations of black/queer people.

In the epigraph that opens this chapter, Hemphill locates a "primordial loneliness" in the "scrotal sack," suggesting the (re)production of alienation and isolation that might attend the experience of social death. Yet he positions "loneliness" against "annihilation," and locating "loneliness" in the "scrotal sack" might alternatively gesture toward its (re)productive potential. Hemphill's image of the "scrotal sack" suggests an engagement with the sexualized processes of racial Othering described by Frantz Fanon. Fanon argues that Western imperial visual logics have turned the black man into "a penis." He also references "scores of Negroes hanged by their testicles," alluding to the history of lynching, and the attendant sexualized violence of castration.[6] By centering the image of the scrotal sack—that which must be severed from the black male body to reduce the imagined sexual and economic threats that black males pose to white supremacy—Hemphill points to the oblique position of black gay men as inheritors of the legacy of antiblack violence. The scrotal sack, a contradictory symbol of both heterosexual reproduction and the commodification of blackness, operates as a site of rupture for Hemphill, as his nonprocreative desires render him as both inside and outside the legacies of sexualized domination that structure black cultural memory. Gay identification and positive serostatus relegate black gay men beyond the "boundaries of blackness," but the disproportionate impact of AIDS situates these men within a historical legacy of black defeat that has been actualized through the domination of black sexuality.[7] That the scrotal sack hangs like "solid bells" suggests nonfunctionality, indexing how processes of "secondary marginalization" render black gay men's suffering as beyond the pale of recognition as antiblackness, and how those processes prevent them from registering even a "sonic of dissent"—audible expressions which black performance scholars have deemed as articulations of subjectivity and a "freedom drive" in the face of black fungibility.[8]

By positioning "loneliness" against "annihilation," Hemphill suggests that loneliness is a collective political feeling. The "primordial loneliness" located in the scrotal sack indexes a "structure of feeling" *between* black gay men who lack a grammar of suffering and a sonic of dissent but who sense,

in their vulnerability to illness and death, an inheritance of a legacy of sexualized antiblack violence.[9] Hemphill's expressions of loneliness capture
black gay men's collective political longings for futures beyond the forces of
antiblackness and antiqueerness that have doubly marked their bodies for
(social) death. In so doing, he advances a vision of collectivity and futurity
inconsonant with not only Afro-pessimist thought but also the queer antisocial thesis advanced most prominently by theorists Leo Bersani and Lee
Edelman. The antisocial thesis in queer theory, which emerged as a response
to the AIDS epidemic, positions queerness as "the social order's death
drive," opposing hegemonic conceptions of the political organized around
"reproductive futurism."[10] In its rejection of futures based in institutionalized forms of relationality, antisocial queer theory shares an affinity with
the Afro-pessimist theories advanced by Wilderson and Sexton.[11] Though
Afro-pessimism and antisocial queer theory remain incommensurate, they
both figure black queerness as a site of social death.[12] Reading Hemphill's
loneliness for its (re)productive potential signals my critical ambivalence
toward such negative theorizations of black queerness.

Because Essex Hemphill invokes loneliness in myriad ways throughout
his work—it is a politics, a style, a feeling, and a social relation—my invo-
cation of the term is necessarily elastic. As a form of negative affect, loneliness shores up the alienation, isolation, and pathologization of black gay
men during the 1980s and early 1990s. But loneliness is also a form of
bodily desire, a yearning for an attachment to the social and for a future
beyond the forces that create someone's alienation and isolation.[13] Therefore, this chapter theorizes loneliness as black gay longing to demonstrate
how the queerness of blackness is located, not only in histories of racial
and sexual violence that continue to fix blackness as a site of social death
and pathology, but also in black literary and cultural imaginings of futures
beyond the forces of antiblackness.

In what follows, I first elucidate what Hemphill identifies as a "functioning self," an articulation of racial and sexual selfhood that rejects black
liberationist psychologists' constructions of black gay psychic damage at the
same time that it acknowledges the psychic damages accrued from living
as a racial and sexual minority in the age of AIDS. I closely read Hemphill's elegies to Joseph Beam, a black gay writer and activist who was his
contemporary and who died in silence of AIDS while fighting to end the
silence around gay men's lives. I focus on Beam's death to demonstrate how
black gay political longing exceeds the body's undoing, and lives on in the
published works of black gay intellectuals. I then analyze a speech given
by Hemphill at a gay writers' conference to illustrate how his public dis-

play of emotion documents the traumatic yet largely unremarked impact of AIDS on black gay men in LGBT and queer studies scholarship, while it also archives the present absence of AIDS within larger discourses of anti-black violence. Finally, I show how Hemphill's poetry embodies black gay men's collective longing for black family and community, and their yearning for forms of intimacy outside the pathology that the black racial family embodies.

Writing the "Functioning Self"

In a 1994 interview with Don Belton, Hemphill prompts us to contemplate the subjectivities of black gay men during the 1980s, and to think differently about risk. He shares with Belton his belief that the "dangerous places black gay men are often willing to go in the name of love or desire" prepare them for radical social action.[14] He insinuates that the pleasures and dangers associated with gay cruising and public sex would prepare black gay men to intervene in a space as hostile as Louis Farrakhan's 1995 Million Man March.[15] Even though the dangers of public sex might have prepared black gay men for the possible physical dangers of activism in hostile environments, the multiple fronts on which these men were fighting for racial and sexual freedom must have taken a psychic toll.

In her study of emotion in AIDS activism, sociologist Deborah Gould discusses the affective states of gay and lesbian communities in the 1980s: "In the early years of the AIDS crisis, affective states circulating in lesbian and gay communities—including what in retrospect I would call gay shame, a corollary fear of intensified social rejection, and frustrated desire for some sort of reciprocal recognition—had tremendous political import."[16] Because black gay and lesbian, as well as bisexual and transgender, communities experienced "intensified social rejection" as racial minorities, their cultural specificity warrants further thinking about the "affective states" that were important to black gay cultural activism.

Heather Love offers a framework for theorizing loneliness as a structure of black gay feeling. In her examination of Radclyffe Hall's *The Well of Loneliness*, Love argues, "In her portrait of Stephen's 'loneliness' Hall offers us a portrait of a complex and historically specific structure of feeling." Because of Stephen Gordon's extreme visibility in the novel, loneliness is less structured by the epistemology of the closet, and becomes a matter of ontology: "Loneliness afflicts Stephen's being; it is deeply inscribed in her body." But loneliness, Love argues, also "describes a condition of singularity, of oc-

cupying an unprecedented and uncharted place in the order of creation."
This is also true for Hemphill and others who felt that their unprecedented
public visibility as black gay men was deeply inscribed in their bodies
and psyches. Like Stephen Gordon, for whom the scientific discourses of
inversion were "sedimented in both the psyche and the body," Hemphill
and others negotiated (scientific) discourses of race, homosexuality, and
HIV/AIDS as embodied experience.[17] Foregrounding black people's failed
claims to personhood, however, requires consideration of how Hemphill
and his contemporaries failed to signify as proper subjects in any of these
categories. In their attempt to articulate black gay male politics, Hemphill
and his contemporaries exist in the "'not-yet-space' of the unimaginable
subject" that is "far from existing in a space of knowability and coherent
identity."[18] Loneliness serves as a proxy for a felt sense of black gay embodiment as uncharted terrain in the 1980s.

Loneliness also expresses a shared sense of being, marked by suffering
without public recognition. Life during the 1980s, particularly in urban environments like Washington, DC, created the literal experience and feelings
of abandonment for black gay men. They were disproportionately affected
by the AIDS epidemic and urban violence, causing them to lose loved ones
and friends en masse. Many black gay men returned home after being rejected by white gay communities, only to be rejected within black communities as well. Sexual discrimination by potential lovers who feared infection
also proved to be a potential source of loneliness. Situating black gay men's
experiences of trauma and loss as stemming from a lack of state protection, the absence of community and familial advocacy and support, and
institutionalized sexual discrimination marks their loneliness as psychic and
social, individual and collective.[19]

Essex Hemphill's expressions of loneliness expand our perspective of
black queer bodies from their association with risk and abjection to include
their passions and longings, and the role of the erotic in black queer politics. Roderick Ferguson proposes that we rethink Audre Lorde's deployment
of the erotic "as a social practice and a technique of the self." Ferguson
locates Lorde's work within a transnational conversation about sexuality
post-1960s that saw sexuality as a site of knowledge. He argues that Lorde's
work "ask[s] us to reengage the post-1960s world as one in which various
movements attempted to rehabilitate sexuality as material for social practice and as a fuel for intellectual production."[20] Hemphill similarly deploys
loneliness as bodily desire to reveal how both erotic fulfillment and sexualized state violence were produced by and inseparable from the global

economic and social transformations occurring during the 1980s. These transformations disproportionately affected urban black people, and produced an even more heightened vulnerability for urban black queer bodies like Hemphill's.

Hemphill understood that his sexuality was formed in and through the urban black communities that he envisioned as the beneficiaries of his work and activism. When asked by journalist Chuck Tarver about debates in black gay communities concerning the need to distinguish between "Black gay men" and "gay Black men," Hemphill responds, "I love my race enough to know that I'm a Black man first and foremost and that my sexuality falls in line after that."[21] His privileging of his racial identity must be understood within the context of the hegemonic black political discourse in the post–civil rights era, which constructed homosexuality as a force of white supremacist domination. This discourse legitimated the marginalization of black gays and lesbians within black culture and politics, and forced many black gay men to live in silence about their same-sex desires in order to belong within their families and communities. In light of the silencing many self-identified black gay men experienced within black communities, Hemphill claimed that the most important aspect of his cultural work was the creation of a "functioning self."

> I would discover that homo sex did not constitute a whole life nor did it negate my racial identity or constitute a substantive reason to be estranged from my family and Black culture. I discovered, too, that the work ahead for me included, most importantly, being able to integrate all of my identities into a functioning self, instead of accepting a dysfunctional existence as the consequence of my homosexual desires.[22]

In this quote, Hemphill is responding to the claims of Frances Cress Welsing, a DC-based black liberation psychiatrist, that black male sexual diversity was a psychological maladaptation to racist oppression, which produced a crisis of survival for the black racial family. Welsing argues that black men, who are frustrated by their failure to meet their true masculine potential under white supremacy, engage in dysfunctional, unsatisfying, obsessive-compulsive patterns in areas like sex, in which they have greater freedom of expression.[23] In his 1991 essay, "If Freud Had Been a Neurotic Colored Woman," Hemphill argues that by couching her homophobia within the discourse of black liberation, Welsing ultimately calls for the eradication of black gays and lesbians.[24]

Hemphill's quest to "integrate all of [his] identities into a functioning self" should be understood as his imperative to publicly resist narratives of psychopathology mapped onto the psyche of the black gay male, on which the black nationalist's quest for healthy black psychology depended. It should also be understood as rooted in his lived experience, as an attempt to "function" despite the social effects of racism and homophobia and the threat of death accrued from being a black gay male in the US racial state. Given this context, Hemphill's "functioning self" must be read in relation to a "dysfunctional existence"—or the forces that render urban black/gay life in Washington, DC, in the 1980s as "dysfunctional," as a social life of social death. Hemphill negotiates the processes of black gay self-making in and through the deplorable structural conditions that undergirded black/gay social life in that time and place. His "functioning self" should then be understood as acknowledging past racial and sexual injuries and pointing to a precarious future. His "functioning self" rejects immobilizing narratives of psychopathology that would prevent his movement toward life, but it does not deny the deleterious psychic and social effects of his lived experience as a black gay man infected with AIDS in a black urban space overdetermined by discourses of deviance and criminality.

Hemphill's attempt to write the "functioning self" is better illuminated in his poem "Heavy Corners." The 1986 version of this poem contained the dedication "To Joseph Beam and I," written for Beam, his contemporary and friend. Robert Reid-Pharr suggests that rather than a clumsy mistake, Hemphill's use of *I* here rather than the grammatically correct *me* marks his "effort to disrupt the distinction between the poet and the community/communiality that he represents," and "make visible those human connections that have been obscured or denied."[25] Hemphill is stressing that the speaking subject of the poem is collectively imagined.

Through this poem's reference to the emotional "heavy[ness]" of street "corners," Hemphill again maps the contradictions of black gay men's psychological and sociological location onto the black urban landscape, attesting to the interplay between his "functioning self" and "dysfunctional existence." The theme of war in the poem alludes to both the state's warfare on urban black communities and gay men in the Reagan era, and the communities' resistance to social and psychic forces that produce black urban isolation and the devastating impact of HIV/AIDS in black gay communities. Hemphill focuses on the increased psychic and social vulnerability of black men in general, and black gay men in particular, within this historical context.

Don't let it be loneliness
that kills us.
If we must die
on the front line
let us die men
loved by both sexes.

The "us" implies that "loneliness" is a collective feeling for black gay men. Hemphill imagines loneliness as genocidal, having the propensity to "[kill] us," and links the feeling back to, at least in part, the logics of black liberation espoused by Welsing. Loneliness is also experienced "on the front line." The militant imagery of the poem is juxtaposed to feelings that are deemed expressions of vulnerability. Hemphill signifies on Harlem Renaissance writer Claude McKay's poem "If We Must Die," which begins, "If we must die—let it not be like hogs." Marcellus Blount describes McKay's poem as a "bold statement of masculine, racial strategy" and "the first attempt to represent a collective Afro-American self within the tender boundaries of the sonnet."[26] McKay's sonnet provides precedence for Hemphill's writing the "functioning self"; and the juxtaposition of the masculine, collective militancy of the poem's rhetoric to the tender, individualistic form of the sonnet points to why Hemphill may have signified on this poem to address his contemporary experiences of racialized and sexualized state violence. His black gay poetics do not deny the vulnerability of the black gay body and psyche, nor do they allow this vulnerability to impede his articulation of a racial and sexual self. They convey both the debilitating psychic and social effects of violence directed toward black gay men in the eighties, and how black gay expressive culture operates as a collective strategy against state-based and intraracial violence. Writing, as an act of ending the silence around black queer lives, of creation, of living in the face of and beyond (social) death, becomes the ultimate act of creation of Hemphill's "functioning self."

Lonely in the Midst of the Movement

Joseph Beam, a Philadelphia-based black gay activist, died two years after the 1986 release of his best-selling anthology, *In the Life*. His success at publishing an unprecedented collection of black gay literature marked him as the leader of a burgeoning black gay arts movement. He also had been an accomplished journalist, publishing a biweekly record review and feature articles for the *Philadelphia Gay News* and several articles for *Blacklight* magazine. He eventually became the editor of *Black/Out*, the news publication for the National Coalition of Black Lesbians and Gays. In addition, Beam was a community activist, and was especially active in movements for prison abolition, given the disproportionate numbers of black people incarcerated during the War on Drugs.[27]

Beam began writing to prisoners in 1979, most likely inspired by the nationally circulating lesbian- and gay-themed newspaper *Gay Community News*, and its Prisoner Project, which began corresponding with and advocating for the rights of incarcerated lesbian and gays in 1975. Beam maintained his most sustained correspondence with Percy "Ombaka" Tate, a black man incarcerated in the Louisiana State Penitentiary, who was working on an anthology of prison writing. Ombaka first wrote to Beam after discovering a letter Beam had written to another prisoner, whose cell Ombaka had recently moved into. Their three-year correspondence was sustained by their shared identification as writers, their shared oppression as black men trapped in physical and emotional prisons, and their erotic bond, born out of loneliness and sexual desire. Ombaka inspired Beam's cultural work, and would appear in his most noted essay, "Brother to Brother: Words from the Heart." In a letter to Ombaka dated September 22, 1985, Beam writes that despite all the popularity he had garnered because of the forthcoming publication of *In the Life*, "he had never been this lonely in his life. Popular Joe. Everyone likes what he writes, but he sits home alone on Saturday nights. He masturbates. He is dying of 'crib death.'" On December 27, 1988, three days before his thirty-fourth birthday, Beam did in fact die a "crib death"—and the cause of death was listed as AIDS.

After his death, Beam's mother, Dorothy, continued the work he had begun on another anthology project, *Brother to Brother: New Writings by Black Gay Men*. Dorothy Beam, who had supported her son during the publication of *In the Life*, noted in an interview with the *Gayly News* that her work on his second anthology project was about working through her loss and about "making sure the credit for her son and fellow writers [wasn't] lost."[28] Dorothy wrote to potential anthology contributors listed in Beam's files and gathered the works they sent to her. Beam's father, Sun, picked up the manuscripts at the post office, photocopied them, and mailed them to Essex Hemphill in Washington, DC. Eventually, Hemphill moved in with Dorothy to complete the project—performing domestic tasks in exchange for housing, while Dorothy cooked and paid for the administrative costs of the anthology.[29]

In an interview in the LGBT-themed magazine *Frontiers*, Hemphill explains how the social conditions of black men's lives prompted the creation of *Brother to Brother*. He writes that it was produced in the "context of confronting AIDS and the death around us. It's almost like a fierce resistance that says, 'Before I die, I'm going to say these things.'" He describes the anthology as "37 men who were willing to come forth, [even] posthumously. We're trying to say everything we can."[30] Given the political urgency of the AIDS epidemic and the disproportionate number of deaths in the black gay community, *Brother to Brother* registers as a response to the racist and heteropatriarchal state power that would usher these men to their premature deaths. Yet Hemphill frames its creation as "fierce resistance," wherein the queer vernacular term *fierce* modifies public resistance associated with blackness, along with the direct-action protests of predominantly white LGBT organizations like AIDS Coalition to Unleash Power (ACT UP).

Fierce usually denotes positive appraisal of someone's aesthetic style. Madison Moore theorizes fierceness as "a spectacular way of being in the world—a transgressive over-performance of the self through aesthetics." He continues, "Because of its transgressive potential and deep connection to showmanship, fierceness allows its users to fabricate a new sense of self that radiates a defiant sense of ownership through aesthetics, and in this way fierceness becomes a social, political, and aesthetic intervention."[31] Hemphill's claim that black gay men are willing to "come forth, [even] posthumously" marks their intervention as spectacular in its self-proclaimed transcendence of death. Highlighting the spectral nature of their aesthetic practices gives them a "sense of ownership" through their ability to publish an anthology that might lessen the power the AIDS virus had over their bodies.

While Hemphill's deployment of fierceness might suggest that 1980s and 1990s black gay cultural aesthetics are solely a form of public defiance, Kevin Quashie argues against reading black expressive culture as exclusively public. Instead, he proposes that signifying can express a "compilation of moments of consciousness" that "transcends the focus on public drama and reinforces the importance of the inner life as a part of expressiveness."[32] Quashie's emphasis on "the importance of the inner life" prompts black queer scholars to consider how black gay writers like Hemphill simultaneously reflected on their experiences of state-based violence and intraracial cultural stigma as sources of emotional pain, but also to remember that black gay literature does not render black gay men's lives as fully knowable.

Hemphill addresses the unknowability of black gay men's lives in another elegy to Joseph Beam, "When My Brother Fell." In the beginning stanzas, Beam is imagined as a fallen soldier, leader of a band of "able brothers" (l. 15). The first four stanzas celebrate the life and legacy of Beam, attempting to archive the loss experienced by those whom his life had affected.

The speaker then addresses Beam directly: "It is difficult / to stop marching, Joseph, / impossible to stop our assault" (ll. 36–39). He now stands in for Beam on the "front lines" (l. 14), attempting to fill a space within the imagined military formation that Beam has previously filled. He states that there are continued "tributes and testimonies / in [Beam's] honor" that "flare up like torches," and that "Every night / a light blazes for you / in one of our hearts" (ll. 40–45).[33]

The themes of loneliness and love in the fifth stanza stand in stark contrast to the image of war carried throughout the rest of the poem.

> There was no one lonelier
> than you, Joseph.
> Perhaps you wanted love
> so desperately and pleaded
> with God for the only mercy
> that could be spared.
> Perhaps God knew
> you couldn't be given
> more than public love
> in this lifetime.[34]

At first glance, it might look as though the speaker is suggesting that Beam's lack of companionship in his private life has caused him to plead with God to let him die. An alternative reading, however, would suggest that Beam's loneliness cannot be understood outside the psychic and embodied contradictions of being black and gay, of Beam's inability to achieve a "functioning self." Key to understanding the deployment of the term *loneliness* is the speaker's implicit disparagement of the NAMES Project AIDS Memorial Quilt, which includes Beam's name in one of its panels.[35] The speaker criticizes the quilt, whose mission is "to preserve the powerful images and stories within [it]" as an expression of "public love": although publicly listing Joseph Beam's name, it could not archive his private, internal struggles.[36]

In the interview mentioned above, Hemphill contrasts his openness about his own HIV status with Beam's "decision" to keep his status a secret until his death. When the interviewer asks him about his status, Hemphill replies, "It's something I haven't even begun to articulate yet. At the most I've come forth in public and said, 'Yes, I am too,' and I've said that because other men have come forth. Joseph [Beam] already showed us one way, and that's not the way I want to go, with the secrecy—though I don't judge him for that."[37] In a published letter to Beam, fellow black gay writer-activist and friend Colin Robinson reveals that none of Beam's close friends knew exactly how he died—if it was suicide, drug overdose, or AIDS—though AIDS was the official version. And in the introduction to his first edited collection of black gay poetry, Assotto Saint (born Yves François Lubin), another friend and contemporary of Beam's, notes that his body was discovered in an advanced stage of decomposition.[38] Beam's dying in silence, especially as a leader of a movement to end the silence around black gay men's lives, reveals how the public efforts of black gay artists and activists to transform their social worlds could not always alleviate their individual psychic pain. Hemphill uses the image of Beam's loneliness in the midst of the movement to speak to these contradictions.

Hemphill's remark about his own serostatus as something he has not begun to articulate speaks to the "crisis of truth" posed by the historical trauma of AIDS. Cathy Caruth argues that historical trauma poses such a crisis by asking how "we in this era can have access to our own history, to a history that is in its immediacy a crisis to whose truth there is not simple access."[39] Caruth is concerned with how traumatic experiences disrupt history and memory. She argues that the psychological impact of extremely violent events produces fissures and gaps in the narratives of the traumatized, thereby rendering certain aspects of the traumatic past as unrepresentable and unspeakable.[40] Hemphill expresses his frustration with projects of public commemoration, because they often elide the overwhelming affective flows that produce trauma's antiarchival impulse.

When I stand
on the front lines, now
cussing the lack of truth,
the absence of willful change
and strategic coalitions,
I realize sewing quilts
will not bring you back
nor save us.

It's too soon
to make monuments
for all we are losing,
for the lack of truth
as to why we are dying,
who wants us dead,
what purpose does it serve?[41]

For Hemphill, "sewing quilts" and "mak[ing] monuments" might too easily dismiss the ongoing effects of the trauma of AIDS, and too quickly turn political grievances into commoditized grief.

Marita Sturken's concept of "screen memory" is useful here, as the NAMES AIDS quilt, while operating as a site for innumerable projections of memory and history, can also eclipse countermemories and modes of grieving that disrupt nationalist projects of public commemoration. Public memorials often seek to provide closure and consign violent historical events to the past. In describing the names inscribed on the Vietnam Veterans Memorial Wall in Washington, DC, Sturken notes that listing these names without paying attention to racial and class hierarchies can produce narrow, nationalist models of multicultural inclusion. Her focus on the disproportionate number of blacks and Latinos from working- and middle-class backgrounds represented on the wall parallels the disproportionate effects of the AIDS epidemic in racial minority and poor communities. Though the quilt's multiple patches seek to account for personal memories and individual histories, these patches cannot stand in for the bodies eviscerated by state and cultural neglect, nor can they be a substitute for the cultural particularities that are diminished by the quilt's neoliberal, multicultural narrative. It is the bodies lost to and injured by violence, Sturken argues, that act as sites of conflict to the narrative of closure that the memorial enacts.[42]

Beam's body, found in such an advanced state of decomposition that the final cause of death could not be determined, acts as an alternative archive of memory that exceeds the quilt's flattening of difference, and refuses calls for healing that would compel survivors to forget the ongoing effects of the state's war on gay men and urban black communities. In March 1989, his mother, Dorothy, sent a letter to Robinson about the impact her son's death had on (black) lesbian and gay communities across the globe. More than twelve hundred people had attended Beam's memorial service, and Dorothy Beam had received roughly fifteen hundred letters from the United Kingdom, Mexico, Canada, various African countries, and every state in America expressing dismay and regret about his death: "The lesbian and gay community is trying to cope. There is an emotional and physical loss among many gay communities. Many are saying, where do we go from here? To whom do we turn? Our spokesperson is dead. How can we carry on his important work?"[43] The import of Beam's life and work to these global counterpublics cannot be easily stitched into the national fabric. Hemphill's inclusion of the lines "I realize sewing quilts / will not bring you back / nor save us" seeks to account for this unrepresentable loss. Memorializing Joseph Beam through the quilt was an act of "public love" that could not archive the political impact his death had on burgeoning black gay movements; nor could it archive his struggles to achieve a "functioning self," which would compel him to die in silence, even while leading the public mission to end the shame and silence in black gay men's lives.

Citing Essex Hemphill's poem "For My Own Protection," which begins with the lines "I want to start an organization / to save my life" (ll. 1–2), Beam writes in the introduction to *In the Life*, his first edited anthology of black gay men's writing, that the anthology is meant to be "the beginning of that organization." He continues, "The words and images here—by, for, and about Black gay men—are for us as we begin to end the silence that has surrounded our lives, as we begin creating ourselves, as we begin to come to power."[44] However, *In the Life* did not save either Beam's or Hemphill's life, nor did it end the silence in Beam's. Beam even notes that *In the Life* is meant to "speak for brothers whose silence has cost them their sanity."[45] Hemphill's poem suggests that Beam's psychosocial distress shapes his desire for death, but his desire stems from a longing for black subjectivity beyond the traumas of everyday black (gay) life and (social) death. If the lived experience of blackness locks the black subject into representations of Otherness and a psychic life of social death, then Beam's "plead[ing] with God" for death, "the only mercy / that could be spared," operates as a yearning for psychic stability and social freedom beyond the constraints of his abject black queer body and psyche. Contesting the idea that understandings of death are shared by everyone within the imaginative space of the nation, Sharon Holland insists on diverse imaginings of death: "Perhaps *some* people are ready to die because the space imagined—the place of death—is not a dead space but a living space."[46] Beam's loneliness, his pleading with God for mercy through death, can be read as his desire to be in a "living space," where blackness does not equal (social) death and being black and queer does not require "silence" that will cost the subject his "sanity."

Hemphill's abrupt inclusion of the lines "There was no one lonelier / Than you, Joseph," and of Beam's wanting "love / so desperately," therefore registers Hemphill's political longing for futures beyond the forces of antiblackness and antiqueerness while also documenting the monumental and inexplicable loss occasioned by the death of Joseph Beam. Hemphill's constructions of loneliness speak to the impossibility of black gay being in the age of AIDS, as his and Beam's deaths confirm, and black gay longing, as embodied in *Brother to Brother*. The anthology documents this impossibility of being, even as it yearns for a future where black gay life and culture will not only survive but thrive.

Essex Hemphill's Tears

In a video recording of a speech he gave at the 1990 OutWrite conference, themed "AIDS and the Responsibility of the Writer," Essex Hemphill reads a draft of what will eventually become part of the introduction to *Brother to Brother*. His speech garners laughter and applause as he discusses how the infamous images of black male nudes by white gay photographer Robert Mapplethorpe, and the site of the black male penis alone, could "obtain the rapt attention withheld from him in other social and political structures of the gay community."[47] Yet Hemphill is visibly filled with mixed emotions: anger, confidence, and a bit of "Snap! Queen" performance.[48] He moves quickly through his speech, but chokes up as he begins to remark on how baths, certain bars, bookstores, and cruising zones in the 1980s "were more tolerant of black men because they enhanced the sexual ambiance." He stumbles on the word *ambiance*, causing the ASL interpreter to stop and look at him. He reads more slowly after this moment, and stops periodically to wipe away his tears. After an unusually long pause, the audience cheers him on, encouraging Hemphill to continue. He wipes his eyes and gives a thumbs-up, saying, "There is so much to say." Then he continues to the end of his speech.

This speech has been debated within queer theory. Queer studies scholar John Champagne argues that Hemphill's tears foreclosed criticism of his reading of Mapplethorpe's photographs as perpetuating racist stereotypes of black male sexuality. Champagne, who had attended the conference, labels the politics of Hemphill's reading of Mapplethorpe "a politics of tears, a politics that assures the validity of its produced explanation by appealing to some kind of 'authentic,' unique, and (thus) uninterrogatable 'human' emotion or experience."[49] In response to this claim, black queer studies scholar E. Patrick Johnson maintains, "Champagne's own 'bravura' in *his* reading of Hemphill's tears illuminates the ways many queer theorists, in their quests to move beyond the body, ground their critique in the discursive rather than the corporeal." As to the significance of Hemphill's tears, Johnson asks, "What about the authenticity of pain, for example, that may supersede the cognitive and emerges from the heart—not for display but despite display? What is the significance of a black *man* crying in public?"[50]

Hemphill's public expression of vulnerability as a black gay man both confirms and exceeds the norms of gender. His speech extends the gendered forms of racial self-fashioning evident in his prose and poetry. As Johnson remarks, Hemphill's tears seem to come "despite" the audience's audible support for his speech. Contrary to Champagne's reading of the tears as foreclosing criticism of his reading of Mapplethorpe, Hemphill in fact received thunderous applause and laughter. He reads the Mapplethorpe images only in order to convey to the audience what he terms "white gay conscious-ness" during the 1980s. He uses the reference to exemplify how "the post-Stonewall white gay community of the 1980s was not seriously concerned with the existence of black gay men except as sexual objects." Mapplethorpe's images serve as visual texts that analogize a larger white gay political vision. Hemphill's remarks about how the penis becomes the identity of the black male speaks to how black men are viewed in "the context of a gay vision." Furthermore, he remembers how black gay men approached the white gay community "in the struggle for acceptance to forge bonds of brotherhood, bonds so loftily proclaimed as *the vision* of the best gay minds of [his] gen-eration" (my emphasis). Again, "vision" emerges, not only to signal visual representations of black men as sexual objects, but also to construct linkages between these representations and black men's role within a gay *political* vision of a more egalitarian future. Hemphill states that in the context of the 1980s, the "most significant coalitions" between white and black gay men "ha[ve] been created in the realm of sex."[51] Yet from his lived experience, sex as a ground for interracial politics had failed.

For Hemphill, the black gay male is maintained within the dominant white gay political vision as a sexualized object, as a source of pleasure and an object of desire whose sexual labor will never be enough to grant him full citizenship within the white gay community. The discourses of gendered and sexualized difference that have marked black culture as unassimilable within a larger American democratic vision have contributed to black gay men's sexual objectification and fetishization within a white gay political vision. Hemphill's speech reinserts the "minds and experiences" of black gay men who have endured such sexual exploitation and racial discrimination. The rejection he experienced in the 1980s by the white gay male community propels him toward a commitment to community building among black gay men and within the broader black community.

Hemphill's speech was clearly written for a black male audience, but he was the only black speaker on the panel, and the video of this talk shows that his audience was predominantly white. The title of the anthology is *Brother to Brother*, and the ending of the speech is addressed to "brothers" and regards "our" communities. That no "brothers" are visible in the video gives added context to Hemphill's crying. His public tears display his loneli-ness in giving a speech to his "brothers" in 1990, at the height of the AIDS epidemic, when the black gay community had been decimated. AIDS had turned a celebration of black gay cultural production into an occasion for mourning.

Hemphill's tears serve as a proxy for the unquantifiable and inarticulable forms of grief accumulating from the experience of living as a racialized and sexualized subject in America.[52] Circumscribed by cultural stigma, which normalizes violence done to the black body, Hemphill's grief stems from not only his brothers' disappearance but also their disappearance without proper recognition. His tears perform public mourning for a collective grief that has not been and can never be consoled. Similarly, Fred Moten discusses Mamie Till Bradley's decision to publicly display her son Emmett Till's mangled body after he was brutally slain in an act of racial violence, contending that the open-casket display was prompted by the ease with which the impact of racial violence goes unacknowledged. Moten calls this the "disappearance of the disappearance of Emmett Till," and asserts that his open casket performs "an abundance of affirmation in abundance of the negative."[53] Hemphill's tears flow, "despite display," to affirm a loss that can never be quantified—a loss obscured by the ubiquity of discourses of black cultural pathology. His tears point us toward a past and a future of racial and sexual grief that no cultural practice of memorialization can relieve. The positive critical reception of Hemphill's work, and the celebratory occasion that the OutWrite conference promised, failed to register the traumatic loss on which *Brother to Brother* depended for its production and consumption.

Holding Blackness at a (Queer) Distance

In the poem "Commitments," Hemphill illuminates the immaterial labor that subtends the quest for a "functioning self," of what it means for black gay men to literally and metaphorically "return home."

> I will always be there.
> When the silence is exhumed.
> When the photographs are examined
> I will be pictured smiling
> Among siblings, parents,
> Nieces and nephews.
>
> . . . .
>
> I am the invisible son.
> In the family photos

> Nothing appears out of character.
> I smile as I serve my duty.[54]

Using the image of the family photograph in the poem, Hemphill deploys the trope of visibility to explore the silent suffering of black gay men in the home. He describes ordinary black family life captured in photographs of holidays and barbecues. He names the blood relations and expectations of marriage that position the speaker as the sexual Other. The speaker poses in the photos so that "nothing appears out of character" (l. 34). As a black man, he must mask his nonnormative sexuality, which has been used as a symbol of black culture's inherent pathologies. His psychic pain is masked by the fact that he must also "smile as [he] serve[s] [his] duty" (l. 35).

In the photos described in the poem, the speaker's "arms are empty, or around / the shoulders of unsuspecting aunts / expecting to throw rice at [him] someday" (ll. 16–18). It is implied that what is absent from his arms are the "smallest children" that "are held by their parents" in the photos (ll. 14–15).[55]That the speaker lacks offspring signals the lack of his fulfillment of his gender role in the kinship network—to produce progeny for carrying on the family name. His empty arms also signal his sexual difference and failure to perform and affirm the mandates of compulsory heterosexuality. The speaker's longing arms reveal a private desire submerged under the collective political desire for black men to lead and produce the black nation, and the collective necessity to resist narratives of black cultural deviance that continue to mark the black racial family as nonnormative.

Robert Reid-Pharr argues that the trope of the black family does the political work of neatly and visually dividing up blacks and whites "at a glance."[56] Hemphill emphasizes the visual, and structures the poem around the photographic images of a black family during the holidays, suggesting that "Commitments" is a meditation on American notions of racial difference. The photographs tell the lie of America in that they reproduce the fictive notion of black racial difference. This is not to say that racial blackness does not have material effects on black bodies or shape black culture. Rather, it affirms that racial difference is still produced through the tyranny of the visual, and that the "epidermalization" of blackness as inherently pathological maintains racialism and by extension antiblack racism in its myriad formations.[57]

Frantz Fanon's theorization of blackness as constantly "discovered" by self as pathological being resonates with Hemphill's "Commitments," as the speaker of the poem meditates on his present absence in the photographic images of the black racial family. Fanon writes, "I was responsible not only for my body but also for my race and my ancestors. I cast an objective gaze over myself, discovered my blackness."[58] Similarly, the speaker envisions himself as the "invisible son" in the family photographs. The term *invisible son* invokes Fanon's claims that the black man exists in "a zone of non-being" and is "responsible for [his] race and [his] ancestors."[59] I contend that the black gay man, named only as the "invisible son" in the photograph, sees himself as "being for Other," as his retention within the family as the psychosexual Other bolsters black racial claims to normativity and subjective wholeness.[60] This man as "invisible son" in the black family serves as the Other on which racial/sexual injuries of slavery are projected. Slavery has been constantly "discovered" as the cause of the black family's persisting pathologies and, as Hortense Spillers argues, subjected black bodies to "gender undecidability."[61] The black gay man remains a sign of the history of such undecidability, particularly of failed heteromasculinity.

In addition, the black gay man figures as a threat to the biological and political future of the black racial family, that mythic construction that, albeit pathologized, makes black folks feel at home in America.[62] The lost object's (the black gay man's) return to the black family renders the "invisible son" visible while he bears all his discursive baggage. The photographic image allows the speaker to cast an "objective gaze over [himself]," discovering blackness as pathological object of the American nation, and furthermore, discovering its linkage to the production of black queerness as the sexual Other retained within the black nation. Looking at his smiling presence in the photo, the speaker sees his subjection under the black nation's quest for "masculine, whole subjectivity."[63] The image allows him to interrogate the black racial family and the black queer subject as the phobic object of both white American and black cultural nationalisms.

Yet the speaker's gay longing enables him to rediscover his relationship to blackness through bodily desire, and the image of "empty arms" or arms "around / the shoulders of unsuspecting aunts" symbolizes Hemphill's black gay longing. The image suggests a metaphorical longing to embrace the black racial family, as symbolized in the "shoulders of unsuspecting aunts" that preclude the possibility of embracing a same-sex lover. The speaker further proclaims that his arms are "so empty they would break / around a lover" (ll. 26–27). His arms are empty in photos taken at Thanksgiving and Christmas, and the Thanksgiving turkey is seen to be "steaming the lens." Whereas the "hazy smoke of barbecue" was, in a prior stanza, "in the background of the photographs," that the turkey is now "steaming the lens" implies that the optic gaze has become blurred rather than the object of the gaze. Upon closer scrutiny, the very traditions, like the turkey, that the black racial family coalesces around are clouding the speaker's gaze. Whiteness, which requires black assimilation but depends on narratives of black pathology for its dominance, reveals itself as structuring the speaker's frame of vision. Through the image of the longing arms, Essex Hemphill's poetry asks readers to "rediscover themselves through a different sense of their bodies, one that bypasses the gaze entirely by beginning from a different sensory location, the sense of touch."[64]

The speaker's longing arms can be filled only by the birth of the text itself. In the introduction to *In the Life*, Joseph Beam anthropomorphizes the written text as a male child: "Together, we, the contributors gathered here, have fathered a child—and it's a boy. He is strong and healthy and eager to be in the world."[65] The speaker can finally fill his "empty arms" with the "smallest child" as embodied in the text, thus providing an alternative structuring for black intimacy. Hemphill's work embodies racial and sexual longing, of empty arms unfulfilled by a lover's embrace, even too fragile for such an embrace, relieved only as his writing "touches" others "across time."[66] His poetry and prose refuse to refuse the pathology of the black racial family and community, yet yearn for forms of intimacy outside the constrained space and time of biological life and (social) death that the black racial family embodies. His embodied texts produce alternative forms of black intimacy across time and space in their ability to empower future readers, as a testament of these men's radical will to live in the face of death, and by allowing their visions for richer black futures to live on. Contemporary (black queer) readers can at last reach across time to wrap their arms around them.

Positing loneliness as black gay longing suggests that acknowledging the specificity and ubiquity of antiblackness does not require a distancing from black political desires for futures beyond antiblackness. Recognizing the centrality of injury to black gay community formation means accounting both for its debilitating effects and for how cultural production and activism enabled black gay men, as subjects of injury, to imagine richer subjective and social lives. As such, black gay writing in the 1980s and 1990s moves us beyond the antirelationality and nihilism embedded in Afro-pessimism and antisocial queer theory and toward an aesthetic and political vision of community and futurity that exceeds the black gay body's undoing. Furthermore, these writings offer a glimpse of how black gender and sexual difference is lived *differently* under regimes of antiblackness. This body of work prompts scholars to take more seriously the continuities *and discontinuities* of violence directed toward black queer and transgender people within larger structures of antiblackness.

THREE

Postmortem Politics

The Other Countries Collective and Black Gay Mourning

Isaac Jackson founded the Blackheart Collective, an artists' collective for black gay men, in 1980. During the 1970s, he noted the strong presence and creative activity of black lesbian feminists in New York City, but regretted that nothing like this was happening for black gay men.[1] At the time the host of a late-night radio show on WBAI, Jackson met musician Fred Carl at the Oscar Wilde Bookshop, one of the first US bookstores dedicated to lesbian and gay authors and texts. Carl worked at Oscar Wilde and soon joined Jackson as a founding member of Blackheart. Then Carl met architecture student Tony Crusor at a meeting of the Committee of Black Gay Men, an NYC-based support group. All three men expressed dismay at the committee's respectability politics, which they felt would not nourish their creativity as self-identified black gay artists.

Consequently, Jackson posted a flyer at Oscar Wilde calling for the formation of a black gay artists' collective, and the group soon held its first meeting. Black gay writers Assotto Saint, Michael Mintz, Arthur Wilson, Edmund Livingston, Phillip Brian Harper, and Salih Michael Fisher, among others, were in attendance. Though the group was initially composed of artists who worked in a variety of forms, many members were writers and some were published. During this period, black gay writers were marginalized in the white-dominated gay publishing industry, as literary venues such as the *New York Native* newspaper and *Christopher Street* magazine rarely published the work of people of color. Inspired by the literary production and political visibility of lesbians of color, who as Kevin McGruder argues "had a strong presence in New York City and a vibrant social network that hosted readings at area cafes, organized rallies and demonstrations," Blackheart's members decided that they would focus their creative energies on producing a literary journal.[2] The result was *Yemonja*, a fifty-six-page journal of black gay men's writings released in the spring of 1982. Two years later, the collective published a second journal, *Blackheart 2: The Prison Issue*, which included writings by prisoners and about the effects of the carceral state on black gay men. Blackheart went through a process of formal incorporation after the second journal was released, with Jackson becoming its president and Audre Lorde a member of its board of directors. Under Jackson's direction, it released a third journal, *Blackheart 3: The Telling of Us*, in 1985.

Though many factors contributed to the dissolution of the Blackheart Collective, AIDS played the most prominent role. Member Cary Alan Johnson recalls that black men began dying of AIDS in large numbers in 1983, and that he lost his partner, singer and dancer Robert Melvin, in 1984. Though at first many black men denied the impact of AIDS on their community, believing that it affected only those among them who interacted sexually with white gay men, the deaths of so many black gay men forced them to reckon with the epidemic's devastating effect. Johnson believes that the members of Blackheart lacked the "emotional connection" to one another to withstand the trauma of AIDS, and so the group dissolved shortly after the release of its final journal in 1985.[3]

In September of that year, however, former member Daniel Garrett called an organizational meeting for a new writers' group. Then in June 1986, he, Colin Robinson, and Isaac Jackson from Blackheart distributed flyers advertising a new writers' workshop for black gay men called the Other Countries Collective. The name Other Countries was inspired by James Baldwin's 1962 novel *Another Country*, his first novel to include a black male character who explicitly expresses same-sex desire. Significantly, this character, Rufus, commits suicide early in the story, and the rest of the narrative is driven by his death. His suicide exemplifies how death often haunts black gay cultural production. In the tradition of Baldwin, who influenced many of the writers participating in the black gay cultural renaissance of the 1980s and 1990s, death and mourning were as important to the work of Other Countries as were desires for community and visibility.

This chapter explores the significance of death and mourning in the development of black gay men's cultural production and activism at the height of the AIDS epidemic, examining the Other Countries Collective in particular. In the context of AIDS and its massive, yet largely unremarked, impact on black gay men in New York City, death and mourning became key parts of these men's everyday lives and worlds, as well as generative sites for cultural development and collective self-preservation. Death and mourning also fueled their activism. In what follows, I provide an overview of the

history of Other Countries, focusing especially on its major components—
the writers' workshop, poetry performances, and major publications. Then
I read elegiac poems and prose from the collective's second publication,
Sojourner: Black Gay Voices in the Age of AIDS (1993), to outline how black
gay aesthetic forms were imbricated in historically and culturally specific
practices of mourning. Finally, I draw from my interviews with surviving
members of the group to discuss how mourning has been a central aspect
of black gay activism, examining in particular an uprising that occurred at
the funeral of Donald Woods, one of Other Countries' most prominent
members.

In my focus on black gay mourning, I contribute to the scholarly discourse on what has been called "melancholic mourning." Sigmund Freud
distinguished between mourning and melancholia, which he presented as,
respectively, "normal" and "abnormal" forms of grief.[4] Literary and cultural
studies scholars have revised Freud's conceptualization of melancholia
as pathological and brought into stark relief the normalizing impulses of
mourning, noting that these formulations exclude nonnormative subjects
and miss the productive possibilities of integrating mourning and melancholia. Instead, scholars such as Sara Ahmed, Ann Cvetkovich, Douglas
Crimp, Michael Moon, Jahan Rahmanazi, and José Muñoz have presented
"melancholic mourning" not as pathological but as aesthetically, culturally,
and politically productive for racial and sexual minority subjects.[5]

Building on and extending these theories, this chapter explores the case
of Other Countries as an alternative archive for theorizing "melancholic
mourning." For its black gay artist members, melancholia was not syn-
onymous with the dominant Freudian vision of melancholia. Rather, the
perpetual deaths of friends and loved ones at the height of the AIDS epidemic, coupled with black men's experiences of racism and homophobia
in the public and private spheres, produced a historically and culturally
specific form of melancholic mourning, animated by a desire for collectivity, community, and empowerment. As such, Other Countries' politics
of melancholic mourning are more in line with Jonathan Flatley's concept
of "affective mapping." Flatley suggests that we rethink melancholia not
only as a mood state but as "something one does." For him, Freud's theory
of melancholia is an allegory for the experience of modernity, an experience constitutively linked to loss. Flatley argues that aesthetic practices can
change one relation of loss into another, and change one's "mood" from
depressive to antidepressive. By identifying the social origins of their emotional lives and identifying with others with whom melancholia might be
shared, Other Countries' aesthetic practices "ma[de] possible the conver-

sion of a depressive melancholia into a way to be interested in the world."[6] The group's modes of collectivity and cultural production attuned black gay men to the shared historicity of their affective experiences, and awakened a "counter-mood" that indexed their interest in alternative ways of being in the world. Through historical and cultural analysis of Other Countries' community-building efforts, aesthetic production, and political activism, I demonstrate how melancholic mourning was productive for black gay men in the early years of the AIDS epidemic.

Moreover, I read the melancholic memories of survivors of the early era of AIDS as a form of resistance to black/gay liberalism in the contemporary moment. Black queer scholars have demonstrated how the trauma of AIDS, particularly the domestication of gay male desires that resulted from its devastation, provided gay men with an entryway into modernity as liberal gay subjects. In contrast, Dana Luciano argues that the mournful body holds the power to resist the progress of modernity.[7] Building on these claims, I demonstrate how black gay men's collective memories of the uprising at Donald Woods's funeral and their sorrowful memories of the early era of the AIDS epidemic act as forms of black/queer optimism. By contesting the erasure of the ongoing epidemic from public discourse and by refusing to consign to the past the associations between blackness, queerness, and death, their collective memories act as a disruption to contemporary forms of black/gay liberalism, thereby producing a more interesting, radical, and transformative present.

"In the Upper Room"

In reflecting on the first session of the Other Countries Collective's writers' workshop (fig. 2), Cary Alan Johnson recalls his simultaneous emotions of excitement about the prospect of meeting so many black gay intellectuals and fear that they were all going to die: "My god how exciting it all was. Daniel [Garrett] was this brilliant nerdy guy with a vision and all these other fascinating boys. . . . But at that point it was clear a lot of us were going to die. Hold on to some beauty was a lot of what Other Countries was about. Everything that was being denied to us—purpose, youthfulness, future, love, faith, all we were losing on a daily basis—was in that room."[8] Johnson feels that the collective was as much about surrounding oneself with what these men embodied, however ephemeral, as it was about the writing.

Black gay men became involved with the Other Countries writers' workshop in myriad ways. Allen Wright initially learned about the collective from Chicago's local gay newspaper before moving to New York City. After

Figure 2. The Other Countries Collective. *Front row, left to right:* James Purcell, Carlos Segura, and Cary Alan Johnson. *Back row, left to right:* David Frechette, Allen Wright, Redvers JeanMarie, L. Phillip Richardson, Colin Robinson, Guy Mark Foster, Rodney Dildy, Roy Gonsalves, Charles Pouncy, Ali Wadud, and Robert Bell. Photo courtesy of Kent Grey.

he arrived in New York, a friend who knew of his interest in writing provided him with further details about the group's formation. Wright began attending the workshop shortly thereafter. G. Winston James learned about the collective during his junior year at Columbia University. He received information about its writers' group from attending meetings of Gay Men of African Descent (GMAD), a local black gay organization founded in 1986 and dedicated to the empowerment of black gay men through the creation of opportunities for fellowship and support. He then joined Other Countries, recalling later that he "quickly felt a sense of belonging and an awareness of the group's importance to me as a writer and the importance of belonging to a community of black gay men."[9] Having moved from Oakland, California, to New York City in 1988, Marvin K. White also joined the group after participating in GMAD. In my interview with him, he describes learning about the group as his "first exposure to a tribe of people called black gay poets."[10] White began workshopping poems at Other Countries, and because of this he had a poem ready when Assotto Saint issued a call for contributions to his groundbreaking collection, *The Road Before Us* (1991), at a later GMAD meeting.

The workshop structure varied over time, but early sessions featured thematic presentations by former Blackheart Collective member and Other Countries cofounder Daniel Garrett. Garrett provided members with excerpts from the writings of Michel Foucault, Derek Walcott, Shulamith Firestone, Audre Lorde, and others, which the group would read in advance and then discuss during the weekly workshops. Writers also arranged a week in advance for their work to be peer reviewed and discussed during the upcoming workshop. Attending members would give their "first impressions," and then the evening's moderator would offer more in-depth commentary. The skill level of workshop attendees varied between those who had never presented their work in a public venue and "serious" writers whose primary aim was to improve drafts of their work with the help of more seasoned writers.

The "seriousness" of someone's writing and dedication to the craft became a source of tension within the group. Opening Other Countries to amateur writers was aligned with its political aims, which included outreach to and fellowship with the local black gay community, but this clashed with the group's interest in cultivating a sophisticated black gay aesthetic and a rich body of literature worthy of preservation. According to White, the reward for paying one's membership dues and attending the workshop regularly was to be published in an anthology or to be invited to perform with the group. But divisions within the group based on raw talent and dedication to the craft of writing guaranteed that not everyone was granted this prize.

Another essential part of the workshop experience was the after-hours fellowship. Participants socialized over dinner, either at a nearby restaurant or at a member's home. James remarks on the feeling of the group as both social gathering and writers' workshop: "There really was a sense that these men were not only fellow writers, but kindred spirits, in some cases friends."[11] Wright describes the after-hours socials as an alternative to the more "established places" for the formation of queer publics.

> The two-hour workshops gave way to more hours at dinner in a local restaurant. . . . We'd go to someone's home and continue the conversations, the flirtations. There was music, a little dancing, laughter, an opening into ourselves and each other that was new and real and, yes, exciting, so different and so welcome. It was something that hadn't existed in the established places we'd been going to find each other: bars, bathhouses, parties, parks, orgies, dance clubs, tearooms. None of those things gave us the space to share ourselves without apology, more completely, or potentially so, for even that potential was exciting.[12]

Wright's critique of the "established places" raises questions about how sites of queer world-making in New York City might have produced their own forms of institutionalization, marginalization, and discipline.[13] The workshop's after-hours social spaces fostered forms of eroticism not organized primarily or exclusively around genital pleasure and bodily desire. This opened up erotic possibilities for black gay men to be with each other in ways that included but extended beyond sexual contact.

In a similar vein, the poetry section of Other Countries' first published journal, *Other Countries: Black Gay Voices* (1988), begins with Donald Woods's "In the Upper Room." Dedicated to the men of Other Countries, the poem attempts to "nail down the moment / the deliberate embrace" (ll. 21–22) of black gay men's collectivity, describing it as "the smelly new / act of love" (ll. 23–24).[14] The "Upper Room" in the poem's title refers to the collective's physical meeting space at the Lesbian and Gay Community Services Center in Greenwich Village. According to Wright, the first workshops took place in a room on the top floor of the center's east wing, ironically a former restroom decorated by pop artist and AIDS activist Keith Haring.[15] James describes the location as a "practical and community matter," because the room rental fee was cheap, and the room itself was "a fixed place to meet in a neighborhood and locale that felt relatively safe (if not empowering) for gay people." Indeed, White remembers that his train ride from Harlem to "The Center" was transformative in that it allowed him to peel away the layers of performance necessary to negotiate the black spaces of Harlem.[16] He believes that for him—and he imagines that this applied to others as well—meeting at the center operated as a mode of escape to a space that allowed for a diversity of gender and sexual expressions, yet one's relationship to black family and community did not have to be compromised. Kevin McGruder mentions that the center's central location was convenient for participants who lived either uptown or downtown, and strategic for soliciting participation from center visitors. The West Village location was also practical because it provided a meeting space with multiple nearby restaurants and bars where members could engage in their ritual of socializing after each workshop.

The "Upper Room" in the title of Woods's poem also gives the space a sacred dimension, as the Upper Room in the Christian tradition is the site of the last supper Christ shared with his disciples before his crucifixion. Like the disciples anticipating Christ's death, White anticipated the death of this generation of writers, many of whom were already dying of AIDS. He describes his encounter with the more established writers of the group— Donald Woods, B.Michael Hunter, Assotto Saint, and Roy Gonsalves—in ways that also evoke expectations of death and loss. And he describes his experience in the group overall as "learning how to write while these men were learning how to die."[17] He recalls that Saint, anticipating the deaths of workshop members, would hand out forms and pamphlets on how to arrange and organize one's literary estate. Part of White's responsibility as a member of Other Countries was to care for ailing members; he remembers an occasion when Saint asked him to take some soup to Woods when he had become too sick to leave his home.

Woods's layered spatial metaphor of sacred communion before death and the meeting's location within New York City's best-known gay district also captures the competing aims of the workshop: to establish a private space for creative (self-)expression, yet assert the presence and significance of racial difference in New York City's gay community. The commitment to meeting at "The Center" attests to the latter. Other Countries began meeting there in 1986. But in 1992, Center of the Rainbow, "the first ever creative arts and community meeting center serving the lesbian and gay people of color community and general public," emerged as a new home for queer artists of color and associated cultural organizations.[18] The board of directors of Other Countries held its first meeting at the new space in September of that year. Yet the members of the writers' collective committed themselves to alternating their meetings between their new home and the newly renovated Charles Angel/People of Color Room at the Lesbian and Gay Community Services Center, which was dedicated to "the struggle against racism, sexism, and homophobia."[19] Claiming its space within the center signaled Other Countries' commitment to making its presence felt within the larger gay community, while meeting at the Center of the Rainbow highlighted its specific commitment to lesbian and gay people of color.

In many respects, Other Countries was committed to the politics of public presence, public visibility, and public expression. But the men of the collective also expressed their desire for privacy, though they were well aware of the public, politicized nature of any space where black men gather for collective self-expression.[20] Black lesbian writers and activists had deployed spatialized tropes of privacy and intimacy to assert their black feminist politics, reconfiguring domestic tropes such as "the kitchen table" that have historically confounded articulations of black womanhood and excluded gender and sexual minorities from the boundaries of the black family and community.[21] During its 1989 performance to commemorate the life of Joseph Beam, Other Countries articulated its desire for a space of intimacy. The dramatic performance consisted of three voices reading lines from Beam's introduction to *In the Life*.

Voice 1: We have few traditions like those of Black women.

Voice 3: No kitchen tables around which to assemble.

Voice 2: No intimate spaces in which to explore our feelings of love and friendship.

Voice 1: We gather in public places:

Voice 1: barbershops,

Voice 2: lodges,

Voice 3: fraternities,

Voice 1: and street corners,

Voice 2: places where bravado rather than intimacy [is] the rule.

Voice 1: We assemble to *do* something rather than *be* with each other.

In deploying feminized tropes of intimacy, the men of Other Countries resisted the gendering of private space as feminine and public space as masculine. While scholars from Elliot Liebow to Melissa Harris Perry have politicized black male–centered spaces such as the street corner and the barbershop, they have been less attentive to quotidian spaces where black gay men have gathered to, as Harris Perry argues, "develop understandings of their collective interests and create strategies to navigate the complex political world."[22] This performance suggests that the traditional spaces where black men gather to develop political strategies tend to emphasize "bravado" rather than "intimacy," thereby reproducing a masculinized notion of black politics. Other Countries' rejection of the imperative to "*do* something" rather than "*be* with each other" critiques notions of black male collectivity solely defined in and through more conventional forms of resistance.[23] The group members' desire to simply "*be* with each other" gestures toward a retreat from the gendered political demands of "doing something," at least momentarily, in order to explore their shared experiences as black gay men and as black men more broadly.[24] Exploring feelings of love and friendship between men threatened gender binaries that were hegemonic in black communities. The members' yearning for the privacy of the "Upper Room" grew out of the hope that it might shield them temporarily from the insidious and overt forms of racism and homophobia that they negotiated daily.[25] Their performance in commemoration of Beam expressed a longing for privacy in the face of the scrutiny that historically was placed on black male intimacy, and a yearning for a space in which to express other ways of *being* black and being black with one another.[26]

Envisioning themselves as more than just a writers' group, the men of the Other Countries Collective imagined the Upper Room and the after-hours socials as spaces to grieve and heal collectively. For Daniel Garrett, the workshop was developed in part to collectively grapple with the psychic weight of racial and sexual difference. He captures this in his essay, "Other Countries: The Importance of Difference," which describes the creation of Other Countries as an effort to ameliorate, or at least collectively acknowledge, the social conditions that produced his melancholy, a feeling he imagined to be shared among other black gay men.

> It would be dishonest to pretend that my interest in beginning Other Countries was merely intellectual, as it was not. In a relatively short period of time (two years), I had been disappointed by what I perceived as my parents' inability to grow with me past my childhood years; disappointed by two close male friends who refused to accept my sexuality (before this, I had begun to see friends as family, as life); disappointed by my failure to find a lover among the men I was meeting, men committed to the pleasure of anonymous, promiscuous sex; disappointed as well by less personal things: a young Black male landlord's exploitive dishonesty and incompetence; the homophobia encountered during a brief stay in Harlem; being mugged twice by groups of young Black men, once at gunpoint; and, importantly, the poverty of vision and power of Black organizations. This disappointment had produced anger, pain, contempt, and fear. Fear. The workshop would be a way of re-connecting with something I thought might still be a vital force.[27]

The writers' workshop, for Garrett at least, was a way to "heal some of these wounds"[28] accrued from his life experiences, which had been affected by his daily, oftentimes violent, negotiations of the public sphere as a racial and sexual minority. But Garrett left the collective in 1989 owing to internal disagreements among the leadership about his creative vision for the group. Nonetheless, the workshop format had opened up a space for dialogue among black gay men, a "re-connecting with something." That "something" acts as a placeholder, holding open the possibilities for a "vital force" to emerge from that space. If the "Upper Room" provided a space of privacy, intimacy, sanctuary, and mourning for black gay men, then their performances set out to transform the public sphere that Garrett identified as critical to the social production of black gay melancholy.

"Creative Empowerment"

The Other Countries Collective insisted on creativity as "an indispensable element of organizing people politically."[29] In light of this, its members put their poetry to work, adapting the printed word for performance so that the group could "take its work into the culture's communal spaces—most notably gay bars—and provide audiences in these spaces with rare reflections on their lives."[30] The members dubbed their work in black gay communities "creative empowerment," encouraging people "to think, act and express themselves autonomously."[31] Their performances covered a range of issues relevant to black communities, and they performed at locations where the presence and solidarity of black gay men were in demand. Other Countries artists presented works in a diverse array of venues, including national universities such as Rutgers and Yale; local and regional black gay nightclubs like Tracks in New York City and Nob Hill in Washington, DC; gay bookstores such as Giovanni's Room in Philadelphia; and black cultural venues such as the Schomburg Center for Research in Black Culture and the Studio Museum, both in Harlem. By 1988, the group had reached over 2,500 men and women and entertained, educated, and affirmed audiences ranging in size from 1 to 800.

The Other Countries Collective achieved its goals of communicating with wide-ranging audiences by presenting literature as a legitimate form of entertainment. The group experimented with genres, once holding a weekend workshop with award-winning dancer and choreographer Ronald K. Brown and writer and activist Craig G. Harris; this event integrated movement and literature as performance art. Other Countries did not see literary activity as separate from other forms of black gay popular culture. Instead, it drew from the performative aspects of literature and integrated it into popular cultural expressions.

One performance in particular exhibits the group's attempt to present literature as inseparable from other black gay popular cultural forms. In 1988, it held a performance entitled "Libido Lit: 101" at the Tracks nightclub. The event featured readings of erotic literature by prominent black gay writers Essex Hemphill, Samuel R. Delany, and Assotto Saint and was hosted by Joe Simmons, a popular black gay porn star and Robert Mapplethorpe model. Given the absence of popular media representations of black gay men as erotic subjects and people with AIDS, the performance offered what Other Countries cofounder Cary Alan Johnson calls "a witnessing." The appearance of AIDS in the immediate aftermath of the gay sexual revolution of the 1970s threatened to once again shroud black gay male sexuality in shame. Johnson notes that black gay men's public performances of erotic literature affirmed their sexual agency at the height of the epidemic.[32] Furthermore, the dominance of media images presenting people with AIDS as white gay men meant that these performances served as alternative spaces for black gay men to mourn their communal losses.

The "Libido Lit: 101" event, which served as a fund-raiser for the group's first publication, illustrates the challenges Other Countries faced as it tried to negotiate its relationship to the larger black gay community.[33] During the show, Simmons read "Confection," a poem written by group member Steve Langley: "i am / chocolate candy / a handful of cookies / the goods you are / forbidden to eat."[34] During the performance, audience members began to loudly express their disappointment, because Simmons was not removing his clothes, which they apparently expected him to do—partly because he was a porn star, partly because the event was held in an erotically charged nightclub, and partly because the poem incited their desires for "forbidden" fruit. Hemphill and Delany attempted to speak over the audience, but when the music was shut off the crowd grew only more annoyed. One person shouted at the white-bearded Delany, "Get off the stage, Santa Claus!" Saint shouted back at the crowd to no avail, and then he expressed himself in a more distinct way. Saint was clad in a tight red and black zebra-print mini-dress, accessorized with a wide, waist-cinching tri-clasp bodice belt and matching black pumps. He was made up, but wore no wig. Tired of the crowd's jeers, he turned around, lifted his skirt, and defiantly showed his ass.

Allen Wright describes "Libido Lit: 101" as "disastrous, but not failed."[35] One of the reasons that he does not regard the event as a failure is that it encouraged the audience to articulate its sexual desires and its sexual politics. In trying to capture the collective feeling of the audience at the event, Wright highlights the importance of black gay men's erotic lives in the context of the AIDS epidemic: "Yes, there is a monster out there devouring us from the inside out, but tonight, we are alive and strong and our desire for each other is good and real, needs to be seen, told and remembered. . . . 'And tonight we dance!' was the response from our audience."[36] The clash at this event demonstrates how Other Countries' vision of literary and cultural politics collided with the broader black same-sex-desiring community's privileging of nightlife as a mode of erotic expression.

If the collective initially understood performance as its most powerful and immediate strategy for *communicating* with new audiences, highlighting the audience's response to "Libido Lit: 101" demonstrates both the benefits and the limits of this approach. In his autoethnographic reflections on the significance of urban black queer club spaces in the late 1980s and 1990s, Jafari Allen argues that the club became "the central institution of Black queer communion": "Here we assert bodies, putatively dangerously riddled with disease and the threat of violence, not only as instruments of pleasure but also as conduits of profound joy, and perhaps spiritual bliss and transcendent connection."[37] The audience's rejection of Other Countries' performatory event, or more accurately, the music being turned off, disrupted the

possibilities of "pleasure," "joy," and "connection" that the Tracks nightclub
created weekly. Moreover, Simmons's recitation of poetry and his refusal to
take off his clothes shifted attention toward the cognitive and away from
the bodies circulating on the dance floor, which Allen believes is "a unique
place to lose the mind one uses all week."[38] As a mode of communication,
club performance allowed audiences to speak back and articulate how expressions of bodily desire and dance were also powerful forms of "creative
empowerment" in the context of the epidemic.

The group also staged a series of three annual performances for World
AIDS Day at the Studio Museum in Harlem. On December 1, 1989, it per-
formed "Acquired Visions," which it later presented at Syracuse and Yale
Universities. Other Countries members next performed "Seeing Through
AIDS/Seeing AIDS Through" at the museum on December 1, 1990. And the
third in this series of performances, given in 1991, was "Behavioral Change:
A Prescriptive Performance for the Second Decade of HIV," which Other
Countries also presented at SUNY-Oswego, Rutgers-New Brunswick, and
the Lesbian and Gay Community Services Center, the site of the collective's
weekly writers' workshops. "Behavioral Change" featured an ensemble cast
of group members reading selected AIDS-themed poetry by workshop participants. As the final performance of the series, "Behavioral Change" signaled a shift in the group's thinking about the AIDS epidemic. The show
opens with a dialogue about black gay men's sexual and emotional lives
after enduring a decade of the epidemic.

Part 1.
Shoot, I'm glad men are reclaiming their bodies enough to want to fuck like crazy
    again. Lemme just touch it one time Mister Man!
VOICE: Safely of course?
(Whips out string of condoms) Just doing my part for our boys in uniform.

Part 2.
Well if that's what we've come to, then I want no part of it. We have been doing these
    AIDS shows for 3 years. And let's face it, we've done terror and mourning and
    fear. . . . So now that we're in the second decade of this shit, what's different? All
    that other stuff was important, but what's different—more specifically, how have
    we changed?[39]

The initial conversation alludes to the discourses of safe sex that emerged
during the early years of the epidemic, and references how the epidemic
changed gay men's sexual practices so that risk became much more of a

central factor.[40] The figurative voice of safety then haunts the conversation, emphasizing the discourses emerging both inside and outside the gay community that disciplined gay men's everyday sexual choices. But the second voice "want[s] no part of it." The trauma of AIDS had produced "terror and mourning and fear" as a structure of feeling for black gay men. Reading the subtitle of the performance as "prescriptive" alongside the group's introspective focus on its own transformation reroutes understandings of the virus outside medicalized and psychologized discourses, so that solutions for psychic healing are determined by the community itself. After entering the second decade of the epidemic, Other Countries called for a shift in the conception of behavorial change that included the question of how the black gay community had changed. In this context, the "behavioral change" of the title is less about transforming black gay men's sexual practices and more about working through the melancholic subjectivity produced in the context of the epidemic.

The members of Other Countries sought to shift the institutionalized discourse pertaining to HIV/AIDS, especially in regard to its psychic and social impact on black gay men's lives. In his abandoned preface to *Sojourner*, Colin Robinson notes that the group's performance series at the Studio Museum held significance, as it gained the members "entry to one of the gatekeeping institutions of black culture."[41] He remembered that group members were hesitant about being labeled the "voices of AIDS" within black cultural discourse, suggesting that the label threatened to confine black gay subjectivity to an abject state of suffering or an agent of contagion that threatened the black community. According to Allen Wright, who toured with the group, the "Behavioral Change" performance was considered too provocative for the Studio Museum, and so the group was not invited back.[42] Other Countries' efforts to represent its members as complex subjects must have exceeded the categories prescribed for them within the black public sphere. That the group even risked alienating this audience attests to its unwavering commitment to the performative power of poetry to transform the lives of its own members, the lives of its community, and society more broadly.

In its epilogue to "Behavioral Change," the Other Countries ensemble performed a call-and-response poem that highlights the specificity of its members' position as racial and sexual minorities within the fight against AIDS.

> Men are writing lies
> Can a poem be a demonstration
> For poems

A wafer sailing through the air at St. Patrick's
Their intentions grand
A cadaver in the street
But they can't make change with words they are
I sit
Silent and their words lie
and want our words to change the world
about the deafening din of silence
Careful
Men can't make change with poems
Fear pins our anger to the page
The show-up does not suffice
Sit still
Men don't make change at all
let the words take action
but regurgitate and rehash the shit
Publish them into the world
let them go where I am afraid
Stand and give testimony[43]

This poem offers a critique of direct-action protests by groups such as the AIDS Coalition to Unleash Power (ACT UP)–New York. It expresses Other Countries' anxieties about the political activities of ACT UP, which had become famous and infamous for protests like the "Stop the Church" action, which is alluded to in the line "A wafer sailing through the air at Saint Patrick's," and various "political funerals," which are conjured in the line "A cadaver in the street."[44] However, mass media attention to ACT UP, a predominantly white organization, regularly reaffirmed the subjects of AIDS as white gay men, thereby erasing black gay male bodies from this symbolic field.

The poem further alludes to how fear—specifically spatialized, territorial fear—prohibited black gay men's participation in such public demonstrations. In reflecting on his involvement in the leadership of ACT UP–New York, black gay activist Allan Robinson considers how things might have fared if the majority of those involved in the organization had been black and Latino: "I think Black and Latino men and women really have to process on becoming involved in civil disobedience. When I got arrested at Stephen Joseph's [New York City's Health Commissioner, 1986–89] office, I wondered how the cops would have responded to ACT UP if we had all been Black and Latino."[45] Robinson's reflection reveals how the political climate, particularly the history of civil rights demonstrations, the rise of the carceral state, and the longstanding role of police power as a violent force in black and Latino women's and men's lives, provides the material context for understanding why blacks and Latinos must "process" their roles in public AIDS activism. This climate produced "fear" that "pin[ned their] anger to the page." In light of this fear, the poem asserts the performative power of "words" to "take action" and "go where [they are] afraid." Thus, Other Countries' poetry performances exposed a desire for self-preservation, even as its members yearned to transform the dominant cultural discourses that produced black gay men's fear and invisibility. Public performance became the central mode of expressing the group's complex political subjectivity, as well as a mode of testifying to the traumatic impact of HIV/AIDS in black gay men's lives.

"Toward a Black Gay Aesthetic"

In his essay "Other Countries," Daniel Garrett titles one of its subsections "Toward a Black Gay Aesthetic." There Garrett links the marginalization of black gay men in US society and Western literature to the development of black gay aesthetic forms. He states that black gay literature acts as historical documentation, social validation, and an expression of black gay men's cultural values. For Garrett, literatures of cultural difference serve as non-Western forms of historiography: "The development of Black literature, women's literature, Gay literature, and now Black Gay literature is not so much a rewriting of history as an additional writing of it; together these various literatures, like our various selves, produce history."[46] His vision of literature as polyvocal history operates in a similar vein as Elsa Barkley Brown's construction of the politics of difference in women's history. Brown uses black women's art to conceptualize histories of difference as "everybody talking at once." Contesting normative notions of history that understand the politics of difference as chaotic and thereby opt for narratives told from singular perspectives, she argues that "the events and people we write about did not occur in isolation but in dialogue with a myriad of other people and events."[47] In a similar fashion, Garrett maintains that black gay aesthetics must be understood as always in dialogue with dominant Western literature, women's literature, black diasporic literature, (white) gay literature, and the various formations that fall in between these categories, especially black lesbian literature. They are also dialogically produced through the variety of experiences *within* the black gay community, particularly those concerning regional, ethnic, class, and gender difference. What emerges under the rubric of a black gay aesthetic is an attention to this difference, a conversation

between men who have individually struggled against multiple marginalizations. Garrett states, "Because we have struggled so hard *individually*, we do
not always listen to the wisdom our brother has found."[48] But this type of
listening is what he and other participants in the black gay cultural renaissance wanted to promote. The feeling of intimacy offered within the space
of the workshop and the values contested through the collective writing
process created a dialogue between men that became critical to black gay
aesthetic forms.

The formation of a black gay aesthetic was also produced through intergenerational dialogue. As I have mentioned, these writers drew heavily from
their black lesbian feminist contemporaries, but they also looked to earlier
black gay culture. In his study of black gay literature in the 1980s and 1990s,
Simon Dickel demonstrates that black queer predecessors in the Harlem
Renaissance and especially James Baldwin in the protest era greatly influenced the aesthetics of this body of literature.[49] In fact, Other Countries
dedicated its first literary collection, the journal *Other Countries: Black Gay
Voices* (1988), to James Baldwin, Richard Bruce Nugent, and Bayard Rustin,
all of whom died in 1987, the year before its publication. *Other Countries*
celebrates the lives and mourns the deaths of this earlier generation of black
gay men. In the context of the AIDS epidemic, however, the conversation
also shifted from an intergenerational dialogue to an intragenerational one.
In his abandoned preface to the second Other Countries collection, board
member Colin Robinson remarks that only five years after producing the
collective's first volume, ten of the men who had made Other Countries
possible were dead from AIDS, and at least four others were living with or
dying from the virus.[50] While Other Countries dedicated the first volume
to an earlier generation of black gay men, the editors dedicated the second volume, the book-length *Sojourner: Black Gay Voices in the Age of AIDS*
(1993), to their own generation.[51] In the same preface, Robinson notes that
the collection is about "the celebration of a community and communal
rituals which both structure our failures in the face of HIV and fortify us to
transcend this epidemic."[52] Despite the immediacy of the traumatic impact
of the epidemic, he states that *Sojourner* is also "grounded in a vision, captured in former Other Countries board member Reginald Jackson's image
of a boy in the darkness of a basement in Boupaloupa, Mississippi, reading
Baldwin by flashlight."[53] Thus, *Sojourner* was equally inspired by the "challenge . . . of leaving something valuable and permanent of [their] Black Gay
lives for future generations."[54]

This vision of futurity, of future generations, alongside the historical context of the premature deaths of black gay men during the AIDS crisis, shaped

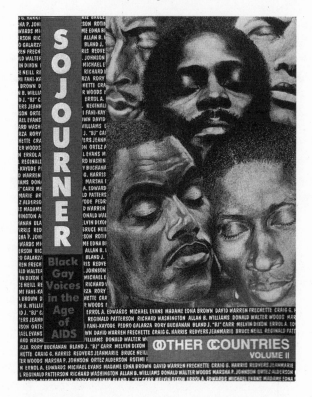

Figure 3. Robert D. Sims, *Visionaries*; etched drawing used on
the cover of *Sojourner: Black Gay Voices in the Age of AIDS*, edited
by B.Michael Hunter (New York: Other Countries Press, 1993).
Photo courtesy of B.Michael Hunter Estate.

black gay men's aesthetic production. *Sojourner* reflects this historically informed vision in both its content and its presentation. Its cover features
Visionaries, an etched drawing that depicts overlapping faces of black men
with their eyes closed (fig. 3).

The closed eyes and overlapping faces in this artwork speak to the simul-
taneity of Other Countries members' private reflections on their pleasures,
fears, and losses and the collective, outward-looking political vision embodied by the group. This cropped image is surrounded by the names of black
gay men lost to AIDS. The book also includes a page listing the names of
those directly affiliated with the group, beneath the heading "We Remember
Your Names"; a three-page black insert lists hundreds of additional names
beneath the heading "Standing on the Shoulders of Ancestors." *Sojourner*
permits readers to visualize the impact of the virus on the black gay community, as well as acting as a repository of memory for a very immediate

history of loss. The volume thus fulfilled the group's mission of developing, disseminating, and preserving the community's diverse cultural and intellectual expressions, particularly the preservationist aspect. G. Winston James notes in his interview the distinction between black gay men writing in journals at home and black gay men having their work published in an anthology "whose physical presence can be disseminated widely and potentially permanently."[55] Accordingly, Other Countries concentrated its efforts on publishing *Sojourner* in order to achieve archival permanence, documenting the complexities of black gay life and death in anticipation of the volume's discovery by future generations of black gay boys and men.

The list of names on the insert makes visible the relationship between the group's reverence for the dead and its poetics. Akasha (Gloria T.) Hull has demonstrated that black women poets such as Lucille Clifton and Dolores Kendrick have relied on "the transmission of female ancestral energy as a vital force in their lives and poetry," which she calls the "ancestral muse."[56] Many of the contributors to this second Other Countries volume also channeled the "ancestral muse" in their work. Robert Vazquez-Pacheco's poem "Necropolis," for instance, illustrates the significance of remembering the dead to black gay poetics.[57] The poem begins with the line "my life is populated with the dead." It continues with twenty-six more lines describing New York City as a haunted landscape. The spacing of the poem, one column featuring the narrative and the other a list of twenty-nine names, represents the proximity between the poem's speaker and the dead that populate his life. He implies that the souls of dead men haunt him and the city in order to express their demand to be remembered.

my life is populated with the dead	Joe
they follow me down streets	Jeff
huddle round me in elevators	Alan
sit behind me in movies	Stewart
or next to me in cabs	Daniel
spiritmen unquiet souls	Larry
they clamor for attention	Vito
demanding remembrance	Ray
new york necropolis	Anthony
monuments to dead times	Robert
and dead men	Darnell
i move through their city	Don
their voices whispering	Warren
remember remember remember	Jose[58]

The haunted landscapes of the "new york necropolis" transform the act of memory into a negotiation between the living and the dead. For Vazquez-Pacheco, the ancestors "clamor for attention / demanding remembrance." Whereas Western theories of trauma suggest that the extremity of mass violence forces the psychic repression of traumatic memory, in the poem the "ancestral muse" forces the subject to remember. The dead themselves refuse to be forgotten, ironically becoming "the vital force" of memory.[59] Furthermore, the constancy of death prohibits forgetting. In a personal reflection on the epidemic, Allen Wright observes, "News of another death now comes with such frequency that my mourning is constant. I imagine the spirits of the departed waiting in line until they can be properly grieved."[60] Wright's statement implies that New York is populated by "spiritmen" because they have yet to be properly grieved. The forgetting of black gay men lost to AIDS in dominant discourses of African American trauma and (white) queer trauma might explain "their voices whispering / remember remember remember."

In Marlon Riggs's "Letters to the Dead," he summons the ancestors as witnesses to his own body's deterioration. Riggs calls on the dead to witness his body as a site of "impending catastrophe," and to observe how his infected body has become a critical site of knowledge production. He writes to his friend LeWayne, recently lost to AIDS, about how his own confrontation with mortality aided in transforming his silence into speech.

> Sweet LeWayne, who first lost sight, then life, to the raging virus, were you nonetheless my witness? Did you see over the ensuing months of my recuperation what happened to my kidneys, my sight, my tongue? Did you see how slowly, gradually, my kidneys once again started to work, how slowly, gradually I began to see the consequences of silence, and how as a consequence of this insight, my tongue unhinged from the roof of my mouth, dislodged from the back of my throat, slipped-free?[61]

LeWayne witnesses, from beyond the grave, Riggs's shifting consciousness. Riggs's repetition of "slowly, gradually" syncs the slow time of his body's recovery with the development of his consciousness about the costs of silence for black gay men. The image of the tongue unhinging and slipping free demonstrates his belief in the power of the "gay voice" to preserve and sustain black gay cultural memory despite the body's undoing.[62]

Riggs further elaborates on silence as a form of discipline by calling on abolitionist Harriet Tubman as witness.

And don't you now see the chilling parallels between the means by which we were held captive in your time, and the methods of our enslavement today? Don't you see the chains, my Harriet, sweet Moses, the chains not so much of steel and law, but more insidious: the invisible chains, linked over centuries, of silence and shame? In this latest crisis, our new master is the virus; his overseer—silence; and his whip—shame.[63]

Riggs creates continuity between the trauma of antebellum slavery and the contemporary trauma of AIDS. The link he establishes "over centuries" is composed of "silence" and "shame," which he believes to be captive forces for those with a seropositive status. For Riggs, silence and shame are means of continuing the psychic discipline on black gay men whose bodies are already being held captive by AIDS. Therefore, he proposes that speaking out about and thinking with the infected body offer agency to those affected by the epidemic.

Speaking out occurs not only through speech but also through bodily performance.[64] Other Countries' poetics also explore how bodies perform in space, particularly in black spaces in which only certain performances of blackness are acknowledged and sanctioned. Marvin K. White's poem "Last Rights" exemplifies how queer black performances can transform black sacred space. The poem narrates the story of a black gay man who has been displaced by his lover's family during a funeral ceremony. It speaks to a largely unremarked struggle of (black) gay men during the AIDS epidemic who were discriminated against by funeral homes, churches, and families that refused to funeralize the bodies of men who died of AIDS. And when churches did funeralize these men, pastors would often condemn their souls to hell.

Many black churches now have HIV/AIDS ministries, but the existence of these ministries can serve to obscure this embattled past. E. Patrick Johnson has argued that black gay men have historically been "cut off from their people" when "those people—family, friends, church members—fail to provide an affirming and supportive environment in which their humanity is acknowledged, particularly during those times of bereavement."[65] In White's poem, the deceased's lover recalls his performance of mourning at the funeral.

> When I learned of Gregory's death
> I cried silently
> But at the funeral

Giiiiirl I'm telling you
I rocked Miss Church
Hell I fell to my knees twice
Before I reached my seat
Three people had to carry me
To my pew[66]

The lover's performance of what seems to be excessive mourning earns him the attention of not only his lover's biological family but also other presumably gay men in the church, which becomes audible "When someone in the choir / Sang out 'Work it girl / Woooooork it'" (ll. 26–28). Later in the poem it becomes evident that this performance earns him his "rightful place" alongside the family when he is "ushered into the waiting limo / Which sped me to [Gregory's] family's house," and it also brings affirmation to "someone in the choir," the space where black gay men historically have been praised for their talents, yet needed to remain discreet so as not to be cut off from their people. Through his performance, the lover queers the sacred space of the black church and its prescribed performances and creates a space of belonging for black gay men.[67]

"Our Black Gay Stonewall"

White's poem ends with reconciliation and incorporation, but the historical reality of this experience was much more complex. He states in an interview that "Last Rights" was inspired by the very real threat of erasure at black gay men's funerals—that not only their bodies but also their life stories would be buried.[68] The "controversy" over Essex Hemphill's funeral in 1995 exemplifies this threat. At the funeral, his family stated that he had given his life over to the Lord, and his friends and contemporaries from the black gay cultural movement understood this statement as a form of erasure.[69] Controversies like that of Hemphill's funeral greatly impacted black gay communities, who held their own memorial services for the deceased.

In her tribute to black gay writer James Baldwin, black lesbian feminist writer and activist Barbara Smith theorizes the significance of the funeral to black gay and lesbian politics. Smith writes about how Baldwin's blackness was affirmed by the many speeches and performances given at his funeral, while his gay identity was negated. This is why she suggests that "we must always bury our dead twice," gesturing toward the separate memorial services held for the deceased by black lesbian and gay communities. Smith explains why naming Baldwin's gay identity at the funeral matters.

Not only would this news have geometrically increased the quotient of truth available from the media that day in general, it also would have helped alter, if only by an increment, perceptions in Black communities all over the world about the meaning of homosexuality, communities where those of us who survive Baldwin as Black lesbians and gay men must continue to dwell.[70]

Smith highlights the significance of visibility for intraracial black politics, making black bodies intelligible as sexual minorities in black communities. She demonstrates that the funeral acts as a space in which the meanings of blackness and homosexuality can be contested and refashioned. This refashioning, she argues, might affect the material realities of black lesbians and gay men who must continue to negotiate the silence and melancholy produced from hegemonic understandings of homosexuality as negation and abjection in black communities.

The distinction between mourning and militancy was a source of political debate in gay communities during the AIDS crisis. Various movement factions debated whether or not public memorials were enough or if the focus should be on political mobilization. Douglas Crimp argues that during the height of the epidemic, "mourning became militancy" in the context of the violence of omission and the silence of families who desecrated memories of the dead.[71] The events surrounding Donald Woods's funeral attest to the blurred distinctions between mourning and militancy during this moment. Woods was a prominent figure in the black gay cultural scene and the New York arts community more broadly. In his 1992 obituary in the *New York Times*, he is celebrated as the executive director of AIDS Films, a nonprofit company that produced education and prevention movies, and as the public affairs director of the Brooklyn Children's Museum. The obituary lists his participation in Arts against Apartheid, the Hetrick-Martin Institute for gay and lesbian youth, and the Brooklyn Arts Council. It also includes his work in Marlon Riggs's documentaries *Tongues Untied* and *No Regrets*. But cardiac arrest is what the obituary reports as the cause of Woods's death, with no mention of his sexuality or his struggle with AIDS.[72] After experiencing the continued erasure of Woods's contributions to the black gay community during the funeral, Assotto Saint got up in the middle of the service and announced that Woods was out, was gay, and had died of AIDS, not a heart attack.[73] Saint incited Woods's friends, many of whom were dressed "inappropriately" in shorts, to stand in solidarity with him. In my interview with writer Marvin K. White, he describes this uprising as "Our Black Gay Stonewall," affirming its mythic proportions in black gay cultural memory.[74]

The erasure and subsequent uprising at Donald Woods's funeral held significance for many other survivors from Other Countries that I interviewed. In my conversation with Allen Wright, he highlights the loss of erotic possibilities, as traditional black funeral practices figuratively scrubbed black gay men clean of their so-called deviant desires.

> With Donald Woods's death, we came together to remember a beautiful man with a loving spirit who was also a brilliant poet and performer. . . . Yet at the funeral, the pastor led a service for someone none of us recognized. We came together in a kind of joy to remember Donald. It was a reunion of poets, writers, musicians, artists, dancers, activists, all who knew or at least appreciated each other's works that had been created over the years—all together out of a love for Donald. But the person being eulogized that day was a stranger to us, a pale and diluted version of the person we knew, admired, and deeply missed. There was nothing to suggest that the man in the closed coffin had freed himself enough to have ever fallen in love with another man, shared a life with another man, planned to grow old with another man, had no shame of his loves, wrote beautifully of them, and was widely loved in return. We sat politely out of some sense of respect for his parents and other relations, for the pastor and whatever relationship we had to (or thought we should have) to the black church. But we knew too that in doing so, we were acting in collusion with the lie. The truth of his life was wrapped in their shame and denial. Our silence supported that terrible fiction of a life that needed to be scrubbed clean of his true loves and of us.[75]

Wright's remarks reveal how funeral services so often sanitized the lives of black gay men who had devoted their artistry and activism to black gay communities. Yet the black church and the black family as cultural institutions commanded the "respect" of members of that community who were a significant part of Woods's life, forcing them to "collu[de] with the lie." Again, shame and silence become disciplinary forces, this time perpetuating a fictive boundary between black homosexuality and heterosexuality, as well as maintaining the fiction of the black family and the black church as solely heterosexual institutions. The predominance of cultural erasure occurring at black gay men's funerals during the epidemic obscures how black sexuality and black spirituality writ large have been marked as nonheteronormative and thus unassimilable within the dominant public sphere. Rather than embrace the queerness of blackness, black cultural institutions participate in the false promise of racial normativity that comes from subscribing to the state's binary gender and sexual codes.

G. Winston James's narrative demonstrates how the funeral operates as a site of denial, with biological families and clergy silencing the complex truths of black life.

> In the case of Essex Hemphill, Donald Woods, and perhaps many others, those moments, in my opinion, were controversial, not because they were simply examples of competing memories between those of biological and chosen family members and friends, but because they were deliberate attempts on the part of biological families and clergy to deny the complex truths about the individuals who had passed—particularly the truth of sexual orientation—and to silence the voices of friends who wished to share and celebrate publicly [at funerals and memorials] the ways in which they knew and remembered the deceased.[76]

As Colin Robinson describes in a follow-up interview, black funeral practices, at least in certain Christian traditions, are centrally concerned with getting the loved one into heaven; they are about restoration. However, for James, restoration to the black family and to the black church means denying the diversity of black genders and sexualities and silencing the voices of the gender- and sexually variant black communities to which the deceased belonged. These communities tell other stories about blackness, stories that, if not recovered, might be buried along with the dead. As the examples of Hemphill's funeral and Woods's obituary demonstrate, the hegemony of heteronormativity in black communities means that these are not stories to be passed on.

Robinson reports that Woods's cultural contributions were rendered as vague. He also points out how the black funeral links black authenticity to notions of respectability.

> In Donald's case, two events were planned—the family planned a church service at which they sought to create the proper Donald they wanted to hold up among people of judgment and send to heaven, a Donald whose inconvenient sexuality was to be muted and did not belong at the center of a respectable service, who wrote poems "to inspire" and led a "social justice" organization. . . . . I don't know what's black about it other than perhaps we want to have respectable funerals and have no problem with the violence that inflicts on others.[77]

Silencing black gay cultural memory is, in Robinson's formulation, a form of psychic violence. His narrative points to a long history of capitulatory black politics of inclusion and respectability that have distorted memories of various genders and sexualities in black culture.[78] His narrative also illustrates how racial normativity has depended on the violent excision of "other" memories, a forgetting of black gay culture and the public efforts of black LGBT people to transform the meaning of blackness, gender, and sexuality. The space of the funeral becomes a site of mourning for the loved ones lost to AIDS and for a lost history, one critical to black gay self-fashioning.

Despite their knowledge of the upcoming alternative funeral service for Woods, Assotto Saint and other members of the black gay community, by rising to their feet at Saint's request, refused to capitulate to the mandates of "respect" demanded by the family and the church at the traditional services for Woods. And Saint's actions at this funeral horrified and embarrassed Woods's family.[79] I mention this to add that this debate over black memory is not one-sided. The competing memorial claims on Woods raise questions: To whom does the body (as a repository of memory) belong? How do we account for black gay men's varying degrees of black cultural belonging when determining to whom their bodies and memories belong? Multiply determined subjects become problematic to cultural memory when multiple constituencies make historical claims on them. White's reference to "Our Black Gay Stonewall" attests to this point. Regardless of the presence of people of color at the center of the Stonewall rebellion, White's formulation points to how this history has been reappropriated so that the primary recipients of freedom are imagined as white lesbians and gays. Black gay men must make claims to an alternative history of sexual freedom, understood as a struggle against the erasure of their histories and memories within black culture. In this alternative history, the black family is cast as the primary site of regulation.

More than abstract claims to memory, claims to property also arise during funerals. If the biological family has control over the deceased's estate, it also determines what becomes available to the archives and by extension to official history. This makes Saint's training in the writers' workshop on how to execute one's literary estate all the more significant. Even beyond intellectual property, it is also important to note that Woods was buried in a plot that Saint controlled. This speaks to a longer history of black gay men footing the bills for funerals that they were oftentimes banned from attending. In his ethnography of gay black men in Harlem, William G. Hawkeswood discusses how these men often paid for the funerals of family members and friends in the early years of the epidemic. Most of these deceased had been

IV drug users who were largely invisible as AIDS victims, since AIDS became a national concern only when it began to affect white gay men.[80]

That same "something," the "vital force" that Daniel Garrett imagined as queer possibility in the "Upper Room," compelled members of the Other Countries Collective to go to the traditional services and let their grief be heard in that space. The uprising at Donald Woods's funeral demonstrates how black gay mourning might disrupt the emergence of black/gay liberalism. Scholars such as Rinaldo Walcott, Robert Reid-Pharr, and Dagmawi Woubshet have credited the mass deaths associated with the AIDS epidemic with cleansing gay men of their messy desires, thereby offering them entry into modernity as liberal gay subjects.[81] However, the uprising at Woods's funeral and the power of that uprising in black gay cultural memory act as a refusal of the discourses of respectability and the disciplinary mechanisms of shame and silence necessary to the production of black/gay liberalism. If black/gay liberalism depends on a forgetting of the queer past and the stigma and shame of AIDS and its (ongoing) impact on black communities, then the power of remembering "Our Black Gay Stonewall" holds open a space for those to whom narratives of stigma, shame, and deviance continue to cling, as well as the possibility for a more radical present.[82]

The Other Countries Collective offers a historical case study for thinking about black gay men's collective mourning as a mode of black/queer optimism. The inconsolable grief of black gay men makes optimism more interesting in its affirmation of the "not-yet-past" of AIDS. In the face of "end of AIDS" and "not-about-AIDS" discourses suggesting that the crisis ended in the mid-1990s and that today's most pressing concerns in US politics and culture are *not* about AIDS, black gay men's melancholic mourning of the losses during the early era of AIDS fracture such narratives of closure.[83] Because many of these men are long-term survivors of HIV, their melancholic mourning attests to the fact of HIV/AIDS as an ongoing site of local and global political struggle. Moreover, black gay mourning acts as a mode of refusal to the neoliberal forces that seek to distance liberal black/gay subjectivity from the historical intimacy of blackness, queerness, and death, an intimacy that helped shape a more radical vision of politics in the early era of AIDS. The politicized nature of their melancholic memories allows us to imagine more radical possibilities amid an increasingly liberal black/gay political agenda.

Black gay mourning, in this instance, accounts for cultural loss even as it acts as a productive force. Though the traumatic impact of AIDS produced negative affects such as fear, shame, disappointment, and grief, the negative affects associated with the traumatic impact of AIDS also became a "vital force" in the production of cultural community, black gay aesthetics, and political activism. Furthermore, mourning provided a way to contest the cultural forces that sought to erase black gay men's artistic and political contributions, and to enlarge the subjective and political possibilities for these men in the present day.

FOUR

"The Future Is Very Uncertain"

Black Gay Self-Making in Melvin Dixon's Diaries

Perhaps I just don't understand how to be human.

—Melvin Dixon

On October 7, 1991, after purchasing a copy of psychiatrist Elisabeth Kübler-Ross's famous treatise on the five stages of grief, *On Death and Dying*, Melvin Dixon wrote in his diary: "Perhaps I am preparing for my own transition."[1] Dixon, a black gay fiction writer, poet, translator, and scholar, had recently learned from his doctor that he had only three T-cells left, so he may have written this passage in anticipation of his own AIDS-related death. The diary entry comes only months after one announcing the death from AIDS of his partner, nonprofit executive Richard Horovitz.[2] After the final entry on November 8, 1991, mentioning his move from Provincetown, Massachusetts, to Washington, DC, to be closer to friends and family for much-needed emotional support, Dixon's diary abruptly ends. More than half the notebook pages are blank.

Dixon died of AIDS in October 1992. His death might prompt us to interpret his diaries as a straightforward exploration of his struggles with and against the virus. But such a reading ignores the constellation of life events that made Dixon vulnerable to AIDS in the first place. As I discuss in the introduction to this book, centering the experiences of black gay men and their multiple forms of exclusion—from white gay communities, heterosexual black communities, and the nation-state—requires a broad analytical framework that sees the death of a generation of black gay writers from AIDS as "resulting from a constellation of life experiences as well as from a discrete happening."[3] This chapter situates Dixon's diaries within a longer history of antiblackness and antiqueerness that leaves its traces in the feelings of uncertainty and self-doubt that structure Dixon's black gay diasporic consciousness.

Situating Dixon's diaries within a transatlantic history of antiblack and antigay violence allows us to view the afterlife of black/queer diasporic trauma as part of the rupture between self-knowledge and identity for black/gay diasporic subjects. As Rinaldo Walcott argues, "The history of the trans-Atlantic slave trade produces a tremendous amount of self-doubt for many, many black people who were born in the Americas."[4] Walcott suggests that the traumatic ruptures of black diasporic history and memory produce a phenomenological experience of not-knowing, of uncertainty and self-doubt for blacks in the West. These feelings are signaled by Dixon's repeated use of the uncommon and formal adverb *perhaps*, as in "Perhaps I just don't understand how to be human."[5] Here Dixon assumes that there is a normative way of being human, and that someone can and must possess the knowledge and capacity to achieve normativity. However, histories of empire and enslavement in the Americas mark black people as outside the category of the human. And while we might categorize gay identity as a neocolonial subject position rooted in the historical and cultural specificities of the West, in the context of heteronormativity embedded within the US nation-state and the embrace of Western norms of gender and sexuality within black American communities in the post–civil rights era, Dixon's gay identity also marks him as vulnerable to the heterosexualizing colonial violence that still structures US state forms and everyday social relations.[6] His ambivalence about his capacity to know how to be human is symptomatic of the traumatic ruptures in cultural knowledge produced by the transatlantic slave trade.

Yet Dixon's "perhaps" also denotes ontological and political possibility, indexing how thinking and writing hold the power to disrupt the coloniality of black gay being. His diaries are a space within which we can investigate his relationship to identity categories like race, sexuality, and the human. This line of inquiry challenges Ross Chambers's notion that AIDS diaries defer the responsibility of making sense of the diarist's life to future witnesses.[7] For black gay men, whose suffering and death from AIDS remain unremarkable, and whose archival permanence is threatened by the racialized, gendered, and sexualized structure of the archive, deferring the responsibility of making sense to future witnesses is not an option. Following the work of Ernesto Javier Martinez, this chapter explores how Dixon's diaries operate as "queer race narratives of intelligibility." His diaries are preoccupied with "the everyday labor of making sense of oneself and of making sense to others in contexts of intense ideological violence and interpersonal conflict." They embody what Martinez calls the "germinative capacity" of life writing for "making sense" of black gay social life in the West.[8]

This chapter briefly sketches Dixon's biography in order to establish the cultural, social, and political significance of his life writing. It offers an overview of this archive, and asserts its relevance as a site for theorizing black gay self-making. It then considers how Dixon's diaries challenge the gay historical accounts of the 1970s, 1980s, and 1990s that focus on sexuality as a singular axis of political struggle. I begin my study of Dixon's diaries during the seventies and early eighties to highlight the insidious traumas of racism and homophobia that increased his vulnerability to AIDS, and show how his diaries challenge the generic boundaries of the AIDS diary. I then trace a shift in those diaries after 1984, when he first suspected that he had the virus, demonstrating how AIDS, as a form of black diasporic trauma, shifted Dixon's thinking. Finally, building on my analysis of the text as a site of theorizing black gay being, I focus on the episodic structure, dated entries, and uncertain ending of the diary to demonstrate how the black gay cultural imagination reorients black gay social life toward futures beyond the time and space of biological life and social death as represented by each entry.

In his focus on what Chambers terms "textual survival," Dixon contests black and queer theories that regard social death as the dominant interpretive framework for theorizing black gay social life. Chambers argues that representation and the possibility of rereading that representation allow for a kind of "textual survival": "But representation is also a means whereby, through the possibility of reading it opens up, a dying subject can anticipate the possibility of a certain form of textual survival, the condition of which, as we've seen, is the death of the author." Chambers illustrates the importance of life writing as a "condition of survival" that extends the possibility of witnessing beyond the author's demise.[9] In the face of uncertainty and impending death, Dixon accelerated his literary output in pursuit of precisely this type of survival.

Diaristic Writing as Praxis of Self-Making

Melvin Dixon was born May 29, 1950, in Stamford, Connecticut, to Jessie and Handy Dixon. He earned a BA from Wesleyan University in 1971 and an MA and a PhD in American civilization from Brown University in 1975. After completing his dissertation about US slave narratives, he began his scholarly career as an assistant professor of Afro-American studies at Fordham University from 1975 to 1976. After the Afro-American Studies Department dissolved to program status, Dixon took a position in the English

Department at Williams College from 1976 to 1980. He later became an associate professor of English at Queens College of the City University of New York, where he was promoted to full professor in 1986. He held a joint appointment at CUNY Graduate Center, a visiting position at Columbia University, and a Fulbright Senior Lectureship at the University of Dakar.

Throughout Dixon's career as a creative writer, scholar, and translator, he explored the relationship between geography, memory, and identity. His first published collection of poems, *Change of Territory* (1983), details a black gay man's search for his racial and sexual heritage. Keguro Macharia argues that Dixon's literal and figurative journeys "recapitulate the racial and sexual diasporas of Claude McKay, Langston Hughes, and James Baldwin."[10] In his celebrated scholarly text, *Ride Out the Wilderness* (1987), Dixon demonstrates how African American writers have used imaginative texts to make placed-based claims for more positive identity constructions. He "examines the ways in which Afro-American writers, often considered homeless, alienated from mainstream culture, and segregated in negative environments, have used language to create alternative landscapes where black culture and identity can flourish apart from any marginal, prescribed 'place.'"[11] This work can be read alongside the long tradition of black scholars such as W. E. B. Du Bois and E. Franklin Frazier, who have theorized black identity in relationship to space. In his critically acclaimed first novel, *Trouble the Water* (1989), Dixon explores family reconciliation through the story of Jordan Henry, a young black professor of history living in New England, who returns to his family's place of origin, Pee Dee, North Carolina, to confront its troubled legacy in the community and to face the consequences of his long absence. Dixon's translations from French of Genevieve Fabre's critical text, *Drumbeats, Masks, and Metaphor: Contemporary Afro-American Theatre* (1983), and *The Collected Poetry of Leopold Sedar Senghor* (1991)—Senegalese president, poet, and cultural theorist—exemplify his critical engagement with transatlantic black thought and cultural production. Many of the poems in his posthumous collection *Love's Instruments* (1995) continue his themes of geography, memory, and identity, but focus heavily on the losses of the early era of the global AIDS pandemic. As Dagmawi Woubshet notes, "In these powerful poems, Dixon consistently figures himself as a double mourner, grieving the deaths of others and his own approaching death; and in some he employs African American spirituals to convey his own sense of dying."[12]

Dixon struggled to balance his life as a creative writer with his critical work as a scholar. In his diaries, he often mentions how his academic career stifled his commitment to being a creative writer. No text attests to his commitment to this craft more than his most celebrated novel, *Vanishing Rooms* (1991), which took Dixon over fifteen years to publish. The novel is set in the 1970s and follows black gay dancer Jesse after his partner, Metro, a white gay man, has been raped and murdered by a gang of white ethnic youths. After Metro's death, Jesse seeks comfort in the arms of Ruella, a black woman and his partner at the dance studio. The novel alternates between the narratives of Jesse, Ruella, and Lonny, one of the white youths who killed Metro. It uses dance performance, the urban landscape, and metaphors of spatial confinement to explore the psychodynamics of race, class, gender, and sexuality, and how they separate and bind together the lives of these characters. When Dixon submitted the novel for consideration, Toni Morrison, then an editor at Random House, rejected it for publication. Commenting on an early draft, Morrison states that Dixon's characters are defined by their sexuality: "Somehow sexuality is not only what they do, it is what they are and that is not enough for me."[13]

While the majority of scholarly attention has been directed toward *Vanishing Rooms* and his posthumously published AIDS poetry, Dixon's diaries serve as one of the most extensive historical accounts of black gay life during the 1970s, 1980s, and early 1990s. They extend the field of black queer studies, which has traditionally treated novels, performance, and film as the primary sites of scholarly inquiry. Besides the posthumously published journals, notebooks, and poems of black gay writer Gary Fisher, which have received scant scholarly attention, to my knowledge no other diaristic accounts of black gay life during the seventies and eighties have been published. In Dixon's early diaries, we find not only his intimate feelings, philosophies of everyday life, and social, cultural, and psychological struggles but also the beginnings of many of his acclaimed published works. His first poetry emerges in 1969 in diaries he kept during his sophomore year at Wesleyan University, and in that same year he wrote his first collection of poems, which he titled "Seasons of the Soul," in a diary he called the Blue Book. The ideas for his acclaimed novels *Trouble the Water* and *Vanishing Rooms* appear in his diaries in the mid-1970s. The diaries also document his travels between the United States, Africa, Europe, and the Caribbean, situating Dixon as a witness to many important historical events, including black rebellions against police violence in Hartford, Connecticut, in 1970, and the General Strike against rising costs of living and low wages in Paris in 1973. From 1984 onward, Dixon's diaries document his struggles against AIDS—what it meant to lose friends and loved ones, including his partner, as well as his concern about his own fate and the life of his cultural work.

Figure 4. Cover of Melvin Dixon's diary, 1970. Excerpts from the diaries of Melvin Dixon,
© Melvin Dixon; used by permission of the Estate of Melvin Dixon.

They offer one of the only autobiographical accounts of black gay struggles against HIV/AIDS, amid a plethora of published literary and filmic accounts of the early era of AIDS centering on white gay men.

Dixon's diaries consist of a series of fifteen notebooks that he kept at various stages of his life. His journal entries are often one or two notebook pages in length, and consist of beautifully written, polished prose, often labeled with time, date, and location. Some evidence suggests that Dixon reread his diaries to reflect on experiences and to track his emotional and professional development. A few of the notebooks have their own titles. He titled the notebook he kept in the summer of 1970 while working for the Urban League "An Un-American Summer: Journal of the Adventures in an Urban Summer of Qualified Life aboard the Unsinkable U.L.G.H. (Urban League of Greater Hartford)" (fig. 4).

The length and style of the title conjure the writings of African descendant people in the eighteenth- and nineteenth-century Atlantic world. In addition, the title positions Dixon's contemporary struggles for racial and sexual freedom along a historical continuum with black writers who had to negotiate the complex and intertwined geographies of slavery and (un)freedom in the antebellum world. His use of the metaphor of a ship to describe the Urban League of Greater Hartford, his conjuring of writers of the early black Atlantic world, and his notation of the date, time, and location in his diary entries indicate an emerging black queer diasporic consciousness that seeps beyond the boundaries of the US nation-state.

Dixon believed that his summer work with the Urban League was "a real test of his commitment to the black community and himself."[14] He worked in its housing department, conducting community investigations and analysis on the living conditions of Hartford's residents. He visited four black women who expressed disappointment with rising rents, lack of repairs, and black urban disenfranchisement in a time of rapid political and economic change. He noted the Urban League's emphasis on "systems change," meaning "that by working through the system one can effect social change in America and that counter-institutions were a last resort." Dixon disagreed with this political philosophy, noting that "the system is not designed for black admission and promotion to decision-making positions," and thus "there is very little one can do to change the American system."[15] His time with other college students at the Urban League helped shape his political consciousness, and his Dominican friend, Nilo, challenged the geopolitical boundaries of his politics. Dixon's sexual marginality shaped his belief that black Americans "have to get it together here (U.S.) among ourselves and our varying ideologies (keeping in mind, however, our international brothers) before we can expand fully our program of liberation for black people throughout the world."[16]

Dixon's diaristic account of his experience at the Urban League aligns with Paul Gilroy's conceptualization of "the ship" as a crucial figure of black Atlantic modernity. For Gilroy, the ship registers a "desire to transcend both the structures of the nation state and the constraints of ethnicity and national particularity" that "have always sat uneasily alongside the strategic choices forced on black movements and individuals embedded in national political cultures and nation states in America, the Caribbean, and Europe."[17] Moreover, the ship conjures the trauma of the Middle Passage, and the forms of racial, gender, and sexual terror that are central to the development of black diasporic consciousness. Dixon's conflict regarding the geopolitical boundaries of black American politics and his engagement with Nilo demonstrate his desire to acknowledge and exceed national and sexual particularity, while his assertion of the dispossession of black people within the American system and his bearing witness to the deplorable housing conditions of black people in Hartford index the antiblack violence that is central to Western modernity. By deploying the image of the ship, Dixon demonstrates how the local and national dimensions of his experiences are in fact shaped by global flows of information, while positioning the diary as a form of black diasporic cultural production and a site for the development of a black diasporic consciousness rooted in a shared sense of national dispossession.

Beyond their important historical, cultural, and political valences, Melvin Dixon's diaries serve as an important site for theorizing black gay self-making. Black feminist scholars have theorized the diary as a genre that disrupts the fictive divide between privacy and publicity. As Akasha (Gloria T.) Hull argues, "Diaries are most often and most interestingly written in times of change and turmoil, or, as it is often put, in times of mobility—most often thought of as geographic, but just as plausibly psychic as well."[18] Dixon's diary writing charts this geographic and psychic (im)mobility, and the diary serves as a space to confront the global forces of racism and homophobia that would render black gay male identity as "ungeographic."[19] Joanne Braxton further complicates raced, classed, and gendered definitions of the diary that would deem the genre privatized and feminized. In discussing the diaries of Harlem Renaissance poet Charlotte Forten Grimké, Braxton writes, "Although the diaries were intended to be private, the diarist's autobiographic act relates to the development of a public voice in the move to objectify and take control of experiences through the writer's craft." Moreover, she theorizes the diary "as a tool for the development of political and artistic consciousness and as a means of self-evaluation" as well as "a retreat from potentially shattering encounters with racism and a vehicle for the development of a black and [gay] poetic identity, a place of restoration and self-healing."[20] As a black gay middle-class male diary writer, Dixon's male and class privileges enable him to keep a diary, but racism and homophobia structure his diaristic writing such that "self-evaluation" becomes a public, political act and "a retreat from potentially shattering encounters with racism [and homophobia]."[21]

Dixon's journals span twenty-five years, but sometimes days, weeks, months, and even years ensue between entries. Though he expresses his commitment to journal writing, he makes no apologies for these temporal gaps, explaining that uncertainty in his life facilitates his silence. His entry for May 22, 1977: "I offer no apologies for my waiting so long for committing my thoughts and actions to these pages. Largely my silence is due to uncertainty. Everything seems to be in a state of flux, change, mutability . . . and I'm unsure mostly of myself."[22] He defines uncertainty as a negative emotion related to the "pain of having no center," and he repeatedly reflects on how the journals are in part an attempt to construct what he calls "self-ness" and "self-(ful)ness."[23] Dixon's deployment of the diary as a creative tool for moving from the "pain of having no center" to a sense of "self-(ful)ness" locates diaristic writing among the cultural forms used by black gay men to achieve what Essex Hemphill called a "functioning self." Diaristic writing offered Dixon an alternative to writing fiction and literary criticism. The genre allowed him to "feel through and write through" his sense of disloca- tion.[24] He describes diary writing as a compulsion; his entries often emerged from the necessity for him to write against sadness, frustration, loneliness, and the feeling of "doom that creeps up on [him] and locks [him] up inside its terror."[25] These entries oscillate between reporting his experiences, ac- complishments, and ideas for creative writing projects and reflecting on his personal and professional successes and failures. On December 5, 1973, he wrote, "Being committed to a journal requires an honesty with 'felt' experi- ence. But I don't want to report the experience—that's too journalistic, but even detailed reporting is sometimes necessary to understand the feeling felt, the lesson, however painfully, learned."[26] Dixon's diaries foreground the labor of self-examination that subtended the presentation of a black gay self through literary and cultural forms, along with the psychological struggles necessary for attaining black gay men's archival permanence through writ- ing and publishing. They capture the immaterial and unquantifiable forms of social and psychological damage that circumscribe black gay person- hood, and demonstrate how writing operates as a method for alleviating that damage.

Disidentifying with White Gay Life

Placing Dixon's diaries at the center of gay culture and politics in the 1970s and 1980s challenges some of the prevailing assumptions that govern gay historiography of this period. Often, gay histories of the seventies, eighties, and nineties have failed to interrogate the whiteness of gay culture and poli- tics, including literary cultures. Charles Kaiser's *The Gay Metropolis* (1997) mentions only one African American woman's experience in his chapter on the 1970s, and he mentions no African Americans in his chapters on the 1980s and 1990s. Like most academic, public, and popular accounts of AIDS activism, Kaiser excludes black gay men from the historical record. In a particularly telling passage reflecting on the devastating cultural losses of AIDS, he describes the deaths of four of the seven white gay members of the literary collective Violet Quill as "typical."

The AIDS epidemic would cause more pain and loss than anyone within the gay community had hitherto imagined possible. And the deaths among art- ists would ravage the creativity of American culture for at least a generation.

A typical disaster was the decimation of the Violet Quill, a group of seven novelists formed at the end of the 1970s.[27]

While the deaths of many members of the Violet Quill were a great loss, Kaiser's perspective is embedded with racial bias. His claiming these deaths as "typical" of the devastating impact of AIDS on "the creativity of American culture" reveals the unmarked whiteness in his conceptualization of that culture. Furthermore, his claim that the pain and loss of AIDS were unimaginable elides how histories of enslavement, colonialism, and national exclusion have depended on the physical deaths of racial minorities from disease, and how discourses of illness have worked to mark people of color as ineligible for US citizenship.[28] James Baldwin notes how white gay people feel cheated because they are born into a society in which they are supposed to be safe, and the anomaly of their sexuality puts them in danger, unexpectedly.[29]

In contrast to Kaiser, Dixon's diaries reveal a sense of danger and concern with the imminence of death that is present in the entries even before he became infected with AIDS. When read as a site of black gay memory in the post-Stonewall era, his diaries represent this moment not as one of pride and pleasure, as it is historically and popularly imagined, but as evidence of the persistent negativities of post-Stonewall gay life. As I mention in chapter 3, the presence of people of color at the center of the Stonewall rebellion does not mean that its historical narration as a major turning point in LGBT political struggles against state-based violence extends to lesbian, gay, bisexual, and trans people of color. Black poor, queer, trans, and disabled people's ongoing struggles against state-based violence trouble the centrality of Stonewall in the American imagination.

On Christmas Day in 1971, at the tender age of twenty-one, Dixon wrote in his diary, "Death you look so sweet today."[30] His seduction by death comes after a long conversation with his mother about love, loneliness, and friendship, and her suggestion that marriage and God might offer comfortable alternatives to Dixon's despair. Dixon also grappled with the meaning of blackness, particularly in black art, during the post–civil rights era. As a dancer, actor, and playwright at Wesleyan University in the early 1970s, he launched the Black Repertory Theater, where he experimented with multiple genres of creative expression. He performed a dance routine that was very similar to the dance between Jesse and Ruella in *Vanishing Rooms*. In the novel, Jesse is ridiculed by his peers at the cafeteria's "black table" for dancing at a black protest on campus. Although Jesse's dance serves as a form of black activism, as a black male who dances in tights and leotards and walks with a "swish," he threatens to represent blackness as gender and sexually deviant.[31]

But during his college years, expressive culture did little for Dixon as a mode of self- and community-making. The Black Repertory Theater served as a means of community building, and it garnered Dixon a degree of respect among fellow black students, but he did not find it emotionally fulfilling. People would ask him what new play he was writing or directing, but his college peers hardly ever inquired about his personal life or well-being. The production of black theatre, as a privileged cultural and political enterprise in the black arts movement, may have placed limits on Dixon's expressions of personhood. He wrote in his diary on May 1, 1972, at 3:00 a.m.: "What I had created [the Black Repertory Theater] finally destroyed me somewhat. . . . Perhaps I just don't understand how to be human."[32] He feared that the task of representing black people and marshaling their cries for revolution through performance would limit, rather than promote, his ability to embody the full range of his personhood, and his access to the fundamental human need to be loved.

This longing was fulfilled by neither the arts nor the radical sexual politics of gay liberation. On November 6, 1973, Dixon commented on his exhaustion with the urban gay male sexual revolution, which has been a central site of memory for contemporary queer theory and politics (fig. 5).

> I don't feel sexual, just [need] someone to talk to. My utmost desire is to be held. Not fucked, sucked or cruised. Just gently, and affectionately held, embraced. Covered with fire from someone's hot flesh—who wants me, needs me—not so much sexually, but humanly, tenderly, soft but firm. How tired I am of the "hardness" of being gay . . . of being crass, brutal, "erect." I've probably gone impotent already because what I'm searching for is not between sheets, nor atop a luncheon table in polite and shady conversation.[33]

For Dixon, the texture of gay male life during this erotic revolution was too "hard." He draws from the multiple connotations of this term—its psychological association with being emotionally difficult, its gendered association with an emotionless masculinity that prevents intimacy, and its sexualized meaning of being sexually aroused. Dixon describes gay male culture during this moment as "crass" and "brutal," challenging Lauren Berlant and Michael Warner's claim that gay male promiscuity during this era was a "common language of self-cultivation, shared knowledge, and the exchange of inwardness."[34]

Racialized fantasies of the black male penis as wholly constitutive of

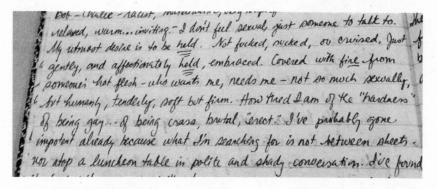

Figure 5. Diary entry, November 6, 1973. Excerpts from the diaries of Melvin Dixon,
© Melvin Dixon; used by permission of the Estate of Melvin Dixon.

black male identity give further meaning to Dixon's disidentification with the "hardness" of gay identity. In his discussion of race in the works of white gay writers of the Violet Quill collective, David Bergman argues, "over and over in the works of the Violet Quill, race is aestheticized." Bergman reads the inclusion of African American men in 1970s and 1980s white gay litera-ture and culture as historically significant because it stood in contrast with then-dominant views of maleness and beauty. He maintains that the Violet Quill's celebration of black male beauty stands in contrast to aesthetic ide-ologies that found no beauty in (black) men, or in "large, aggressive, well-armored men." Edmund White of the Violet Quill believed that aesthetic and erotic modes had the possibility of eluding racism, because "they can exist independently of the social, cultural, and economic framework when both sexual desire and the Beautiful are pursued without a sense of respon-sibility."[35] However, black gay writers like Dixon did not have the luxury of irresponsibility in the development of their aesthetic and cultural pro-duction. For black gay men, the invisibility and representational distortion produced by black heterosexism and white (gay) racism meant that their aesthetic production often had to be geared toward creating positive identity constructions that would render their lives visible and valid.[36]

Given this context, Melvin Dixon's ruminations about his own impo-tence register as both a failed physiological response and as what Keguro Macharia calls "quitting," exemplifying Dixon's refusal to withstand the racialized "toxicity" and subsequent "exhaustion" that subtend gay iden-tification.[37] In light of Dixon's refusal to acquiesce to the normative social protocols of gay identity, the diary operated as a space for him to make sense of his experiences. On February 3, 1974, he wrote, "Language is my work-

shop. There I search for the tools to make some sense of my experiences."
Here he expounds on the power of language, and of poetry in particular, for
"working out the pain of not knowing, not understanding."[38] Dixon's pain
was exacerbated by his not knowing or understanding how to be black and
gay in an era in which gay identity and politics were dominantly expressed
through whiteness, pleasure, and pride. The space of the diary offered him a
way to privately explore, critique, and reimagine what it meant to be a black
gay man beyond its dominant meanings in the public sphere.

Making Sense of Black Gay Life

In his discussion of "felt intuition" as a method in black queer studies, Phillip Brian Harper describes the uncertainty and speculative rumination that
characterize minority experience. Harper argues that minority experience
produces uncertainty and speculation because it "continually renders even
the most routine instances of social activity and personal interaction as possible cases of invidious social distinction and discriminatory treatment."[39]
He explains how people who inhabit marginalized bodies must constantly
speculate about how their very presence transforms social space. Marginalized people constantly encounter unknown persons who may treat them in
a certain way, discriminate against them, or exclude them because of their
race, class, gender, ability, and/or sexuality. Harper describes this kind of
speculation as exhausting and debilitating, because one cannot predict an
unknown person's reactions, and because the meaning of the event that
sparks one's speculation can never be truly resolved. Although Dixon's diaries explore matters of love, friendship, creativity, and belonging that might
be considered as universal concerns, they are primarily concerned with
questions of race and sexuality as sites of ruminative speculation. Moreover,
his many inquiries regarding his occupation of the category human index
the failures of any claim to universality, and instead render his speculative
life writing as an effect of the various histories, discourses, and material
struggles that shape black/gay embodiment in the late twentieth-century
United States. Focusing on his cultural particularity reminds us of the ways
that race and sexuality are bound up with notions of the human, acting as
disciplinary forces that categorize racialized, gendered, and sexualized bodies into and/or outside hierarchal genres of human being.[40]

Dixon's diaries can be read as a black gay site of memory through their
interplay between uncertainty, speculation, and exhaustion. And though
this reading may compel us to rethink his "slow death" as beginning before
his HIV diagnosis, he took up this labor of making sense in order to move

toward life.[41] His commitment to the task of making sense was in some ways about his diaries' future witnesses, of bearing witness to other minorities who might encounter these diaries after his death. On December 9, 1971, Dixon wrote, "I know I will die young because I seem to have little strength to exist in this cold world—on its own terms. I am not so brave to commit a final suicide. So I die a little each day through sex and promiscuity, alcohol, and heavy eating. Yes I die a little each day hoping all the while to be born again."[42] Though this statement registers how death and narratives of cultural pathology shaped Dixon's consciousness, he could not have imagined at the time of this writing that he would pass away at the age of forty-two. His primary task was to make sense of these categories for himself. He embarked on this project of speculative knowledge production because, as Harper argues, "not to proceed speculatively, is to speak plainly, not to live."[43]

Moreover, Dixon's multiple marginalizations made his complex personhood illegible to the institutions that he navigated. He had to privilege one aspect of his identity over others in these institutional contexts: either black identity (for publishers and readers of his early fiction, and within the academy as a black student and as a professor of African American literature) or gay identity (in the white gay publishing industry in his later fiction and poetry, in white gay subcultures, and as a person with AIDS). The speculative space of the diary allowed him to make meaning of his multiply determined identity, precisely because diary writing operated outside the demands of institutional legibility. Some of Dixon's earliest recollections of institutional illegibility and geographic dislocation coincide with his time as a professor at Williams College from 1976 to 1980. He deeply regretted his decision to move to Williamstown, Massachusetts, claiming that the town disconnected him from the broader community of "black and Third World People." He expressed his desire to leave and "get back to [his] own values."[44] Dixon's sexuality compounded his feelings of isolation. On February 16, 1979, he wrote, "In Williamstown—no room for a black person, no room for a gay person. No room for me." He further recounted the significance of place to black gay self-making, claiming that he felt "cast out" of Williamstown, "which refuses to respond to my need for emotional/sexual contact." Because of his feelings of racial and sexual displacement, Dixon frequently visited the "bar/bath scene" in New York City on the weekends, where he enjoyed "intense, although fleeting and sometimes anonymous contacts."[45]

Seeking reprieve from sexual isolation, Dixon faced racial exclusion during his travels to popular US lesbian and gay destinations such as Provincetown, Massachusetts. On August 23, 1970, he was refused accommodations at a hotel in Provincetown after the "ol' white lady" who owned it found out that he and his four friends were black. She feared that they would be too loud.[46] On another trip to Provincetown on July 26, 1985, he wrote, "Provincetown is not a great place to be alone . . . I've seen only two black couples of gay men since I've been here. Single black men seem only interested in whites. And then the whites are 90% interested in whites—except, of course, if you show much basket—then you're only the stereotypical stud. So what's a lonely lady like me to do?"[47] Dixon's racial-sexual alterity in these New England towns produced a sense of psychic immobility, and his deep engagement with the texts of African diasporic writers allowed his imagination to "wander" in the face of racial, sexual, and economic forces that sought to curtail his movement.[48] On August 8, 1976, Dixon expressed his desire to be a wanderer like Claude McKay and live off his writings.[49] He cited Langston Hughes as another black queer wanderer whom he deeply admired. His longing for racial and sexual intimacy eventually compelled him to return to New York City, and accept a job teaching English and creative writing at Queens College. This move mirrors the migrations of Hughes and McKay to New York City during the Harlem Renaissance era. Dixon's literal and figurative wandering, both domestic and abroad, demonstrates how the transnational flow of bodies, ideas, and cultural and political artifacts shaped US black gay cultural movements in the 1970s, 1980s, and 1990s.

While living in Europe, Dixon faced forms of racism similar to those that he had experienced in the United States. He documented the racial discrimination he encountered trying to secure housing and attempting to enter gay cultural spaces, calling European racism "more subtle and undercover than White American racism."[50] He recalled an experience of housing discrimination in Paris in which a white property owner stated that he did not want *etrangers* living in his property, which Dixon interpreted to mean "black people."[51] After requesting entry into one gay club, the doorman replied "C'est prive," but Dixon believed that *private* was a code word for "whites only." Several gay clubs in Amsterdam also denied him entry. Though his experiences of racism in Europe were similar to those he experienced in the United States, especially when involving black gay men's exclusion from white-owned gay bars and restaurants in urban centers, Dixon found European antiblackness more tolerable, because it was coupled with anti-American sentiment. Describing his experiences in Europe, he stated on Monday June 28, 1971, "Being gay, being black, being in Europe is rough."[52]

Dixon grappled with the heterosexism embedded within the structures of the university as both a student and a professor. In 1974, while working on his PhD in American civilization at Brown University, he discussed his discomfort with his creative writing mentor at the time, African American poet Michael S. Harper, who had been teaching at Brown. Dixon felt that he could not discuss his homosexuality with Harper, "because he'd reject me and my work, yet how central this is to my work."[53] Though he feared Harper's rejection of his homosexuality and the homosexual content of his creative writing, it was Harper who first told him that he was avoiding something in his writing. After reading Dixon's short story "The Boy with Beer" in 1974, Harper directed him to be more assertive about his position on homosexuality. Speculating about what might have been missing from his work, Dixon stated in his diary entry of January 26, 1978, "Maybe it was a confrontation with my real feelings, anger, hurt, is this a protection?"[54] This "protection" stemmed in part from his failure to confront the negative affects associated with the structural impossibilities of embodying black and gay identities simultaneously.

The university disciplined the forms of writing that would legitimate his status as a student and his job security as an employee, and its structures of disciplinarity aided in the creation of what Dwight McBride calls "straight Black studies."[55] After publishing the short story "The Boy with Beer" and two poems in Joseph Beam's anthology, In the Life (1986), Dixon asked a few of his black gay colleagues at Queens College, where he was a professor at the time, to publish a review of the collection. Both colleagues refused: one, who was pre-tenure, because of tenure concerns, and the other, who was post-tenure, because he did not want to be "outed" by such a review. The prospect of being "outed" by a publication also contributed to Dixon's sense of un-belonging in historically black institutions.[56] In 1990, he applied for a position at the historically black Howard University in Washington, DC. After the English Department expressed interest in his candidacy, Dixon remarked, "I sent in my vita—but seeing all the obvious citations of gay publications and anthologies and papers read, I doubt if I would be a top candidate."[57] As a student and professor of African American literature and culture, his gay identification and his exploration of homosexuality in his creative work threatened the already fraught legibility of African American letters in the academy.

Melvin Dixon's struggle to negotiate multiple identities is evident in his creative writing. Reflecting in July 1986 on his revisions of "A Choice of Rooms"—which would eventually become the novel Vanishing Rooms—Dixon feared that his characters might be too thin because of his refusal to deal with the black gay protagonist Jesse: "Perhaps I've been avoiding dealing with Jesse. Dealing with my own overly passive personality, perhaps. I don't know."[58] In addition to multiple rejections from major publishers, possibly caused by the novel's representations of queer interracial desire, Dixon's diaries indicate that one of the reasons it took him fifteen years to complete *Vanishing Rooms* was its semiautobiographical nature.[59] As a black gay man in an interracial relationship, Dixon's difficulties with representing Jesse might have stemmed from his limited access to forms of self-knowledge and the absence of complex representations of queer interraciality in popular and political culture of the time. Dixon was an early member of the New York chapter of Black and White Men Together (BWMT), a national political organization that formed in 1980 with the goal of combating racism in the gay community. He wrote *Vanishing Rooms* in part as a response to the organization's political shortfalls. Though BWMT claimed to be interested in eliminating racism, Dixon believed that many of the interracial couples in the group depended on racism to fuel their erotic life.[60] *Vanishing Rooms* can be considered speculative in its ability to invent the aesthetic forms necessary to imagine a liberated black gay subject, as expressed in Jesse's choreography of the queer interracial dance performance and the breaking of the fourth wall at the end of the novel. In this context, this novel becomes an intellectual project that struggles to make some sense of the psychic and embodied contradictions of race, queerness, and desire in the 1970s. Dixon's attempt to represent the complexity and intersectional nature of his identities and desires, and the intersecting structural forces that constricted his possibilities of personhood, might explain the form of the novel, which he described as "three narrators, three singers in a cabaret, each fighting for the microphone, saying 'It's my turn, it's my turn, I've gotta tell my story.'"[61]

Dixon's diaries chronicle the conflict between his calling as a creative writer and his role as a scholar-activist committed to black communities. In a January 26, 1978, entry, he recalled a confrontation with his father about wanting to "use his education to come back to the black community and help."[62] Handy Dixon, an independent painter and contractor, had moved to Stamford, Connecticut, from the Carolinas in the 1940s, a move that would inspire his son's first novel, *Trouble the Water*. He thought that writing would only enhance his son's personal ego, and questioned how a poem in a magazine would improve the black community. Dixon felt that his father never loved him, and his decision to pursue a PhD was heavily influenced by his desire to please him. Reflecting at three o'clock in the morning on his decision to become a professor, he wrote, "I've always felt that I had to be more than I was—overcompensating—because I felt unacceptable—my artistic struggles have been ones in which I want to be recognized as a man, as a creative deserving someone's love and attention."[63] Here we see how

Dixon's desire for recognition and belonging—to be "recognized as a man, as a creative"—operates through a desire for gender and class ascendancy, thereby threatening to reproduce the very structures of domination that rendered him vulnerable in the first place. On December 18, 1974, Dixon wrote in his diaries about bringing his boyfriend, Didier, home to Stamford to meet his family. After his father forbade Didier from visiting the house again, Dixon remarked, "And I took that to mean me, too, since it was a matter of Daddy's unwillingness to deal with the 'situation' as he calls it."[64]

In many ways, Dixon had internalized the state discourses labeling the black family as a "tangle of pathology." Most notably espoused by senator Daniel Patrick Moynihan in his 1965 report *The Negro Family: A Case for National Action*, these discourses blamed blacks for their economic failures because their gender and sexual arrangements did not follow the norms of white middle-class domesticity. The *Moynihan Report* blamed black women in particular for their people's failures to achieve normative citizenship, arguing that their domination of the household produced deviant sons.[65] In a diary entry on October 1, 1972, Dixon discussed his mother's belief that his father had homosexual inclinations before they were married. She also believed that Handy's distance from his son stemmed from his own fears of homosexual desire. Dixon thought that his father's lack of affection for his mother caused her to pay more attention to him, and he surmised that this maternal overaffection combined with the paternal disaffection is what made him a homosexual.[66] Dixon's inability to untangle his homosexual identity from the so-called tangle of pathology that circumscribes the black family shaped his feelings of loneliness, alienation, and despair during his early years as an undergraduate and graduate student, and his life as a creative writer and professor. But much of this would change when the threat of AIDS reoriented his speculation, away from biological and social life and toward the afterlife of his published texts as a mode of living on beyond death.

AIDS, the Racialized Past, and an Uncertain Future

Dixon first mentioned AIDS in his diaries on December 1, 1984 (fig. 6). After he discovered a red rash on each armpit, he feared that he might have contracted the virus.

Troubling times. Uncertainty. Fear of medical problems and bodily failure. Two rashes on either armpit, red, rashy ridge. A lesion that signals AIDS? I get afraid. Worry. Damn myself and awkward walks in the night. I'm careful,

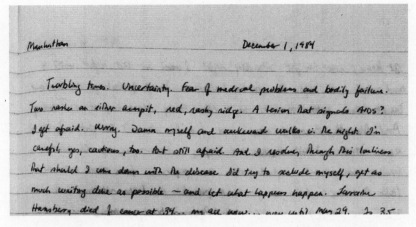

Figure 6. Diary entry, December 1, 1984. Excerpts from the diaries of Melvin Dixon,
© Melvin Dixon; used by permission of the Estate of Melvin Dixon.

yes, cautious, too. But still afraid. And I resolve, through this loneliness that
should I come down with the disease I'd try to seclude myself, get as much
writing done as possible—and let what happens happen. Lorraine Hansberry
died of cancer at 34 . . . my age now . . . now until May 29.[67]

The truncated nature of these sentences indicates the gaps and elisions
of traumatic knowledge. The passage moves from fear to worry to self-
condemnation back to fear. Dixon's self-diagnosis of the rashes and lesions
on his body affirms Paula Treichler's claim that the promiscuous gay male
body acts as the central text on which discursive constructions of AIDS are
inscribed.[68] His subsequent reference to his "awkward walks in the night"
suggests an internalization of the social and scientific discourses that blamed
gay male promiscuity for the spread of AIDS.

While this diary passage highlights how scientific and popular discourses
shaped gay men's understandings of their bodies and behaviors in the early
era of AIDS, Dixon's reference to Lorraine Hansberry's cancer-related death
raises questions about the health effects of racialization.[69] In his tribute to
Hansberry, James Baldwin believes that his dear friend and literary contemporary may have died so young because of the trauma of witnessing
racial violence: "And it is not at all farfetched to suspect that what she saw
contributed to the strain which killed her, for the effort to which Lorraine
was dedicated is more than enough to kill a man."[70] Baldwin believed that
living in the shadow of slavery and bearing witness to Jim Crow racism
facilitated the metastasizing of cancerous cells that ushered Hansberry to a

premature death. Dixon's reference to Hansberry evokes a history of racist violence that has made his gay male body more vulnerable to AIDS. During the early years of the epidemic, blackness operated as a site of blame for the appearance of AIDS in the United States. Paul Farmer describes how US public health officials inferred that Haitian immigrants had brought the AIDS epidemic to America. These researchers believed that unraveling the "Haiti connection" would lead them to discover the disease's epidemiological origins. Because Haitians denied intravenous drug use, homosexual activity, and a medical history of blood transfusions, their contraction of the virus led US scientists to ascribe their illness to the deviance of black culture, especially as regards vodou practices. Haitian immigrants in the United States and Canada were automatically deemed AIDS carriers, leading to anti-Haitian discrimination.[71] Treichler and Farmer demonstrate how racial and sexual ideologies structure social and scientific discourses of AIDS, marking black gay bodies as doubly stigmatized in the North American imaginary.

Dixon's attempt to make sense of AIDS in this discursive context explains why he might have seen himself as a death-bound subject. His diaries demonstrate, however, that his rashes and lesions were not experienced as certainty of an AIDS-related death. It was almost two years after he first discovered the rashes on his armpits that he finally saw a doctor. While viewing a CBS television special, "AIDS Hits Home," in October 1986, Dixon saw someone featured whose skin had dark spots, which concerned him: "The spots on my face make me worried. Especially after seeing someone on CBS with similar 'dark' spots. I'm scared. Yes. And Uncertain . . . about everything." Five days later, he consulted a dermatologist about his spots, but his long history of seborrheic dermatitis cast doubt as to whether the spots were AIDS-related. Dixon also complained about his chronic sore throat, but his primary care physician thought that it was related to sinusitis. By 1986, clear advances in scientific and medical knowledge about AIDS had been made, including testing for antibodies, connecting AIDS to the HIV retrovirus, and treatment through antiretrovirals like AZT, but Dixon's diaries reveal that his fears were not assuaged by medical discourse, nor were they laid to rest by his doctor's diagnosis. From Dixon's perspective, the interplay of bodily inscription (rashes and lesions) and self-diagnosis, media discourses, and medical expertise did not produce a feeling of certainty about his future, but rather reproduced preexisting feelings of uncertainty.

These feelings bring to mind what Lauren Berlant calls "disturbed time." Writing about Essex Hemphill's infamous line, "Now we think / as we fuck," Berlant argues that this line signals the speaker's return to private, domesticated gay life now that the threat of AIDS and death haunts gay men's public sexual encounters.[72] For Berlant, Hemphill's "think[ing]" signals "disturbed time," or "a historical present and not just everydayness because the atmosphere suggests a shift of historic proportions in the terms and processes of the conditions of continuity of life." To be forced to stop and think indexes an optimistic attachment to life that Berlant reads as cruel and naïve, a point that might be affirmed if we take into account Hemphill's premature death from AIDS.[73] Yet such a reading forecloses an analysis of how death has long structured the temporality of black life. In her analysis of black death and mourning, Karla F. C. Holloway presents the African American experience of death and dying as paradoxical in that it is at once anticipated due to its omnipresence, and on the other hand a persistent interruption to the cycles of everyday black life. Holloway posits that black culture is shaped not so much by a disavowal of death as by an embrace of its proximity and interruptions.[74] It is logical, then, to think that for Dixon, black culture's historical intimacy with death produced not a sense of disturbed time but the continuation of a black racial feeling of uncertainty regarding one's attachment to life.

Melvin Dixon's diaries provide an alternative reading of what it means to "think as we fuck." The night he discovered that the spots on his face were "red and raised like lesions," he recalled going to a porn theater for sex and finding blood in his underwear after he returned home (fig. 7a).

> The real terror came this evening. I went to David's cinema . . . I had to go out. I wanted the touch of someone, anyone. I wore Chris's leather jacket and went to David's Cinema on 54th and Broadway to see a porno film. I went to their back room because I wanted the touch of a man's hand on me—on my chest, my balls, my ass. I didn't let anyone suck my cock, but one finger found my behind and probed, then I felt a tongue back there and mouth. I masturbated while the tongue was at work. When I got home I noticed blood in my underwear. That's when the terror struck. Who and *what* was sharp enough to draw blood? And now I am probably doomed. I'm terrified—crazy with fear—and writing this in my journal with careless and shaking handwriting because I'm so shaken up. What the hell do I do? I didn't let anyone penetrate me, and I thought a mouth back there would be safe. How did I happen to start bleeding? Does this mean that I've exchanged body fluids? Am I contaminated? This is how bottom feels.[75]

By associating his feelings of "terror" and "fear" with the "bottom," Dixon's narrative invokes a sense of powerlessness. Darieck Scott uses the term *bottom* as a metaphor for both "the nadir of hierarchy (a political position

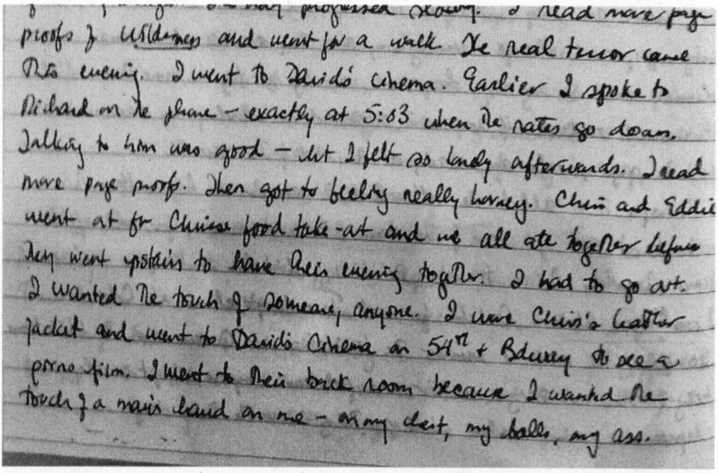

Figure 7 (*a, b*). Diary entry, March 5, 1987. Excerpts from the diaries of Melvin Dixon,
© Melvin Dixon; used by permission of the Estate of Melvin Dixon.

possibly abject)" and "a sexual position."[76] In so doing, Scott probes the
relation between the coercive practices and pleasurable possibilities that
inhere in processes of black racialization. Dixon's discovery of his lesions
compels him to venture into the back room of David's Cinema, because he
"wanted the touch of a man's hand on [him]." His refusal to let anyone suck
his cock, though permitting another man to finger and tongue his ass while
he masturbated, implies a measure of control. The anonymity provided by
the back room of the porn theater allows Dixon to play the bottom (the
sexual position) for a little bit. But the terror struck when he got home.

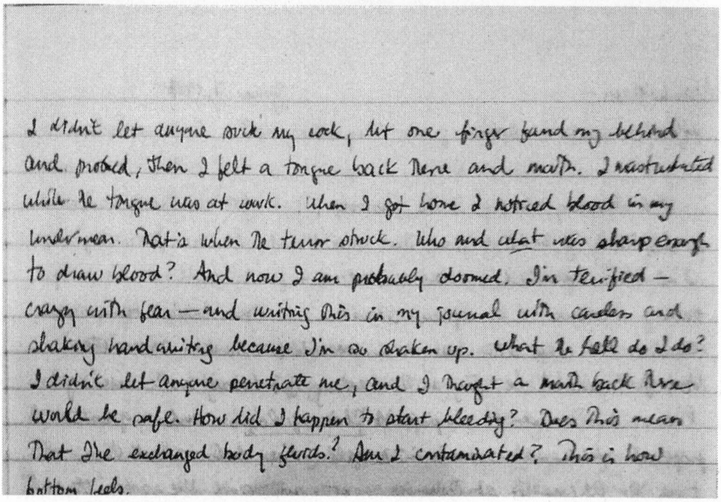

His questions regarding the cause of the bleeding, despite his choice not to be genitally penetrated—a self-identified practice of "safe" sex—align his vulnerability to penetration with Scott's other definition of bottoming. In this sense, Dixon's bottom feelings index the racialization of black bodies as "the nadir of hierarchy." His terror at the sight of blood evidences the embodiment of risk, pathology, and loss produced by the terror of AIDS. But his terror also conjures a historical legacy of defeat that has been actualized through the domination of black sexuality. If Dixon's sense of time is disturbed, it stems, at least partially, from the not-yet-past of slavery that has skewed his life chances long before the appearance of AIDS.

"Textual Survival" and the Form of Black/Queer Optimism

Although Dixon's feelings of being on the "bottom" convey the black gay body's vulnerability to death, that he continues writing after his AIDS diagnosis gestures toward the possibility of black/queer diasporic futures. Rinaldo Walcott argues that the appearance of AIDS in the United States, and its links to Haiti and Africa, brought with it the necessity for a certain diasporic consciousness and sensibility. He proposes that the global AIDS pandemic was particularly significant to diaspora's return, because it brought together antiracist activism and queer activism.[77] In this context, a shift is perceptible in Dixon's consciousness after discovering the signs of AIDS on his body. While the threat of AIDS compounded his racialized feelings of uncertainty, the global AIDS pandemic also occasioned the formation of his black/queer diasporic consciousness. In the years after he discovered the rashes, he channeled these feelings of uncertainty toward writing as a praxis for archiving the self for future generations, evidenced in his emphasis on "get[ting] as much writing done as possible."

Dixon relied on the germinative capacity of life writing as a means of reorienting black queerness toward living and living on. Though his body became increasingly debilitated by the AIDS virus, the threat of impending death mobilized him to complete as many writing projects as possible. On July 17, 1986, while living in Dakar, Senegal, he wrote, "My defense is to write. It is a defense against sudden annihilation, sudden death, despair."[78] Rather than express how it feels to be dying, Dixon mobilized diaristic and other forms of writing to ward off the regime of feelings marking the time of his impending demise. Conscious of how racial and sexual difference confounds the task of bearing witness, he did not rely on the ethical imperative of others to bear witness to his death. Instead, he focused all his energies on completing and publishing his work as a means of "textual survival." As I discuss in the introduction, he was very concerned about the disposability and erasure of black gay life in both black heterosexual communities and white gay communities, which he termed "double cremation." For Dixon, double cremation extended beyond the erasure of black gay history, gesturing toward the structural forces that threaten to render black gay personhood as an impossible mode of being. He charged future witnesses of his published and unpublished works to preserve them as evidence of black gay being, as a site for reimagining black gay personhood beyond its associations with (social) death.

Dixon's emphasis on "textual survival" critiques queer theory's move away from archival recovery of gay and lesbian writing. Jaime Harker argues that queer theory's shift from recuperation and canonization of gay and lesbian writers and toward queering the traditional canon has left many lesbian and gay writers in the margins of the larger literary canon. Her concern is that such exclusions elide analyses of the formal and aesthetic choices made by gay and lesbian writers in particular, and that queer scholars miss how gay and lesbian writers might complicate our understandings of the literary historical periods in question.[79] I would include Dixon and other black gay writers among those marginalized by the rise of queer theory. This is best exemplified by Arthur Flannigan Saint-Aubin's critique of the black gay anthology *Brother to Brother* that was published in the *Journal of the History of Sexuality*. In the article, he uses queer theorist Eve Sedgwick's work to prove that the anthology fails to justify the need for a specifically "black gay male" discourse.[80] However, the exclusion of black gay male writers on the basis of their identity claims does not account for their emphasis on textual survival as a mode of political longing for more complex articulations of black gay personhood. Queer theory's marginalization of black gay male writers created the conditions of possibility for antisocial and antifuture strains of queer theory to emerge and flourish without ethical concerns about whether such queer politics even imagine black gay men, and other black queer and trans people, as political subjects. Dixon's emphasis on textual survival brings into stark relief queer theory's collusion with antiblackness insofar as it disregards his imperative that we "remember [him]." If Dixon is indeed "somewhere listening for [his] name," does he experience the continued exclusion of black gay men's lives and legacies in queer history and memory as a repetition of racial injury?

And while Dixon mobilized writing and publishing to ensure his textual survival, the form of his diaries demonstrates how the black gay literary imagination operates as a site for envisioning futures beyond a death-bound horizon. Ross Chambers argues that AIDS journals substitute the narrative syntax of beginning, middle, and ending with the structure of the chronicle, with its greater immediacy. He notes that the "now this, now that" arrangement of the diary is a contiguous rather than a cohesive series of dated entries. Moreover, he claims that AIDS journals are not oriented retrospectively, like autobiography or other narrative texts of witness. Rather, they look forward, to enunciate a future in which they will be read, and the open-endedness of their chronicle structure implies prospectivity as much as the thematics of survival does.[81] Dixon's diaries evidence a sense of black/queer optimism in the black gay diasporic cultural imagination. Processes of black racialization skewed his life chances from the beginning, and the terror of AIDS compounded the threat of death. But the contiguous arrangement of his diaries presents the possibility of disrupting the racial calculus that marks black subjects for premature death. Whereas the discursive ordering of autobiography might reaffirm normative chronologies that position the black subject on a straight line toward death, the episodic structure and dated entries of the diary temporally fragment that line, offering queer possibilities outside the biological time and space of black social death that each entry represents.

Though the abrupt ending of Melvin Dixon's diaries may generate negative affect for witnesses, both the final entry and the blank pages that follow it operate as a site of ontological and political possibility that inheres in the black gay cultural imagination. Remarking on the ambiguity of the final entry, Chambers notes, "Their end, in spite of the author's death that it signifies, remains *suspended*, as if another entry were always possible and as if to propose some possibility of continuation."[82] The form of Dixon's diaries as prospective rather than retrospective mimics the racialized and sexualized feelings of uncertainty that he experienced as an AIDS-infected, black gay man in the early era of AIDS. Though his final entry marks the end-time of his biological life, the blank pages after it "propose some possibility of continuation." Black/queer optimism can be located in these blank pages. They hold open a space for imagining a more utopian future horizon for black gay subjects which is not fixed by the diary reader's present. The end-time of Dixon's diaries remains suspended, indexing possibilities for futures as each new reader encounters them. The optimism embedded in the form of these diaries allows us to imagine black/queer futures neither bound to the finite temporality of Dixon's life nor yoked to the present of the diary's witnesses.

As a contemporary witness to Dixon's diaries, many of his experiences with family and community in the 1970s and early 1980s resonated with my own. His beautifully written accounts of his struggles against isolation and alienation within black communities, gay communities, and in the academy still resonate. Feeling backward into Dixon's archives helped me make sense of my contemporary experiences as a black gay man. Reading his diaries was difficult labor that required speculation and caused exhaustion. I took many breaks after encountering heartbreaking passages, and I cried after I read the entry coinciding with his partner Richard's death from AIDS. Reading about his agonizing experiences of loneliness during his early years compelled me to stop by a bar or a liquor store immediately after I left the archive. But it was the shift in Dixon's outlook after discovering the rashes on his armpits that inspired this chapter. It seemed that Dixon was much more hopeful once he suspected that he had AIDS, and the source of that hope was writing: "The hope against despair lies with our ability—indeed our insistence—on creativity. Silence equals death. Voice and self-expression mean regeneration."[83]

To me, Melvin Dixon's attempt to write as a mode of making sense of his personhood and as praxis of refusing death as *the* site from which to imagine black/queer politics is his greatest contribution to our thinking about black gay social life. His death from AIDS evidences the fact of black gay social life lived in an antiblack and antigay world—but his writing engenders imaginative possibilities for black gay personhood beyond this fact. Though feelings of uncertainty and self-doubt animate black gay subjectivity in the West, these feelings also evidence a yearning for more complex articulations of racial, gender, and sexual selfhood, and a political longing for more certain futures for black gay subjects in the New World. Dixon's diaries helped me make some sense of my own black gay being as a site of longing amid the everyday violence of racism and homophobia. They shift my thinking away from historical recovery as a practice of emotional rescue necessary for liberal black gay subject formation, and toward an understanding of black gay historiography as both a practice of survival and a method of gathering evidence of being "powerful enough to transform our very existence."[84]

Epilogue

Afterimage

The photograph in figure 8 was taken in October 1985 at radio station WBAI's Manhattan studios. Joseph Beam took it, most likely after his interview at the station about the forthcoming publication of the anthology he edited, *In the Life*. All the men in this photo were key figures in the black gay cultural renaissance. Beam, then editor of *Black/Out*, the magazine of the National Coalition of Black Lesbians and Gays, published a copy of the picture to accompany his editorial "Caring for Each Other." In the editorial, he recalls his days growing up in West Philadelphia, and how he and other members of the community would often be harassed by Slim. Slim was the neighborhood "alcoholic," but when he caused any trouble, neighbors would console him and escort him home instead of calling the police or an alcohol rehabilitation center. The essay is a meditation on placing community responsibility ahead of reliance on the state. Beam believed that *the state* was simply a euphemism for "white people," and that the state has never been concerned about the lives of black people. State apathy, he argues, extends to black gay men and IV drug users dying of AIDS, and he believes "it would be a fatal mistake if we were to relinquish our responsibility for AIDS in the Black community to such an external mechanism."[1] In this context, the photograph of these black gay men in embrace visualizes their ethics of care and their sense of responsibility toward one another and to the broader black community amid the epidemic. Beam concludes the piece with his now infamous line, "Black men loving black men is the revolutionary act of the 80s."[2]

At first glance, the photo is a celebratory moment of black gay community, as the men join in joyous embrace. That they have assembled for an interview for *In the Life*, to which many of them are contributors, captures the movement's aims of asserting more complex articulations of racial, gender,

Figure 8. Key figures in the black gay cultural renaissance, October 1985. *Left to right:* Essex Hemphill, Assotto Saint, Craig G. Harris, Ray Melrose, Daniel Garrett, and Colin Robinson. Photograph by Joseph Beam. Photo courtesy of the Estate of Joseph Beam.

and sexual selfhood through writing and publication. As I mention in chapter 2, Joseph Beam imagined the publication of *In the Life* as fulfilling Essex Hemphill's vision for an organization that would save black gay men's lives in an environment of state neglect and exclusion from black heterosexual and white gay communities.

Though this study focuses on movement activities in two US cities, the men in this photo represent the global reach of Beam's call. Hemphill and Ray Melrose were based in Washington, DC, while Assotto Saint, Craig G. Harris, Daniel Garrett, and Colin Robinson were based in New York City. Beam hailed from Philadelphia, but his father was an immigrant from Barbados. Born Yves François Lubin, Saint was an immigrant from Haiti; Robinson was an immigrant from Trinidad and Tobago. Hemphill, Saint, Harris, and Beam died of AIDS, while the cause of Melrose's death is unknown. Robinson and Garrett are still alive. Robinson is an LGBTQ rights activist in Trinidad, and Garrett lives and works as a writer in his home state of Louisiana.

In the wake of the deaths of many of these figures, the viewer of this photograph must come to terms with the fact that their love for one another was not enough. The photo's reference to both the black gay cultural movements in the late seventies, eighties, and nineties and the deaths of a generation of black gay artists and activists during this same period prompts me to reevaluate the stakes of my reading practice. How do I bear witness to this historical period as a black gay cultural renaissance while not losing sight of the era's haunting, traumatic losses? Remarking on the photograph, Daniel Garrett offers a reading of Beam's photograph that informs my analysis.

> When Joe Beam sent me this photo . . . it helped to remind me how rare that whole time had been. What I've always appreciated about art is this very effect—we are allowed to enter again and enlarge our experience. Something we can come back to again. It is a fact that these artifacts, consumer items in the epoch of capitalism, can be seen as purely western forms, but it is also a fact that we can use whatever there is to make what we need to sustain us.[3]

Like Garrett, I have entered this archive again to "enlarge [black gay] experience." Rather than focus solely on death and loss, I have chosen to focus on the "art" and "artifacts" of this movement as something more than "western forms." This book foregrounds the power of cultural production to "sustain" black gay men amid the ubiquitous forms of violence that targeted them during the late seventies, eighties, and nineties, and to reimagine black gay social life beyond its association with (social) death.

After receiving the photograph, Garrett wrote a poem in response, stating, "Arts calls forth art."[4] I read Beam's photograph alongside Garrett's poem as a form of what Christina Sharpe calls "annotation": "As portraits of Black people circulate in a variety of publics, they are often accompanied by some sort of note or other metadata, whether that notation is in the photograph itself or as a response to a dehumaning photograph, in order that the image might travel with supplemental information that marks injury and, then, more than injury."[5] Sharpe is concerned with the constant public circulation of images of black death, injury, and trauma. Although these images are distributed to invoke sympathy or empathy, they often reproduce the very antiblack logics that they seek to disrupt. For Sharpe, annotation becomes a way of "seeing something in excess of what is caught in the frame."[6] While Beam's photograph does not explicitly depict black suffering, its historical reference to the early era of AIDS reproduces state and media discourses that read black gay bodies as death-bound. Moreover, the photograph's framing of six black men in embrace marks black gay men's resistance to ubiquitous forms of violence that target them through communal forms of care and support, and reminds us of how state neglect and racial and sexual exclusion forced these bodies into the frame. Their embrace and smiles mark this as a scene of subjection for multiply marginalized subjects who were desperately reliant on one another for survival in the absence of state protection. State neglect, racism, and homophobia animate the visual field through which we see this photograph, capturing black gay social life through visual logics that mark these men's bodies for death.

Though the historical context of AIDS positions this photograph within a larger black/gay "album of the dead," I am interested in annotating this image as a way "to make black life visible, if only momentarily."[7] I turn to Garrett's unpublished poem as a way to counter the death-dealing epistemes that circumscribe this historical artifact of the black gay cultural renaissance. The poem, "Beam's Photograph," consists of five stanzas that describe the photograph and its subjects from various perspectives.[8] The first stanza celebrates the occasion of black men being together, especially the moment of black men holding each other in joyous embrace. This stanza also emphasizes the differences between these men, taking on the visual economies that make black men appear as undifferentiated through racialized fantasies that view black masculinity as a singular image of hypermasculinity and hypersexuality.[9] In so doing, it disrupts racialized fantasies of *the black male body*.[10] The stanza concludes with the men in the photo finding freedom through embracing one another, challenging intramural visual perceptions of black masculinity that forbid expressions of physical love between black men and privilege capitalist modes of being that promote individualism and competition.[11]

In the second stanza, the photographic image becomes a metaphor for black gay men's investment in political visibility. Garrett uses synesthesia to emphasize the structural forces that circumscribe black gay representation, claiming that "the slowly burning silence / of self-hatred does not light" the photograph.[12] In her analysis of circum-Caribbean photographic practices, Krista Thompson argues, "The use of light produced through visual technologies generates distinct aesthetic, synaesthetic, physiological, and phemonological effects, creating or denying types of viewership in particular performative and spatial contexts."[13] Garrett reimagines the visual technologies of photography, in particular the visual economy of light necessary for (black) bodies to appear, so that the bodies are being lit not by self-hatred but by the need to share "what one was, is, and desires to be."[14] Politicizing black gay identity becomes a visual technology that reframes these bodies within a different economy of light. In so doing, Garrett's poem denies modes of viewership that would read representations of black sexuality as duplicitous.[15] He directs viewers to see in this image black gay men's collective political longings for richer subjective and social lives. The light of possibility created through the political practice of self- and community-making allows viewers to see the complexity of black gay personhood, at least momentarily, indicated by the list of the photographic subjects' various attributes, such as "Essex's ease, Yves' pride."[16]

The third stanza highlights the political possibilities that are engendered through collective exploration of black gay being. Here Garrett foregrounds a complementary rather than a binary construction of strength and weakness that redefines the terms of black masculinity. Whereas racial, gender, and sexual norms dictate that black men must be strong, Garrett desires from other black men a "strength other than force" and "a tenderness other than grief."[17] In chapter 1, I argue that the affective politics of grief are entangled with social systems of value that are distributed unevenly according to racial, class, gender, sexual, and spatial hierarchies. I show how black gay literature refuses to refuse the narratives of deviance and pathology that circumscribe black/gay social life, while gesturing toward possibilities of black gay being that lie outside value. By asserting his desire for "a tenderness other than grief," Garrett offers a visual reading practice that recognizes black gay male vulnerability without relegating those outside the frame of the photograph as devalued. A tender reading must include those whose images may be lit by self-hatred, and figures like Ronald Gibson/Star, a drag queen prostitute whose life cannot be fully captured under the sign "black gay man." As I note in chapter 2, Beam's silence around his serostatus and the fact that he died alone—his body discovered in an advanced state of decomposition—reveal the limits of political visibility and collectivity as central to the politics of black gay survival. Garrett's disassociation from the Other Countries Collective and his expression of feelings of self-alienation in the poem confirm this point. Reading this photograph through the lens of tenderness allows the viewer to acknowledge black gender and sexual minorities as subject to pain, while countering dehumanizing white supremacist visual logics that do not recognize black suffering.

In the fourth stanza, the speaker of the poem proclaims that the men in the photograph are beautiful, highlighting how the black gay cultural renaissance of the late seventies, eighties, and nineties extends the black arts movement's emphasis on black self-determination and intramural revaluation of black bodies.[18] Garrett's poem departs from black arts movement discourse by acknowledging that the subjects in the photo identify as black men, since heteropatriarchal logics espoused by some black nationalist intellectuals saw gender nonconformity and homosexuality as existing outside the boundaries of blackness.[19] As I mention in Chapter 2, black liberation psychiatrists like Dr. Frances Cress Welsing regarded the eradication of black gender and sexual minorities as necessary for advancing liberatory projects that aim to secure black subjective wholeness. The fifth stanza confronts the state-based and intraracial forces that would require this eradication: "Sometimes just being / is revolutionary."[20] In the face of ubiquitous forms of violence targeting black gay men in the late seventies, eighties, and nineties, these men's attempts to reimagine their personhood through cultural production and their efforts to secure their survival through publishing were nothing short of revolutionary. If Joseph Beam is correct in his assertion that under white supremacy, racial capitalism, and heteronormativity, "black men were never meant to be together—not as father and son, brother to brother—and certainly not as lovers," then black gay being registers as a revolutionary act.[21] As I have argued, being (as opposed to doing and as a form of doing) attends to the micropolitical and intersubjective processes missed when the imperative is to do something. Being captures the processes of individual and collective self-making and self-preservation subordinated to dominant frameworks of political resistance and rebellion. Being offers a more complex way of thinking about the relationship between black gay personhood and forms of structural violence that overdetermine representations of black gay social life.

The final lines of Garrett's poem attend to the labor of black gay self-making in the midst of ubiquitous forms of violence. That the photographer and so many men in this photograph died prematurely indexes the fact of being black and gay in an antiblack and antigay world. The regimes of antiblackness and antiqueerness that ushered these men to premature death attest to the fact that "what is on film / may fade away."[22] Nevertheless, this book decenters death in order to demonstrate how black gay cultural production operates as an alternative archive for imagining black gay personhood beyond the forces of antiblackness and antiqueerness, which I have termed "evidence of being." Because circum-Caribbean photographic practices often inhabit the representational edge of presence and absence, hypervisibility and invisibility, Krista Thompson argues, "they produce a form of excess, a visual superfluity, that points precisely to the limits of vision or what lies just beyond photographic and visual capture." In so doing, these photographic practices "create 'afterimages' that can be seen and felt after the moment of the photograph's production."[23] Beam's photograph represents black gay (social) death and social life, black gay political visibility and historical erasure, and should be included among the circum-Caribbean photographic practices that reveal the limits of vision. However, reading Garrett's annotation alongside Beam's photograph directs our view toward the "otherwise possibilities" of black gay social life, possibilities that lie beyond photographic and visual capture.[24] Garrett's annotation symbolizes an ongoing black gay political vision of community and futurity that exceeds the forms of biological life and social death that the photo represents, while reflecting the labor of black gay self-making and world-making through which a more livable black gay social life becomes possible. His poem reflects this political vision, thereby creating a more optimistic "afterimage" of black gay social life in the 1970s, 1980s, and 1990s.

ACKNOWLEDGMENTS

This book emphasizes the power of collectivity in black gay cultural production, activism, and survival in the 1970s, 1980s, and 1990s. As a work
of black gay cultural production, it too has been a collective effort. Various
people and communities have provoked, critiqued, enriched, and made
space for my thinking about this project over many years. While all the
people who contributed cannot be named here, I would like to acknowledge some of the people, organizations, and institutions that have made
this book possible.

My research has been supported by the Penn Predoctoral Fellowship for
Excellence through Diversity at the University of Pennsylvania. I would like
to thank Heather Love and Herman Beavers for their mentorship during my
time there. I also benefited from the intellectual community that I developed:
Alden Young, Garry Bertholf, and Grace Sanders Johnson were excellent peer
mentors and friends. The Martin Duberman Visiting Scholars Fund at the
New York Public Library supported my archival research at the Schomburg
Center for Research in Black Culture. At Duke University, the Summer Institute on Tenure and Professional Advancement at the Center for the Study of
Race, Ethnicity, and Gender in the Social Sciences provided support as well.
I am grateful to Jeffrey Q. McCune for serving as my program mentor, and to
the many young scholars of color who, as program participants, expanded
my intellectual community. At San Francisco State University, research support from the President's Office and the Office of Research and Sponsored
Programs helped me complete this book. I would like to thank the Woodrow Wilson Foundation for its generous support through the Career En-
hancement Fellows Program, and I am thankful to Dagmawi Woubshet for
his mentorship and generous engagement of my work during the fellowship
period. I am grateful as well to be a part of an awesome cohort of Woodrow

Wilson Fellows. The School for Cultural and Social Transformation and the Ethnic Studies Division at the University of Utah provided much-needed support during the final stages of writing this book. Thanks also go to Doug Mitchell, Kyle Wagner, Mary Corrado, Sandra Hazel, Tyler McCaughey, and the anonymous reviewers at the University of Chicago Press—your support, guidance, and vision transformed my manuscript into a book.

My work has benefited immensely from my engagement with various intellectual communities. I would like to thank several faculty members at the University of Maryland—Psyche Williams-Forson, Christina B. Hanhardt, Keguro Macharia, Michelle V. Rowley, Nancy L. Struna, and Elsa Barkley Brown—for their close readings and careful feedback on earlier drafts. I give my thanks especially to Christina B. Hanhardt for being a tireless advocate, mentor, and friend throughout this process. She has modeled for me what it means to be an intellectually rigorous and politically engaged scholar, and I am grateful for her unwavering commitment and support. Keguro Macharia believed in this book from the beginning, and he read many, many drafts. I am indebted to him for his mentorship, friendship, and intellectual generosity. I have also benefited immensely from being a part of the SPACE writers' collective. Marlon Moore, Treva Lindsey, Riley Snorton, Mecca Sullivan, Angelique Nixon, Marlo David, and LaMonda Horton-Stallings read this entire book, and it would not be the same one without their loving, incisive critique. I would like to thank LaMonda Horton-Stallings in particular for being a longtime mentor; her creative and innovative work continually inspires me to be a better scholar. The Queer Writing Group at San Francisco State University—Nan Alamilla Boyd, Evren Savci, Deb Cohler, Jessica Fields, and Marc Stein—provided very helpful feedback on my introduction. It has been a privilege to be a part of this group of esteemed scholars. Marc Stein has been an exceptional senior colleague, and my work grew immensely from his feedback on several chapters of this book. He and Jorge Olivares also have been great friends. My colleagues in the Department of Sociology and Sexuality Studies at San Francisco State University have been very supportive of my work; special thanks go to Ed McCaughan, Andreana Clay, Jessica Fields, Allen LeBlanc, Marla Ramirez, Valerie Francisco-Menchavez, Alexis Martinez, Clare Sears, Chris Bettinger, and Colleen Hoff. I have also benefited from conversations with colleagues from across campus, especially Tomas Almageur, Javon Johnson, Celine Parreñas Shimizu, Andrew Jolivette, Jacqueline Francis, Laura Mamo, and Martha Kenney. I owe a debt of gratitude to Amy Sueyoshi and Tina Takemoto for their friendship and generosity. Dilara Yarbrough has been an amazing writing partner at the end stages of this book. And becoming colleagues and fast friends with the incomparable Cheryl Dunye has made my time at San Francisco State University a memorable, enjoyable, and meaningful experience.

I am grateful to the senior scholars who have encouraged me throughout the writing process. Thank you to Roderick Ferguson, Robert Reid-Pharr, Cathy Cohen, E. Patrick Johnson, Jennifer Devere Brody, Kevin Mumford, Charles I. Nero, Christina Sharpe, and Marlon Ross—without your work, mine would not be possible. My thanks also to some of the amazing colleagues whose work I admire, and who have encouraged and supported me along the way: Marlon Bailey, GerShun Avilez, Matt Richardson, Erica Edwards, Ernesto Javier Martinez, Mireille Miller-Young, Jennie Brier, Tiffany King, Terrance Wooten, Kwame Holmes, Kai Green, David Green, Brandon Manning, J. T. Roane, Julio Capó, Michelé Prince, Jessica Walker, Cristina Perez, Paul Saiedi, Doug Ishii, Jarah Moesch, Jennie Chaplin, Alex Juhasz, Sarah Schulman, Kenyon Farrow, Charles Stephens, Emily Hobson, Julius Fleming, Jillian Hernandez, Sami Schalk, Dan Royles, Matt Brim, La Marr Bruce, Gabriel Peoples, Lisa Arellano, Stacie McCormick, Ramzi Fawaz, Clifton Granby, Jennifer DeClue, Shante Smalls, Jennifer Jones, Alix Chapman, Jih-Fei Cheng, Elliot Powell, Jeffrey Coleman, Tavi Gonzalez, Aneeka Henderson, Treva Ellison, and many more.

This book depended on the labor of many archivists and activists. I extend my appreciation to Steven Fullwood for his curation of the In the Life Archive at the Schomburg Center for Research in Black Culture. I would also like to thank archivists Miranda Mims and Alexsandra Mitchell for their assistance during my many trips to the Schomburg over the years. My thanks as well to Philip Clark at the DC Rainbow History Archives, and to the many black gay activists who gave me access to their oral history interviews. I am grateful to those who allowed me to interview them, and to those who gave me permission to use works from various estates: Colin Robinson, Cary Alan Johnson, Isaac Jackson, Tony Crusor, Robert Vazquez-Pacheco, Marvin K. White, Kevin McGruder, Johnny Manzon-Santos, G. Winston James, Gil Gerald, Allen Luther Wright, Sur Rodney Sur, Len Richardson, Robert E. Penn, Fred Carl, Ron Simmons, Wayson Jones, Pamela Sneed, Lisa C. Moore, Sharon Farmer, Deanna Dixon, Kent Grey, Becket Logan, Faith Childs at Faith Childs Literary Agency, and many others.

Friends and family have supported me throughout this process. Eddie Perry, Clifton Williams, Jermaine Bozier, Marvin Mabini, Arnita Wofford, and Leo Raffule: thank you for being a friend! Thanks to my family for your enduring support! And to my mom, Justin, Tim, Aunt Frank and Uncle Ernest, Cheryl, and all my aunts, uncles, cousins: I love all of you!

Notable Individuals, Organizations, and Publications

Individuals

Blackberri—Blackberri was born Charles Timothy Ashmore in 1945 in Baltimore. He attended the University of Arizona, but left for California after experiencing racism and homophobia. He began his career as a gospel artist; eventually he became a prominent figure in the gay arts movements of 1970s San Francisco, and appeared onstage and on albums alongside many national recording artists. He released an album, *Finally*, in 1981. Blackberri's work is featured in several important documentaries of the gay arts movement, including *The Word Is Out: Stories of Some of Our Lives* (1979), *Looking for Langston* (1989), and several films produced by Marlon Riggs. He contributed poetry and prose to several anthologies of the black gay cultural renaissance, including *In the Life* and *The Road Before Us*. He continues to live and work as a singer-songwriter and cultural activist in Oakland, California.

Ronald K. Brown—Born in 1966 in Brooklyn, New York, Brown founded the Brooklyn-based dance company Evidence in 1985. The group's performances weave together elements of traditional and contemporary African diasporic dance, contemporary urban dance, and spoken word. Brown has choreographed for several major dance companies, including Alvin Ailey. He lost a partner to AIDS in the early era of the epidemic, and many of his early pieces grappled with black gay experiences of racism, loss, and AIDS during that period. Brown also worked in conjunction with the Other Countries Collective, conducting workshops on interpreting poetry through dance. He continues to work as director and choreographer of Evidence in New York City.

Steven Corbin—Corbin was born October 3, 1953, in Jersey City, New Jersey. He began writing after he dropped out of the film program at the University of Southern California. In 1989, Corbin published his debut novel, *No Easy Place to Be*. The novel is set in Harlem in 1920s, and captures the politics, culture, and sociality of the Harlem Renaissance through three black sisters, whose lives take them in varied, and sometimes competing, directions. Yet it was his subsequent novel, *Fragments That Remain* (1993), that established Corbin as an important voice in the black gay cultural renaissance. The novel confronts the intersections of black family life, colorism, homosexuality, and interracial desire through the story of a prominent black gay actor, Skylar White. *Fragments That Remain* was shortlisted for the Lambda Literary Award for Gay Fiction in 1994. Based on the success of his writing, Corbin taught creative writing at UCLA. His next novel, *A Hundred Days from Now* (1994), grapples with love, homophobia, and AIDS through the story of its black gay protagonist, Dexter Baldwin, and his partner, Mexican-American Sergio Gutierrez. It depicts the hundred days following Guttierez's bone marrow transplant, which was performed to halt the effects of the AIDS virus. Corbin's involvement with AIDS Coalition to Unleash Power informed the novel's unflinching look at the emotional, economic, cultural, and social turmoil produced by the virus. Corbin died of AIDS on August 31, 1995, in New York City.

Larry Duckette, Jr.—Born in 1953 in Washington, DC, Duckette attended Virginia State University, where he earned a bachelor's degree in applied music. With Essex Hemphill and Wayson Jones, he created the performance group Cinque. He also worked with Marlon Riggs on the film *Black Is . . . Black Ain't*. Duckette died in 2001.

Larry Duplechan—Born December 30, 1956, in Los Angeles, Duplechan attended the University of California–Los Angeles, where he studied English. He first pursued a career in music, as a solo singer and a member of a jazz vocal group, but gave it up due to the demands of full-time employment. However, music would become a major feature of his literary works. In 1985, Duplechan published his first novel, *Eight Days a Week*, a humorous account of the life of a black gay musician, Johnny Ray Rousseau, and his search for love and fame in 1980s Los Angeles. Rousseau would be featured in a subsequent novel, *Blackbird* (1986), a prequel to *Eight Days a Week*. *Blackbird* established Duplechan as a major voice in gay African American fiction, and was eventually adapted for the screen in Ian Patrik Polk's 2014 film of the same title. Duplechan continued writing about Johnny Ray Rousseau in *Captain Swing* (1993) and *Got 'Til It's Gone* (2008). In 1989, he published the novel *Tangled Up in Blue*, which grapples with the devastation of AIDS. The novel focuses on a married couple, Maggie and Daniel Sullivan, and their struggles after Maggie discovers that Daniel is bisexual and had been in a relationship with her gay friend, Crockett Miller, who recently tested positive for AIDS. In addition to his novels, Duplechan's work has been published in many anthologies. He lives in Los Angeles with his partner, Greg Harvey.

Rotimi Fani-Kayode—Oluwarotimi (Rotimi) Adebiyi Wahab Fani-Kayode was born in April 1955 in Lagos, Nigeria. In 1966, he and his family moved to Brighton, England, to escape the Biafran War. He moved to the United States in 1976 to attend Georgetown University in Washington, DC, and earned an MFA in fine arts and photography at the Pratt Institute in New York City. While in New York, he befriended Robert Mapplethorpe, who became a major influence on his work, particularly his explorations of queer interracial desire; but Fani-Kayode extended concerns beyond queer sexuality to explore questions of racism, colonialism, exile, war, spirituality, and HIV/AIDS. In 1983, he returned to the United Kingdom, where he continued to develop and display his work. Fani-Kayode, whose work has been exhibited across the globe, died of AIDS in 1989 in London.

Gary Fisher—Born June 19, 1961, in Bristol, Pennsylvania, Fisher attended the University of North Carolina at Chapel Hill from 1979 to 1983, studying English and creative writing. He was a talented, though yet unpublished, poet, fiction writer, and diarist. He died of AIDS in 1994 at the age of thirty-two. After his death, literary scholar Eve Kosofsky Sedgwick edited portions of his journals, poems, and stories as the collection *Gary in Your Pocket* (1996).

Gilberto Gerald—Gilberto (Gil) Gerald was born in 1950 in Panama City, Panama. He graduated with a bachelor's degree in architecture from Pratt Institute in Brooklyn, New York, in 1974. After ten years working as a professional in the field of architecture, Gerald became immersed full time in both the gay and lesbian movement and the community-based response to HIV and AIDS. He is a founding member and the first paid executive director of the National Coalition of Black Lesbians and Gays. A former treasurer and vice-moderator of the Metropolitan Community Church of Washington, DC, Gerald also held these positions on the board of the Metropolitan Community Church of Los Angeles. In 1987, he served as a member of the National Steering Committee for the National March on Washington for Lesbian and Gay Rights. As a co-founder of the National Minority AIDS Council, Gerald served as its first secretary of the board. He was executive director of the Minority AIDS Project in Los Angeles, on the board of directors of AIDS Project Los Angeles, and treasurer of Gentlemen Concerned, which in the late 1980s and early 1990s raised money from the black community for AIDS services in Los Angeles. Gerald also served for two years as director of development for the Black Coalition on AIDS. His essay in *In the Life* documents his struggles to become a naturalized citizen of the United States as an Afro-Panamian national and a gay man. Since 1990 he has worked as a consultant, assisting community-based organizations with their fund-raising, program development, and capacity-building challenges through specialized technical assistance services. He lives in New York City.

Roy Gonsalves—Roy Gonsalves was born in 1960 in Roxbury, Massachusetts. He was a member of the Other Countries Collective, and contributed to several major anthologies of the black gay cultural renaissance. An award-winning poet and fiction writer, his book of stories and poems, *Perversion*, was published in 1990. In addition, Gonsalves was the founding editor of the *Pyramid Poetry Periodical*, a black gay-themed literary journal. He died of AIDS in 1993.

James Earl Hardy—Born December 14, 1966, in Brooklyn, New York, Hardy received a bachelor of arts in communication from St. John's University and a master of science in journalism from Columbia University. After working as a magazine editor and music critic for several years, he began writing novels. He is best known for his *B-Boy Blues* series (1994), best-selling novels that merge black gay and hip-hop aesthetics. Subsequently, Hardy has written and produced several plays, including *B-Boy Blues* and *Confession of a Homo-Thug Porn Star*, the latter a one-person show about the life of Tiger Tyson, an Afro-Latino gay porn star and producer. He lives and works in New York City.

Craig G. Harris—Harris was born in 1959 in New York City, and attended Vassar College from 1976 to 1980. He worked at the Gay Men's Health Crisis as a health educator and HIV prevention and service provider focusing on people of color, and as a media specialist and health educator for the Spectrum AIDS Project in Washington, DC. In 1988, Harris served as executive director of the Minority AIDS Task Force. At various times, he worked as a journalist for *Gay Community News*, *Black/Out*, the *Advocate*, *Outweek*, and *Art and Understanding*, and edited the black gay supplement for the *New York Native* in February 1986. In addition, Harris was a short story writer, essayist, and poet, and published work in several key anthologies of the black gay cultural renaissance, including *The Road Before Us*, *Tongues Untied*, *In the Life*, *Brother to Brother*, and *Sojourner*. Harris was also an activist. After realizing that the closing workshop on AIDS at the 1986 American Public Health Association Conference in San Francisco had no speakers of color, he rushed the stage, grabbed the microphone from San Franciso health commissioner Merv Silverman, and shouted, "I will be heard!" Harris died of AIDS on November 26, 1992.

E. Lynn Harris—Born Everette Lynn Jeter in 1955 in Flint, Michigan, Harris moved with his mother to Little Rock, Arkansas, when he was three years old. His surname was changed upon his mother's marriage to Ben Harris. After attending the University of Arkansas, Harris was a computer salesman for thirteen years, moving between major cities in the South. Then, after suffering depression, he quit his job and found inspiration in his writing. He was unable to find a publisher for his first novel, so he self-published *Invisible Life* (1991) and sold copies of it from the trunk of his car. Based on the success of this sale, he landed a book deal with Doubleday. *Invisible Life* follows the life of Raymond Winston Tyler, Jr., a black man who discovers his same-sex desires in college while dating a female cheerleader. The novel tracks his adulthood in the closet during the early era of AIDS, and his encounters with various other black men who sleep with men but do not identify as gay or bisexual. Ten of Harris's novels, which build on the narrative of his debut novel, appeared on the New York Times Best Seller list. In addition to his fiction works, one of his most important contributions to the black gay cultural renaissance is *Freedom in This Village* (2005), his edited anthology of black gay men's writing from 1979 to 2005. Harris died of heart disease on July 23, 2009, in Los Angeles.

Lyle Ashton Harris—Born in New York in 1965, Harris earned a BA at Wesleyan University and his MFA at the California Institute of the Arts. He also completed training at New

York University and the Whitney Independent Study Program. Harris works in multiple media, including photography, collage, performance, and installation. His most significant contributions to the black gay cultural renaissance were his installation *Face: Lyle Ashton Harris* (1993) at the New Museum in New York, which combined photography, video, and audio to critique masculinity and explore the intersections of race, gender, and sexuality; and his solo exhibition, *The Good Life* (1994), which interspersed his own photos with family photos to critique notions of race, sexuality, and kinship. Harris is associate professor of art and art history at New York University.

B. Michael Hunter—Bertram Michael Hunter was born in 1958 in New York City. He attended Adelphi University and the Northeastern University School of Law. A member of the Other Countries Collective, Hunter served as managing editor of its Lambda Literary Award–winning anthology, *Sojourner: Black Gay Voices in the Age of AIDS*. He was featured in Bill T. Jones's dance performance *Still/Here*. Hunter died of AIDS in 2001.

G. Winston James—Born in 1957 in Kingston, Jamaica, James holds an MFA in fiction from Brooklyn College. He is the author of two poetry collections, *Lyric: Poems along a Broken Road* (1999) and *The Damaged Good* (2006), and the short story collection *Shame the Devil: Collected Short Stories* (2009). With Lisa C. Moore, he coedited the anthology *Spirited: Affirming the Soul and Black Gay/Lesbian Identity* (2005). A former executive director of the Other Countries Collective, James edited the group's third journal, *Other Countries III: Voices Rising* (2007). He lives and works in Ft. Lauderdale, Florida.

Cary Alan Johnson—Johnson was born in 1960 in Brooklyn, New York. He earned a bachelor's degree from Sarah Lawrence College and a master's degree in international affairs from Columbia University. He was a member of the Blackheart Collective. As a founding member of the Other Countries Collective, Johnson coedited its first journal, *Other Countries: Black Gay Voices*. His plays, poetry, and essays are featured in several key anthologies of the black gay cultural renaissance, including *Other Countries: Black Gay Voices*, *The Road Before Us*, and *Brother to Brother*. From 2009 to 2012, he served as the director of the International Gay and Lesbian Human Rights Commission. Johnson lives in Tanzania, where he continues his human rights work concerning LGBT issues and HIV.

Bill T. Jones—Jones was born in 1952 in Bunnell, Florida. He attended Binghamton University, where he began to study dance. With his partner, Arnie Zane, Jones began to perform solo and duet works in New York City and internationally, and in 1982 formed the Bill T. Jones/Arnie Zane Dance Company. In 1994, Jones debuted *Still/Here*, a dance performance grappling with his AIDS diagnosis and the loss of Zane, his dance and life partner, to AIDS. Though well received internationally, the performance became subject to national controversy after dance critic Arlene Croce refused to review it, calling it "victim art." Jones has choreographed over 120 works for his company and others, including Alvin Ailey. He serves as the artistic director of New York Arts Live, and lives with his partner, Bjorn Arnelan, in Rockland County, New York.

Wayson Jones—Born in 1957 in Laurel, Maryland, Jones received his bachelor's degree in music in 1980 from the University of Maryland–College Park, where he studied saxophone, piano, and music composition. From 1980 to 1982, he performed with the dance company Improvisations Unlimited. Jones is a founding member of the performing arts group Cinque, with Essex Hemphill and Larry Duckette. He works as a visual artist based in Washington, DC.

Isaac Julien—Julien was born in 1960 in London. He attended Saint Martin's School of Art, where he studied painting and film. He founded the Sankofa Film and Video Collective, a London-based black film organization dedicated to developing an independent black film culture in the areas of production, exhibition, and audience. A globally renowned filmmaker and visual artist, Julien's numerous works often explore the relations between history, memory, race, and sexuality. His film *Looking for Langston* is an impressionistic exploration of black queerness during the Harlem Renaissance. It incorporates many artists from the black gay cultural renaissance, and is one of the most celebrated works to emerge from that period. Julien lives and works in London.

John Keene—John R. Keene Jr. was born in 1965 in St. Louis. He attended Harvard University and received his MFA from New York University. He was a longtime member of the Dark Room Collective, a Boston-area black writers' group, and contributed a short story to *Brother to Brother*. Keene's most significant contribution to the black gay cultural renaissance is his experimental novel *Annotations* (1995). He has subsequently published a poetry collection, *Seismosis* (2006), and the story and novella collection *Counternarratives* (2015). Keene splits his time between Chicago and New Jersey, where he is associate professor of English and African American and African studies at Rutgers University–Newark.

Randall Kenan—Kenan was born March 12, 1963, in Brooklyn, North Carolina, and raised in rural parts of the state. After graduating from the University of North Carolina–Chapel Hill, he moved to New York City, where he worked on the editorial staff at Alfred A. Knopf. Kenan's many works include *A Visitation of Spirits* (1989), a novel that centers on the life and death of black gay teenager Horace Cross in fictional Tims Creek, North Carolina, and the award-winning short story collection *Let the Dead Bury Their Dead* (1992), also set in Tims Creek. Kenan lives in North Carolina, where he is professor of English at UNC–Chapel Hill.

Glenn Ligon—Born in 1960 in the Bronx, Ligon attended the Rhode Island School of Design and received a BA from Wesleyan University in 1982. He completed the independent study program at New York City's Whitney Museum of American Art in 1985. Ligon's most prominent contributions to the black gay cultural renaissance are *Notes on the Margin of the Black Book* (1991–93), which juxtaposes Robert Mapplethorpe's photographs of black men to textual critiques of the images, and *Feast of Scraps* (1994–98), which constructs a photo album juxtaposing family photos to captioned photos of black gay pornography. He is based in New York City.

Kevin McGruder—McGruder was born in 1957 in Toledo, Ohio. He earned an MBA in real estate finance at Columbia University and a PhD in history at the Graduate Center of the City University of New York. He served on the board of directors of the Other Countries Collective, and also traveled with the group while it performed across the country. In addition, he was the director of the Gay Men of African Descent, founded in New York City in 1986. McGruder is an assistant professor of history at Antioch College in Yellow Springs, Ohio.

Ray Melrose—Born in 1951 in Texas, Melrose studied Russian affairs at Colorado College. He served in the US Air Force from 1971 to 1974, but was given an involuntary honorable discharge after his homosexuality was discovered. During the early 1980s, Melrose served as the president of the DC Coalition of Black Lesbians and Gays. In that role, he founded the Enik Alley Coffeehouse, an arts space he converted from a two-story carriage house behind his home. The place became a central location for the burgeoning black gay and lesbian arts movement in Washington, DC. When Melrose became the manager of the competing dc space in the mid-1980s, many of the performers and artists from the Coffeehouse followed him there, and it eventually became the successor to the original space. The circumstances of Melrose's death are unknown.

Charles I. Nero—Nero was born in 1956, and grew up in a suburb of New Orleans. He was in the first generation in the South to desegregate traditionally white public and private schools, but later attended Xavier University, a historically black Catholic university, where he studied theater and became especially interested in the black arts movement. While working toward a PhD at Indiana University, Nero studied black queer culture, and met with resistance from professors to pursue this area of study. Essex Hemphill contacted him personally to review the landmark anthology *Brother to Brother: New Writings by Black Gay Men* (1991) and later included his essay "Toward a Black Gay Aesthetic: Signifying in Contemporary Black Gay Literature" in that anthology. The essay has been republished many times. Nero also wrote the introduction for the Cleis Press edition of Hemphill's collected writing, *Ceremonies: Prose and Poetry* (2000). He is professor of rhetoric at Bates College, and has published many essays on the intersections of race, gender, sexuality, literature, and culture.

Robert F. Reid-Pharr—Born April 4, 1965, in Charlotte, North Carolina, Reid-Pharr attended the University of North Carolina–Chapel Hill. He received his PhD in American studies at Yale University in 1994. While an undergraduate student, Reid-Pharr was active in the National Coalition of Black Lesbians and Gays, and interned in its Washington, DC, office. He also participated in the Other Countries Collective, and contributed a bibliography of black gay literature, media, and organizations to *Brother to Brother*. He has published four books, including the Randy Shilts Award–winning *Black Gay Man: Essays* (2001), and many essays exploring the intersections of race, gender, and sexuality in African diasporic literatures and cultures. He is the Distinguished Professor of English at the City University of New York-Graduate Center.

Marlon Riggs—Riggs was born in 1957 in Forth Worth, Texas. He studied history at Harvard University, and in 1981 received a master's degree in journalism with a specialization in documentary film from the University California–Berkeley. After graduation, Riggs began working on documentary films and was a journalism instructor at Berkeley, eventually becoming a tenured faculty member there. In 1987, he completed his first feature-length documentary film, *Ethnic Notions*, for which he received an Emmy Award. In 1989, he completed *Tongues Untied*, an experimental, feature-length documentary exploring the lives and experiences of black gay men. The film was subject to controversy after it aired on public television in 1991. Right-wing politicians condemned its subject matter as obscene, and questioned the role of federal money in funding art that was considered obscene. Riggs completed several subsequent works, including *Affirmations* (1990), *Color Adjustment* (1992), *Non Je Ne Regrette Rien/No Regrets* (1992), *Anthem* (1993), and *Black Is . . . Black Ain't* (1994). In addition, he contributed essays and prose to several major anthologies of the black gay cultural renaissance. He died of AIDS in 1994, before completing work on *Black Is . . . Black Ain't*.

Colin Robinson—Born in 1961 in Port of Spain, Trinidad, Robinson grew up in Brooklyn, New York. He is a founding member of the Blackheart Collective and the Other Countries Collective. He coedited Blackheart's third journal, *Blackheart 3: The Telling of Us*, served as managing producer for Other Countries' first journal, *Other Countries: Black Gay Voices* (1988), and contributed to several other black gay journals and anthologies. Additionally, Robinson was the first executive director of Gay Men of African Descent and the New York State Black Gay Network, and was the New York field producer of Marlon Riggs's film *Tongues Untied*. In 2016, he published the poetry collection *He Have His Father Hard Head*. Robinson works as director of CAISO: sex and gender justice, a social justice organization based in Trinidad and Tobago.

Darieck Scott—Scott was born in 1964 in Fort Knox, Kentucky. Raised in a military family, he has lived in various cities around the United States and Europe. He completed his BA at Stanford University, an MA and a JD at Yale University, and a PhD in modern thought and literature at Stanford University. Scott's primary contribution to the black gay cultural renaissance is the novel *Traitor to the Race* (1995), which explores themes of queer interracial desire, homophobic violence, and cultural and political identity. He has subsequently published the edited collection *Best Black Gay Erotica* (2004), the novel *Hex* (2007), several academic essays, several short stories, and the award-winning scholarly work *Extravagant Abjection: Blackness, Power, and Sexuality in the African American Literary Imagination* (2010). He lives in San Francisco, and is associate professor of African American and African diaspora studies at the University of California–Berkeley.

Reginald Shepherd—Shepherd was born in 1963 in New York City. He received an MFA from Brown University and studied at the Iowa Writers' Workshop. Shepherd contributed work to several major anthologies of the black gay cultural renaissance, including

In the Life and *Voices Rising,* and to gay-themed media such as *Gay Community News* and *Fag Rag.* An award-winning poet and essayist, Shepherd published five collections of poetry: *Some Are Drowning* (1994), *Angel, Interrupted* (1996), *Wrong* (1999), *Otherhood* (2003), and *Fata Morgana* (2007). Two volumes of his literary criticism have been published: *Orpheus in the Bronx: Essays on Identity, Politics, and Freedom of Poetry* (2007) and *A Martian Muse: Further Readings on Identity, Politics, and Freedom of Poetry* (2010). Shepherd died of cancer in 2008 in Pensacola, Florida.

Ron K. Simmons—Simmons was born in 1950 in Brooklyn, New York. He earned a PhD in mass communications from Howard University, where he served on the faculty for twelve years. Upon his arrival in Washington, DC, in 1980, he became active in black gay movements. Under the pseudonym Butch, Simmons contributed to *Blacklight* magazine as a photographer and a designer. His academic essay, "Some Thoughts on the Challenges Facing Black Gay Intellectuals," was published in the anthology *Brother to Brother,* and became widely influential. He also served as field producer, photographer, and actor in Marlon Riggs's documentary *Tongues Untied.* Simmons was the long-time director of Us Helping Us, Inc., an AIDS service organization focused on black gay and bisexual men in Washington, DC, where he continues to live.

Adrian Stanford—Stanford was born in the late 1940s, and began publishing in the homophile magazine *ONE* in the 1960s. His poem, "Remembrance in Rittenhouse Square," is about one of Philadelphia's most notable black drag queens, Sarah Vaughan. His work appeared in publications such as *Fag Rag,* the *Drummer,* the *Philadelphia Tribune,* *Spartan,* and *Ampersand,* and would subsequently appear in the black gay anthologies *In the Life* and *Brother to Brother.* Stanford's writing career culminated in the publication of the poetry chapbook *Black and Queer* (1977), considered one of the first collections categorized as black gay literature. His work is credited as one of the origins of the black gay cultural renaissance. Little is known about his life apart from his 1981 murder in Philadelphia.

Marvin K. White—Born in 1966 Oakland, California, White was a member of the Other Countries Collective, and former member of the San Francisco–based performance group Pomo Afro Homos. He contributed work to several key anthologies of the black gay cultural renaissance, including *The Road Before Us* and *Sojourner.* White has published four critically acclaimed collections of poetry: *last rights* (1999), *nothing ugly fly* (2004), *our name be witness* (2011), and *status* (2011). He works as a public theologian in Oakland.

Allen Luther Wright—Wright was born in 1956 in Chicago, and attended the Graduate Center of the City University of New York. As a member of the Other Countries Collective, he performed with the group as it toured the country. His writing also appears in several key anthologies of the black gay cultural renaissance, including *The Road Before Us, Other Countries: Black Gay Voices,* and *Sojourner.* Wright was featured in Marlon Riggs's documentary *Tongues Untied.* He lives and works in Brooklyn, New York.

Ajamu X—Ajamu was born in 1963 in Huddersfield, West Yorkshire, England, to Jamaican parents. After studying black history and photography at Jan Van Eyck Academie in the Netherlands, he moved to London in 1988, and became involved in the city's LGBTQ culture and politics. His first major exhibition, *Black Bodyscapes* (1994), focused on the gender and sexual expressions of black gay men. A recent exhibit, *Fierce: Portraits of Young Black Queers* (2014), continued his traditions of documenting black queer subcultural life. Ajamu served as archive manager of the Black LGBT Archive Project, and co-curated the exhibition Outside Edge: A Journey through Black Gay and Lesbian History (2008) at the Museum of Docklands. An artist, curator, archivist, and activist, he continues to live and work in London.

Black Gay Men's Support, Advocacy, and Arts Groups

Adodi, Inc.—Formed in 1985 in Philadelphia in response to the ravages of AIDS on black same-sex-desiring men, the group continues to promote experiential, intellectual, emotional, and spiritual growth opportunities for same-gender-loving men of African descent. It has several local chapters and sponsors an annual retreat.

Black and White Men Together—The organization was founded in 1980 in San Francisco as a consciousness-raising group and multicultural organization. It continues to be dedicated to eradicating racism in the LGBT community, eradicating racism and homophobia in society, and supporting gay men in interracial relationships. Local chapters have emerged across the nation, some of which include other racial groups and women (Men of All Colors Together and People of All Colors Together).

Black Gay Men United—Based in Oakland, California, Black Gay Men United was a support and advocacy group. It formed in 1987 as a loosely structured, nonhierarchical discussion group in which black gay men met biweekly in members' homes to discuss topics ranging from the personal to the political. The group also planned yearly retreats and organized political and cultural events. Member Marlon Riggs and participating members of Pomo Afro Homos used knowledge developed from this consciousness-raising group to inform their artistic works.

Black Men's Xchange—Founded in 1989 by noted behavioral health expert, social architect, and activist Cleo Manago, Black Men's Xchange (BMX) is a human rights, educational, antioppression, and advocacy organization dedicated to dismantling barriers to well-being, dignity, self-respect, and protection, with a focus on responsive public policy and the prevention of health threats to same-gender-loving (SGL), gay-identifying, nongay-identifying, and bisexual males of African descent. It has chapters in Los Angeles, Oakland, San Francisco, Sacramento, Orange County, Detroit, Denver, Atlanta, Minneapolis, Baltimore, and Philadelphia.

Brother to Brother—The San Francisco–based organization was formed in 1982 and was dedicated to an exchange of information and knowledge, serving as a support and advocacy group for the black community of and by black gay men, exclusively and especially for the cultural, social, and sexual development of black men in all fields—the arts and sciences, commerce, and industry. It met weekly in a potluck setting so that members could construct selves and raise awareness while enjoying one another's company. It distributed a monthly newsletter edited by Bernard Sinkler.

Committee of Black Gay Men—The group was formed to provide support and community for local black gay men, and to combat negative stereotypes of black gay identity. In 1979, fourteen men met at the Third World Gay Conference held in Washington, DC, to discuss, formulate, and implement a plan for a national network by and for black gay men. They established chapters in Washington, DC, New York City, and Chicago. A national conference was held in Atlanta in 1980.

Gay Men of African Descent—A New York City–based organization founded in 1986 by the Rev. Charles Angel, GMAD is dedicated to the empowerment of black gay men through providing opportunities for fellowship and group support. It continues to work for these men's educational, social, and polical mobilization. GMAD dedicates itself to consciousness-raising and the development of the lesbian and gay community, and is inclusive of African, Black, Caribbean, Hispanic, and Latino men of color. The group published a monthly newsletter (first titled *Calendar*, then *Angel Times*, and then *GMAD Newletter*) that ran from 1988 through 1999.

Pomo Afro Homos—Short for Postmodern African American Homosexuals, Pomo Afro Homos was a performance group founded in 1990 in San Francisco by interdisciplinary theatre artist Djola Bernard Branner; actor, director, and producer Brian Freeman; and singer, dancer, and actor Eric Gupton. The group performed multimedia theatre pieces around the country from 1990 until it disbanded in 1995. It faced controversy because of its focus on the lives and experiences of black gay men. The mayor of Anchorage, Alaska, tried to prevent the advertisement of the group's performance, and the National Black Theatre Festival banned it from performing in 1991. Pomo Afro Homos' major works included *Fierce Love: Stories from Black Gay Life* and *Dark Fruit*. Eric Gupton was born in Boston and attended Antioch College. He moved to San Francisco and worked as a journalist and human resource officer to support his career as a dancer. He died of AIDS in 1993. Brian Freeman was born in 1955 in Boston. He was an actor and producer on Marlon Riggs's documentary *Tongues Untied* (1989) and Cheryl Dunye's *The Watermelon Woman* (1996). He lives and works in San Francisco. Djola Branner contributed to several literary anthologies, including Assotto Saint's *Here to Dare*. He continues to work as a theatre artist, creating such shows as *Sweet Sadie*, *Homos in the House*, and *Mighty Real: A Tribute to Sylvester*. In addition, he is dean of the School of Interdisciplinary Arts and associate professor of theatre at Hampshire College in Amherst, Massachusetts.

Unity, Incorporated—The Philadelphia-based grassroots organization focused on supporting the city's black gay men living with AIDS. It was cofounded and directed by

Tyrone Smith and James Roberts in 1989, and continued its work for the better part of a decade.

Us Helping Us, People into Living, Inc.—A community health organization founded in Washington, DC, in 1985, Us Helping Us was established to address the needs of black gay and bisexual men in the context of the AIDS epidemic. Its models of community care developed out of early grassroots organizing against AIDS at the DC gay and lesbian nightclub the Clubhouse. The group was founded by black gay theologian Rainey Cheeks, and black gay activist Ron K. Simmons was the longtime director of the center, which continues to serve the black gay and bisexual communities in Washington, DC.

Black Gay Publications

B&G: Black & Gay; A Different Point of View—The New York City–based journal was published monthly by editor and publisher Joseph Cornell from 1990 to 1992. It included op-eds on cultural and political issues; coverage of local, national, and celebrity news; and film, music, and book reviews, along with a classified advertisement section for job and personal ads.

BGM—A Washington, DC–based literary magazine published bimonthly by Sidney Brinkley's imprint, Blacklight Press, *BGM* (short for Black Gay Male) ran from 1987 to 1991. After the last issue of *Blacklight* magazine was published, Brinkley formed the Blacklight Press and also *BGM*, a magazine for black gay men that featured poetry, fiction, essays, and artwork.

Black/Out—A Washington, DC–based quarterly magazine published by the National Coalition of Black Lesbians and Gays, *Black/Out* began as *Habari-Habari* in 1980, and then became *Black/Out* under the direction of Joseph Beam. It circulated nationally from 1986 to 1989.

BLK—*BLK* was a Los Angeles–based, nationally circulating magazine published by Alan Bell from 1988 to 1994. Bell first produced *BLK* as a newsletter for attendees of his safer-sex club, Black Jack, in the context of AIDS. But the newsletter expanded to offer an alternative, hard-hitting national news source for black gays and lesbians across America.

Moja—A New York City–based newspaper published from 1978 to 1979 by Calvin M. Lowery and William J. Harris, *Moja* is considered to be one of the first publications geared toward a black gay and lesbian audience.

Pyramid Periodical: A Provocative Quarterly for Gay People of Color—This New York City–based journal of black gay poetry and fiction was created and edited by Charles Pouncy and Rodney Dildy and ran from the fall of 1988 to the winter of 1990. It was the successor to *Pyramid Poetry Periodical*, which was founded by Roy Gonsalves. After the fourth volume, the journal's subtitle was changed to *The Provocative Journal for Lesbians and Gay Men of Color*, and the journal began to include work by women.

NOTES

INTRODUCTION

Because of the fragmentary nature of the historical record, some publication dates, group formation or disbandment dates, and other pertinent information may be unavailable.

1. Brian Rafferty, "When Is an End Closure, When Is a Closure a Beginning," *NYQ*, April 19, 1996, 26; box 1, folder 1, Melvin Dixon Papers, Schomburg Center for Research in Black Culture, New York Public Library.
2. Melvin Dixon, "Somewhere Listening for My Name," *Callaloo* 23, no. 1 (2000): 82.
3. Dixon, 82.
4. Dixon, 82.
5. Dixon, 82.
6. Christina Sharpe, "Black Studies: In the Wake," *Black Scholar* 44, no. 2 (2014): 59–60.
7. Cathy Cohen describes the "dual process of secondary marginalization" that black gays and lesbians faced in this era: "Again, I want to emphasize that for many black lesbians and gay men, attempts to silence them and make their presence invisible came not only from black communities but also from racist white lesbians and gay men. Under such conditions black 'queers' faced a dual process of secondary marginalization—one originating within black communities and the other rooted within white lesbian and gay institutions and space." Cathy J. Cohen, *The Boundaries of Blackness: AIDS and the Breakdown of Black Politics* (Chicago: University of Chicago Press, 1999), 94.
8. Dixon, "Somewhere Listening," 83.
9. Dagmawi Woubshet notes that the sorrow songs of slaves are "predominately a genre of mourning" and "were instrumental in encoding escape" and "cyphering the plans of fugitives." Dagmawi Woubshet, *The Calendar of Loss: Race, Sexuality, and Mourning in the Early Era of AIDS* (Baltimore: Johns Hopkins University Press, 2015), 21.
10. I use the term *gay* to preserve the integrity of their identity claims. These writers used the nomenclature "black gay" in several of their texts, including *In the Life: A Black Gay Anthology; Brother to Brother: New Writings by Black Gay Men; Other Countries: Black Gay Voices;* and *Sojourner: Black Gay Voices in the Age of AIDS.* I use the terms *queer* and *same-sex-desiring* throughout this book to refer to those who do not self-identify as gay. I also use *queer* to situate black gay writing within contemporary queer theory, and to describe affects, political feelings, socialities, and geographic sites that produce

alternative ways of being in the world, modes of being, and ways of knowing that disrupt normative identifications.

11. I use the slash in *black/queer* not only to suggest "black and queer" and "black queer" but also to take seriously Afro-pessimism's claims that blackness and queerness can never meet, because blackness is the constitutive outside of queerness.

12. Sidney Brinkley, "Who's Who in Black Gay Politics," *Blacklight* 4, no. 4 (1983): 12. Though coalition building in Washington, DC, and Baltimore was key in the development of black gay politics on a national scale, a group based in the Los Angeles metropolitan area and known as the Association of Black Gays had formed earlier, in 1976. It briefly published the journal *Rafiki: The Journal of the Association of Black Gays.*

13. Discussing the surge in black federal employment after the Civil Rights Act of 1964, Thomas Sugrue argues, "Government became one of the most important avenues for minority employment. Beginning in the 1970s, many employers began to reach out to minority workers out of fear of litigation." Thomas Sugrue, *Sweet Land of Liberty: The Forgotten Struggle for Civil Rights in the North* (New York: Random House, 2009), 537. Marlon Ross discusses the historical conditions in which some black gays and lesbians moved away from black communities. He demonstrates how pre-Stonewall black lesbians and gays, unlike their white counterparts, had no option of moving to urban centers or going slumming in black sectors of these urban centers that whites called home. They did not have the racial or class privilege to be independent from their families and communities. So it was not until the late 1960s and 1970s and the advent of militant black nationalism, which defined itself against sexual Others, and gay liberation, which offered a rhetoric of racial inclusion, that "embracing European American style autonomous gay identity made *some* sense for *some* black homosexuals" [emphasis in original]. Marlon B. Ross, "Some Glances at the Black Fag: Race, Same Sex Desire, and Cultural Belonging," *Canadian Review of Comparative Literature* 21, nos. 1–2 (2000): 203.

14. In the article "'No Blacks'—Racism in the Gay Press," Michael J. Smith gives the example of a Help Wanted ad published in a gay-themed newspaper: "GWM (Gay White Male) for 3–4 day job, help, home fix-up . . . Exp pref but not nec is good worker. Must be clean, dependable." Smith notes twenty ads that he deemed blatantly discriminatory in their suggestion that white gay men are more employable and housable. Michael J. Smith, "'No Blacks'—Racism in the Gay Press," in *Black Men/White Men: A Gay Anthology*, ed. Michael J. Smith (San Francisco: Gay Sunshine Press, 1983), 159–62. For an example of psychopathological representations of black gay men in black popular media, see Alvin Pouissant, "Sex and the Black Male," *Ebony*, August 1972, 117–18. For more on black gay popular representation in the 1970s, see also Bill Sanford Pincheon, "Mask Maker, Mask Maker: The Black Gay Subject in 1970s Popular Culture," *Sexuality and Culture* 5 (2001): 49–78.

15. Sidney Brinkley elaborates on how racial discrimination occurred through the act of carding. Many black gay men witnessed white patrons walk into white-owned establishments without showing ID, while black patrons were asked to show multiple pieces of ID, only to be told that the identification was unacceptable for admission. Brinkley linked this to Jim Crow segregation, because all bars had to serve food, and thus could not restrict admission on the basis that they were restaurants, and discrimination at restaurants had been a highly visible component of civil rights protest. Sidney Brinkley, "The Bottom Line," *Blacklight* 1, no. 2 (1979): 2. Black gay men suffered a disproportionate amount of homophobic street violence in Washing-

ton, DC, in the late 1970s and early 1980s; however, white gay antiviolence activists' focus on sexuality as the single axis of oppression did not permit an analysis of how the convergence of racism and homophobia might render black gay bodies as more vulnerable to violence—a theme I further explore in chapter 1.

16. Jeffrey McCune notes how "the stigma around sexual practices, the mandates of a stable identity formation, and the abjection of non-normative masculinity produce a 'feeling' that prompts many black men to live 'in secret.'" Jeffrey McCune, *Sexual Discretion: Black Masculinity and the Politics of Passing* (Chicago: University of Chicago Press, 2014), ix.

17. In his introduction to *In the Life*, Joseph Beam notes that part of his motivation for developing a black gay anthology was because, by mid-1983, he had "grown weary of reading literature by white Gay men who fell, quite easily, into three camps: the incestuous literati of Manhattan and Fire Island, the San Francisco cropped-moustache-clones, and the Boston-to-Cambridge politically correct radical faggots. None of them spoke to me as a Black gay man. Their words offered the reflection of a sidewalk; their characters cast ominous shadows for my footfalls." Joseph Beam, "Leaving the Shadows Behind," introduction to *In the Life: A Black Gay Anthology*, ed. Joseph Beam (Boston: Alyson Publications, 1986), 13. For more on representations of black male homosexuality in African American literature, see Charles Nero, "Toward a Black Gay Aesthetic," in *Brother to Brother: New Writings by Black Gay Men*, ed. Essex Hemphill (Boston: Alyson Publications, 1991), 229–52; and Robert F. Reid-Pharr, "Tearing the Goat's Flesh: Homosexuality, Abjection, and the Production of a Late Twentieth Century Black Masculinity," *Studies in the Novel* 28, no. 3 (1996): 372–94.

18. For a discussion of homophobic sentiment in dominant black intellectual traditions, see Ron Simmons, "Some Thoughts on the Challenges Facing Black Gay Intellectuals," in Hemphill, *Brother to Brother*, 211–28; and Essex Hemphill, "If Freud Had Been a Neurotic Colored Woman: Reading Frances Cress Welsing," in *Ceremonies: Prose and Poetry* (Berkeley: Cleis Press, 2000), 52–62.

19. Woubshet, *The Calendar of Loss*, 57.

20. Martin Duberman, *Hold Tight Gently: Michael Callen, Essex Hemphill, and the Battlefield of AIDS* (New York: New Press, 2014), 32.

21. Isaac Jackson was born in 1955 in New York to African American and West Indian parents. He works as a harm reduction activist in San Francisco. New Haven, Connecticut, native Fred Carl was born in 1955. He had moved to New York City in the 1970s from Providence, Rhode Island. He works as a professor of music at New York University. Tony Crusor was born in 1958 in Chicago. Though not a writer, he was drawn to the group from his disenchantment with other black nationalist organizations that regulated his masculinity according to norms of gender and sexuality. He works as an architect in New York City.

22. The aftermath of Woods's funeral became the subject of Thomas Glave's O. Henry Award–winning short story, "Final Inning," first published in 1996 in *Kenyon Review*. 18, nos. 3–4 (1996): 116–34.

23. For more on the publication and literary reception of *Brother to Brother*, see Duberman, *Hold Tight Gently*, 176–82.

24. Ross Chambers, *Facing It: AIDS Diaries and the Death of the Author* (Ann Arbor: University of Michigan Press, 2009), 9.

25. Simon Dickel, *Black/Gay: The Harlem Renaissances, the Protest Era, and the Constructions of Black Gay Identity in the 1980s and 90s* (East Lansing: Michigan State University Press, 2012), 9.

26. José Esteban Muñoz, *Disidentifications: Queers of Color and the Performance of Politics.* (Minneapolis: University of Minnesota Press, 1994), 57.

27. Thanks to Cathy Cohen, whose brilliant insights and engagement with my work helped me better articulate this point.

28. In the introduction to *In the Life*, editor Joseph Beam discusses how he was "fed by" the novels, anthologies, and creative nonfiction of the black lesbian writers, as well as the work of Chicana lesbian feminist Cherríe Moraga and white lesbian feminist Barbara Deming. Joseph Beam, "Leaving the Shadows Behind," 13. In an interview in the *New York Native*, the founder of the Blackheart Collective names Cherríe Moraga and Gloria Anzaldúa's anthology *This Bridge Called My Back: Radical Writings by Women of Color* (4th ed., Albany: SUNY Press, 2015) as a major influence on the group's development and aesthetics. Charles Michael Smith, "Black Gay Men Expressing Themselves in Print," *New York Native*, 1983; posted on *Bookmaven* (blog) September 1, 2013, http://urbanbookmaven.blogspot.com/search?q=black+gay+men.

29. Combahee River Collective, "A Black Feminist Statement," *WSQ: Women's Studies Quarterly* 42 (1981): 210–18; Combahee River Collective, "Why Did They Die? A Document of Black Feminism," *Radical America* 13, no. 6 (November–December 1979), 41–46.

30. Christina B. Hanhardt, *Safe Space: Gay Neighborhood History and the Politics of Violence* (Durham, NC: Duke University Press, 2013), 111–14.

31. Isaac Jackson, quoted in Smith, "Black Gay Men Expressing Themselves in Print."

32. Jackson's reference to the "voices of our black sisters" conjures Evelynn Hammonds's similar observations about black female sexuality in general and black lesbianism in particular as a site of negation in white and black feminist and queer discourse. Evelynn Hammonds, "Black (W)holes and the Geometry of Black Female Sexuality," *differences: A Journal of Feminist Cultural Studies* 6, nos. 2–3 (1994): 126–45.

33. Simmons, "Some Thoughts on the Challenges Facing Black Gay Intellectuals," 224.

34. Simmons, 57.

35. E. Patrick Johnson inquires about the utility of Judith Butler's notion of performativity to racialized and classed subjects, "but what is the utility of queer theory on the front lines, in the trenches, on the street, or any place where the racialized and sexualized body is beaten, starved, fired, cursed—indeed, when the body is the site of trauma?" E. Patrick Johnson, "Quare Studies, or Everything I Learned about Queer Studies I Learned from My Grandmother," in *Black Queer Studies: An Anthology*, ed. Mae G. Henderson and E. Patrick Johnson (Durham, NC: Duke University Press, 2005), 129. About Eve Sedgwick's foundational theory of the "epistemology of the closet," Marlon Ross argues that "the fascination with the closet as the primary epistemological device defining sexual modernity—results in a sort of racial claustrophobia, the tendency to bind both intragender desire and modernity within a small but deep closet containing elite European men maneuvering to find a way out." Marlon Ross, "Beyond the Closet as Raceless Paradigm," in Henderson and Johnson, *Black Queer Studies*, 171.

36. Maurice Stevens discusses how race has functioned to otherize bodies that "are the ultimate source of phobia" and "not imagined to possess the psychic interiority necessary for identification and institutional legibility." Maurice Stevens, "From the Past Imperfect: Towards a Critical Trauma Theory," *Letters* 17, no. 2 (2009): 4. In *Wrong Place, Wrong Time*, John Rich elaborates on the racial and gender politics that circumscribe the trauma narratives of urban black male subjects, and how their labeling as "thugs" and "beasts" affect their medical care—sometimes not being treated for

pain, or how their occasional violent resistance to medical care is understood as symptomatic of their inherent deviance. John Rich, *Wrong Place, Wrong Time: Trauma and Violence in the Lives of Young Black Men* (Baltimore: Johns Hopkins University Press, 2009), 6–23.

37. See Daryl Scott, *Contempt and Pity: Social Policy and the Image of the Damaged Black Psyche, 1880–1996* (Chapel Hill: University of North Carolina Press, 1997); Kevin Mumford, "Untangling Pathology: The Moynihan Report and Homosexual Damage, 1965–1975," *Journal of Policy History* 24, no. 1 (2012): 53–73.

38. See Julia and Nathan Hare, *The Endangered Black Family: Coping with Unisexualization and Coming Extinction of the Black Race* (San Francisco: Black Think Tank, 1984); Frances Cress Welsing, *The Isis Papers: The Keys to the Colors* (Chicago: Third World Press, 1991); Pouissant, "Sex and the Black Male."

39. Frantz Fanon, *Black Skin, White Masks* (New York: Grove Press, 2008). Eric Stanley argues that Fanon is useful for thinking about antiqueer violence as "the bodily terror of force" and for considering how "ontological sovereignty also falls into peril under foundational violence," which is "embodied as a feeling of nonexistence." Stanley restages Fanon's figure of "the black" as "the queer," in essence flattening the multiple forms of difference that structure black queer embodiment. For Stanley, "hope of a radical politics to come" becomes visible only "retroactively" through the archives of brutally murdered bodies of queer and trans people of color. Eric Stanley, "Near Life, Queer Death: Overkill and Ontological Capture," *Social Text* 29, no. 2 (2011): 14. I am concerned with how black gay men negotiated the forms of antiblack and antigay violence that multiply marked their embodiments, how they used literary and cultural forms to imagine alternative modes of black gay being; resist the modes of bodily terror and psychic domination that sought to usher them to premature physical, social, and psychic death; and imagine futures beyond antiblackness and antiqueerness.

40. For a discussion of how race is mutually imbricated with heteronormativity, see Roderick Ferguson, *Aberrations in Black: Towards a Queer of Color Critique* (Minneapolis: University of Minnesota Press), 23–27; Cathy J. Cohen, "Punks, Bulldaggers, and Welfare Queens: The Radical Potential of Queer Politics?," *GLQ* 3, no.4 (1997) 452–57.

41. Robert D. G. Kelley, *Race Rebels: Culture, Politics, and the Black Working Class* (New York: Free Press, 1996); Cathy J. Cohen, "Deviance as Resistance: A New Research Agenda for the Study of Black Politics," *Du Bois Review* 1, no. 1 (2004): 27–45.

42. See Kevin Quashie, *The Sovereignty of Quiet: Beyond Resistance in Black Culture* (New Brunswick, NJ: Rutgers University Press, 2012), for an analysis of the hegemony of political resistance as dominant interpretive framework for black culture and black subjectivity.

43. Cathy Cohen distinguishes between defiant acts by those with limited resources to create autonomous spaces absent power from outside authorities, and acts of resistance that require intent to redistribute power in the country. By theorizing being, I suggest that black gay existence and survival in themselves are acts of resistance for black gay men subject to the forces of double cremation—forces that doubly render them as socially dead within modernity. Cathy Cohen, "Deviance as Resistance," 37.

44. Essex Hemphill, "Vital Signs," in *Life Sentences: Writers, Artists, and AIDS*, ed. Thomas Avena (San Francisco: Mercury House Press, 1994), 54–55.

45. Adam Geary, *Antiblack Racism and the AIDS Epidemic: State Intimacies* (New York: Palgrave MacMillan, 2014).

46. Kai Erikson, "Notes of Trauma and Community," in *Trauma: Explorations in Memory*, ed. with introductions by Cathy Caruth (Baltimore: Johns Hopkins University Press, 1995), 185.

47. In his analysis of AIDS and Latino theatre and performance, David Roman argues, "AIDS is experienced as only one component within a complex system of exploitation and oppression." David Roman, *Acts of Intervention: Performance, Gay Culture, and AIDS* (Bloomington: Indiana University Press, 1998), 196. In his ethnography of gay Filipino men in New York City in the early era of AIDS, Martin Manalansan argues that Filipino gay men's diasporic subjectivities extended the bounds of their suffering beyond the nation-state. Martin Manalansan, *Global Divas: Filipino Gay Men in the Diaspora* (Durham, NC: Duke University Press, 2003), 152–83. Horacio Roque Ramírez analyzes the obituaries of queer Latino men published in the San Francisco-based LGBT-themed newspaper *Bay Area Reporter*. Ramírez argues that heteronormativity and normative masculinity circumscribed the lives of many lost to AIDS, ushering their historical trace into obscurity. He further notes how immigration status and language barriers intensified the experiences of AIDS for Latino same-sex-desiring men in San Francisco. Horacio Roque Ramírez, "Latino Gay Histories/ Dying to Be Remembered: AIDS Obituaries, Public Memory, and the Queer Latino Archive," in *Beyond El Barrio: Everyday Life in Latina/Latino America*, ed. Gina Pérez, Frank A. Guridy, and Adrian Burgos (New York: New York University Press, 2010). Irene S. Vernon and Andrew Jolivette beckon us to consider AIDS within a long history of settler colonialism—in which disease was central to the destruction of the Native—and its ongoing traumatic effects on contemporary Native populations. Vernon further demonstrates how Native skepticism of state-sponsored medical programs and the displacement of Natives on reservations further impact their access to care. Irene S. Vernon, *Killing Us Quietly: Native Americans and HIV/AIDS* (Lincoln: University of Nebraska Press, 2001); Andrew Jolivette, *Indian Blood: HIV and Colonial Trauma in San Francisco's Two Spirit Community* (Seattle: University of Washington Press, 2016).

48. Orlando Patterson, *Slavery and Social Death: A Comparative Study* (Cambridge, MA: Harvard University Press, 1982), 7.

49. Saidiya Hartman, *Lose Your Mother: A Journey along the Atlantic Slave Route* (New York: Farrar, Straus and Giroux, 2008), 6.

50. Cohen, *Boundaries of Blackness*, 89–91.

51. Reid-Pharr, "Tearing the Goat's Flesh," 373–74.

52. Calvin Warren, "Onticide: Afropessimism, Queer Theory, and Ethics," Ill-will-editions, 2015, https://illwilleditions.noblogs.org/files/2015/09/Warren-Onticide-Afropessimism-Queer-Theory-and-Ethics-READ.pdf.

53. Pierre Nora, "Between Memory and History: Les Leuix de Memoire," *Representations* 26 (1989): 7.

54. Saidiya Hartman, "Venus in Two Acts," *Small Axe* 12, no. 2 (2008): 4.

55. Hartman, 12.

56. Hartman, 26.

57. Frank Wilderson, "The Position of the Unthought: An Interview with Saidiya Hartman," *Qui Parle* 13, no. 2 (2003): 183.

58. Heather Love, *Feeling Backward: Loss and the Politics of Queer History* (Cambridge, MA: Harvard University Press, 2009), 29.

59. Tina Campt, "Black Feminist Futures and the Practice of Fugitivity," Helen Pond McIntyre '48 Lecture, Barnard College for Women, October 7, 2014.

60. Campt.
61. Jennifer Devere Brody and Dwight McBride, eds., "Plum Nelly: New Essays in Black Queer Studies," special issue, *Callaloo* 23, no. 1 (2000).
62. Karla F. C. Holloway, *Passed On: African American Mourning Stories; A Memorial* (Durham, NC: Duke University Press, 2002), 2.
63. Darian Aaron, "Black Gay Men Reject 'Lifetime HIV Risk Estimate' in New CDC Report," *Georgia Voice* (Atlanta), February 24, 2016.
64. Love, *Feeling Backward*, 29.
65. Heather Love, "Spoiled Identity: Stephen Gordon's Loneliness and the Difficulties of Queer History." *GLQ* 7, no.4 (2001): 496.
66. Roderick Ferguson argues, "Bureaucracy [i.e., the Centers for Disease Control and Prevention] is not simply a structure but a turbine for racial, gender, and sexual discourses that shape the meaning of black queer life and sex." Roderick Ferguson, "To Be Fluent in Each Other's Narratives," in *Black Sexualities: Probing Powers, Passions, Practices, and Policies*, ed. Juan Battle and Sandra L. Barnes (New Brunswick, NJ: Rutgers University Press), 162.
67. Vincent Brown, "Social Death and Political Life in the Study of Slavery." *American Historical Review* 114, no. 5 (2009): 1248; José Esteban Muñoz, *Cruising Utopia: The Then and There of Queer Futurity* (New York: New York University Press, 2009), 35.
68. Shaka McGlotten, *Virtual Intimacies: Media, Affect, and Queer Socialities* (Albany: SUNY Press, 2014), 74.
69. See Cindy Patton, *Globalizing AIDS* (Minneapolis: University of Minnesota Press, 2002).
70. John Drabinski, "James Baldwin's Afro-Optimism," unpublished paper presented on March 19, 2015, at CUNY Graduate Center.
71. Scholars often date the emergence of the black gay cultural renaissance to the publication of Beam, *In the Life* (1986). I date its emergence to the 1977 publication of Adrian Stanford's poetry collection *Black & Queer* (Boston: Good Gay Poets Press, 1977), one of the first books to be categorized as black gay literature. Little is known about Stanford's life apart from his murder in Philadelphia in 1981.

CHAPTER ONE

1. Alethia Knight, "District Police Hunt Common Thread in Slayings of Homosexuals," *Washington Post*, September 30, 1981.
2. Lindon Barrett, *Blackness and Value: Seeing Double* (Cambridge: Cambridge University Press, 1999), 28.
3. Barrett, 28.
4. John D'Emilio argues that the rise in violence in the 1980s, despite the proliferation of activism in the 1970s, attests to the persistence of institutionalized homophobia and heterosexism: "Although lesbians and gay men won significant victories in the 1970s and opened up some safe social space in which to exist, we can hardly claim to have dealt a fatal blow to heterosexism and homophobia. One could even argue that the enforcement of gay oppression has merely changed locales, shifting somewhat from the state to the arena of extralegal violence in the form of increasingly open physical attacks on lesbian and gay men." D'Emilio's claims imply that these murders of gay men are formations of state-sanctioned violence, evidencing a backlash against gains made from LGBT movement building of the previous decade. John D'Emilio, "Capitalism and Gay Identity," in *The Gay and Lesbian Studies Reader*, ed. Henry Abelove, Michéle Aina Barale, and David M. Halperin (New York: Routledge, 1993), 473.

5. Martin Meeker, *Contacts Desired: Gays and Lesbian Communications and Community, 1940s–1970s* (Chicago: University of Chicago Press, 2006), 2.

6. Dick Munn, "Blacklight Fills a Real Need," *Washington (DC) Blade*, December 5, 1979. Microfilm, Library of Congress.

7. Sidney Brinkley, "Rough Trade" (editorial), *Blacklight*, June 1981, 2.

8. Quoted in Bernard D. Headley, *The Atlanta Youth Murders and the Politics of Race* (Carbondale: Southern Illinois University Press, 1998), 69.

9. Brinkley, "Rough Trade," 2.

10. Kwame Holmes, "What's the Tea? Gossip and the Social Production of Black Gay History," *Social Text* 122 (2015): 65.

11. For more on how gossip and rumor figure into the complex entanglements of blackness, queerness, and public life, see C. Riley Snorton, *Nobody Is Supposed to Know: Black Sexuality on the Down Low* (Minneapolis: University of Minnesota Press, 2014).

12. "Under Grace's Hat," *Blacklight* 3, no. 1 (September 1981): 17.

13. It is not clear exactly what forced the police's hand, but activist pressure was surely a catalyst.

14. Quoted in Lou Chibbaro Jr., "AIDS Conference, Black Conference This Weekend," *Washington (DC) Blade*, October 7, 1983, 1.

15. "Under Grace's Hat."

16. Lou Chibbaro Jr., "Latest Murder Prompts Police Appeal," *Washington (DC) Blade*, August 7, 1981, A-5.

17. Quoted in Chibbaro, 17.

18. Holmes, "What's the Tea?,"65.

19. "Cliques" (editorial), *Blacklight*, December–January 1980–81, 5.

20. Lou Chibbaro Jr., "Another Murder Found Gay-Related," *Washington (DC) Blade*, January 18, 1979, 4.

21. For more on the black federal workers and the struggle for racial equality in Washington, DC, in the post–Civil Rights era in particular, see Frederick Gooding Jr., "American Dream Deferred: Black Federal Workers in Washington, DC, 1941–1981," PhD diss., Georgetown University, 2013. ProQuest Dissertation Publishing ISBN: 978-1-303-38940-5.

22. David K. Johnson, *Lavender Scare: The Cold War Persecution of Gays and Lesbians in the Federal Government* (Chicago: University of Chicago Press, 2004).

23. Courtney Williams, interview by Mark Meinke, 2001, Rainbow History Project, Washington, DC.

24. Sidney Brinkley, "Rough Trade," *Blacklight*, June 1981, 2.

25. Holmes, "What's the Tea?," 65.

26. Lou Chibbaro Jr., "Gay Murder Investigators Reassigned," *Washington (DC) Blade*, January 8, 1982, A-3.

27. "Cliques," 5.

28. Barrett, *Blackness and Value*; Terrion Williamson, "In the Life: Black Women and Serial Murder," *Social Text* 33 (2015): 95–114; Lisa Cacho, "'You Just Don't Know How Much He Meant': Deviancy, Death, and Devaluation," *Latino Studies* 5 (2007): 182–208.

29. Grace Kyungwon Hong, *Death beyond Disavowal: The Impossible Politics of Difference* (Minneapolis: University of Minnesota Press, 2015), 16.

30. Hong, 16.

31. Quoted in Jim Marks, "Essex Hemphill, Just a Poet," *Washington (DC) Blade*, February 11, 1983, 21.

32. Quoted in Marks, 21.
33. Quoted in Marks, 21.
34. Essex Hemphill, "Homocide: For Ronald Gibson," *Blacklight* 4, no. 4 (1983): 11.
35. Jack Zipes, *Fairy Tales and the Art of Subversion* (New York: Routledge, 2006), 178.
36. Roderick Ferguson opens *Aberrations in Black* with the image of the black drag-queen prostitute from Marlon Riggs's film *Tongues Untied*, which is based on Hemphill's poem and the life of Ronald Gibson/Star. Roderick Ferguson, *Aberrations in Black: Towards a Queer of Color Critique* (Minneapolis: University of Minnesota Press, 2004), 1.
37. Eric Stanley, "Near Life, Queer Death: Overkill and Ontological Capture," *Social Text* 29, no. 2 (2011): 2.
38. In his discussion of "realness," based on his ethnographic research in ballroom communities in Detroit, Marlon Bailey argues, "Realness requires adherence to certain performances, self-presentations, and embodiments that are believed to capture the authenticity of particular gender and sexual identities. These criteria are established and function within a schema of race, class, gender, and sexuality. Racialized, classed, gendered, and sexualized performances, self-presentations, and embodiments, to a large extent, give realness its discursive power in both the ballroom scene as well as in society at large." Marlon Bailey, "Gender/Racial Realness: Theorizing the Gender System in Ballroom Culture," *Feminist Studies* 37, no. 2 (2011): 377–78.
39. L. H. Stallings, *Funk the Erotic: Transaesthetics and Black Sexual Cultures* (Urbana: University of Illinois Press, 2015), 158.
40. Stallings, 158. For more on the undercommons, see Stefano Harney and Fred Moten, *The Undercommons: Fugitive Planning and Black Study* (New York: Minor Compositions, 2013).
41. Though many versions of the Cinderella fairy tale exist across the globe, Cinderella is categorized by the Aarne-Thompson system of classifying folktales as "the persecuted heroine" who overcomes her oppression. This central thematic of unjust oppression and triumphant rewards guides my use of this particular fairy tale to mark a trace of optimism in Hemphill's imagination. That Cinderella's socioeconomic conditions are produced by the death of her mother/parents (depending on the version) only furthers my point that optimism need not be divorced from painful pasts or uncertain futures.
42. Michael Snediker, "Queer Optimism," *Postmodern Culture* 16, no. 3 (2006): 2.
43. For more on this coffeehouse, see Genny Beemyn, *A Queer Capital: History of Gay Life in Washington, D.C.* (New York: Routledge, 2014), 210–14.
44. Wayson Jones, interview by the author, 2015.
45. The Gay, Lesbian, and Bisexual People of Color List, email listserv, accessed March 8, 2018, http://www.qrd.org/qrd/www/culture/black/essex/random.html.
46. Essex Hemphill, "Without Comment," in *Ceremonies: Prose and Poetry* (Berkeley, CA: Cleis Press, 2000), 75.
47. Wayson Jones, interview by the author, 2015.
48. Jones, interview.
49. Jones, interview.
50. "Essex Hemphill/Wayson Jones Brass Rail," YouTube video, 1:34, posted by Wayson Jones January 2, 2016, https://www.youtube.com/watch?v=avE9kuzn7NQ.
51. Geneva Smitherman, *Talkin and Testifyin: The Language of Black America* (Detroit: Wayne State University Press, 1977), 104.
52. Jan Cohen-Cruz, *Engaging Performance: Theatre as Call and Response* (New York: Routledge, 2010), 1.

53. Cohen-Cruz, 2.

54. Stallings, *Funk the Erotic*, 178.

55. Stallings, 188.

56. Samuel Delany similarly argues, "In a society that prides itself on the widespread existence of opportunity, interclass contacts are the site and origin of what can later be seen as life opportunities." Samuel Delany, *Times Square Red, Times Square Blue* (New York: New York University Press, 1999), 156.

57. Lisa Cacho notes that ascribing value to the devalued dead requires "narrating their lives through the same ideals, morals, and ethics that disciplined them while they are alive." Lisa Cacho, "'You Just Don't Know How Much He Meant,'" 190.

58. Williamson, "In the Life," 108.

59. Barrett, *Blackness and Value*, 84.

60. Hemphill's poem and Cinque's performance continue to reverberate as audiences encounter them in black queer film. In Marlon Riggs's *Tongues Untied*, Essex Hemphill's voice can be heard reciting "Homocide: For Ronald Gibson" alongside the soulful music of Roberta Flack, operating as the soundtrack to the scene of a black drag-queen prostitute walking the streets. Cinque performs "The Brass Rail" as part of one of the photo montages in Isaac Julien's *Looking for Langston*.

CHAPTER TWO

1. Martin Duberman, *Hold Tight Gently: Michael Callen, Essex Hemphill, and the Battlefield of AIDS* (New York: New Press, 2014), 264.

2. Ian Urbina, "Washington Officials Try to Ease Crime Fear," *New York Times*, July 12, 2006.

3. Frank Wilderson, *Red, Black, and White: Cinema and the Structure of U.S. Antagonisms* (Durham, NC: Duke University Press, 2010); Jared Sexton, *Amalgamation Schemes: Antiblackness and the Critique of Multiracialism* (Minneapolis: University of Minnesota Press, 2008).

4. Orlando Patterson, *Slavery and Social Death: A Comparative Study* (Cambridge, MA: Harvard University Press, 1985); Saidiya V. Hartman, *Scenes of Subjection: Terror, Slavery, and Self-Making in Nineteenth Century America* (New York: Oxford University Press, 1997).

5. Jared Sexton, "Ante-Anti-Blackness: Afterthoughts," *Lateral 2: The Journal of the Cultural Studies Association* 1 (2012), http://lateral.culturalstudiesassociation.org/issue1/content/sexton.html.

6. Frantz Fanon, *Black Skin, White Masks* (London: Pluto Press, 2008), 173.

7. Cathy Cohen, *The Boundaries of Blackness: AIDS and the Breakdown of Black Politics* (Chicago: University of Chicago Press, 1999); Darieck Scott, *Extravagant Abjection: Blackness, Sexuality, and the African American Literary Imagination* (New York: New York University Press, 2010).

8. Fred Moten, *In the Break: The Aesthetics of the Black Radical Tradition* (Minneapolis: University of Minnesota Press, 2003), 20–21; Uri McMillan, *Embodied Avatars: Genealogies of Black Feminist Art and Performance* (New York: New York University Press, 2015), 58.

9. Raymond Williams, "Structures of Feeling," in *Marxism and Literature* (Oxford: Oxford University Press, 1977), 128–35.

10. Leo Bersani, *Homos* (Cambridge, MA: Harvard University Press, 1995); Lee Edelman, *No Future: Queer Theory and the Death Drive* (Durham, NC: Duke University Press, 2004).

11. Frank Wilderson argues that in order for "the black" to become a relational figure, he must overcome the hurdles that Fanon poses to the possibilities of black being, meaning his ontological excess and lack of resistance in the eyes of the Other. Thus, any representational claims to black relationality are forms of "structural adjustment" and "borrowed institutionality." Because of the failure of visual representation to "bring the Slave 'into view,'" representations of black institutionality, in terms of black family or community—the locus of visions of black futurity—are not simply impossible but unthought and unimaginable. Wilderson, *Red, Black, and White*, 38. Similarly, Lee Edelman argues that "queerness could never constitute an authentic or substantive identity, but only a structural position determined by the imperative of figuration." Edelman argues that queer theory is fundamentally opposed to politics, and that queerness, as it is figured in cultural representation, effectively constitutes the limits of politics. Queerness becomes visible only when posed in opposition to the social fantasy of a reproductive future that provides the basis for all political visions. Edelman, *No Future*, 24.

12. Afro-pessimists see queerness as a form of relationality that cannot enfold the structural position of blackness as outside the realm of human being. Antisocial queer theory has defined itself against black politics because of its rootedness in collective identity claims and visions of futurity.

13. My theorization of loneliness as both a collective feeling of loss and hope stems from the work of queer affect theorist José Esteban Muñoz. Muñoz theorizes queerness as a utopian communal vision of futurity and hope, and rejects the queer antisocial thesis on the grounds that its romance of the negative distances it from other modalities of difference like race, class, and gender. In "Photographies of Mourning," the second chapter of *Disidentifications*, Muñoz deciphers *Looking for Langston*—which he reads as the central text and connective tissue of the various artistic forms that made up the black queer cultural renaissance—as a "text of mourning" that indexes the centrality of mourning to the everyday lives of black queers who mourn the losses of history, memory, community, and AIDS. For Muñoz, melancholia is central to black queer identity formation in the 1980s and 1990s. My theorization of Hemphill's loneliness contemplates what it would mean to rethink the bodies and texts comprising the black gay cultural renaissance not only as sites of melancholia but also as sites of "utopian longing" in the way Muñoz advances in *Cruising Utopia*. José Esteban Muñoz, *Disidentifications: Queers of Color and the Performance of Politics* (Minneapolis: University of Minnesota Press, 1994), 57–74; Muñoz, *Cruising Utopia: The Then and There of Queer Future* (New York: New York University Press, 2009), 11.

14. Don Belton, "Where We Live: An Interview with Essex Hemphill and Isaac Julien," in *Speak My Name: Black Men on Masculinity and the American Dream*, ed. Don Belton (New York: Beacon Press, 1995), 214.

15. The Million Man March was a massive political demonstration by black men held on Washington, DC's National Mall. The National African American Leadership Summit, a group of civil rights activists alongside members of the Nation of Islam, united to "convey to the world a vastly different picture of the black male" and for self-help and self-defense against the racial and economic injustices plaguing the African American community. However, the march received criticism because of its exclusion of women and sexual minorities. Haki R. Madhubuti and Maulana Karenga, "Million Man March Fact Sheet," in *Million Man March/Day of Absence: A Commemorative Anthology*, ed. Haki R. Madhubuti and Maulana Karenga (Chicago: Third World Press, 1996), 152. See Robert F. Reid-Pharr, "It's Raining Men: Notes on the Million

Man March," in *Black Gay Man: Essays* (New York: New York University Press, 2001), 164–75, for a discussion of gender and sexual politics undergirding the Million Man March.

16. Deborah Gould, *Moving Politics: Emotion and ACT UP's Fight against AIDS* (Chicago: University of Chicago Press, 2009), 24.

17. Heather Love, *Feeling Backward: Loss and the Politics of Queer History* (Cambridge, MA: Harvard University Press, 2009), 107–8.

18. Tiffany Lethabo King, "Post-Identitarian and Post-Intersectional Anxiety in the Neoliberal Corporate University," *Feminist Formations* 27, no. 3 (2015): 130.

19. For an in-depth discussion of how black people battling AIDS were excluded from mainstream black politics, see Cathy Cohen's *The Boundaries of Blackness*.

20. Roderick Ferguson, "Of Sensual Matters: On Audre Lorde's 'Poetry Is Not a Luxury' and 'Uses of the Erotic,'" *WSQ: Women's Studies Quarterly* 40, nos. 3–4 (2012): 297–98.

21. Chuck Tarver, "Untied Inspiration," *Network*, December 1990, http://www.qrd.org /qrd/www/culture/black/essex/blessings.html.

22. Essex Hemphill, "If Freud Had Been a Neurotic Colored Woman: Reading Frances Cress Welsing," in *Ceremonies: Prose and Poetry* (Berkeley: Cleis Press, 2000), 58.

23. Frances Cress Welsing, *The Isis Papers: The Keys to the Colors* (Chicago: Third World Press, 1991).

24. Hemphill, "If Freud," 58.

25. Robert F. Reid-Pharr, "Stronger, in the Life," in *Black Gay Genius: Answering Joseph Beam's Call*, ed. Steven G. Fullwood and Charles Stephens (New York: Vintage Entity Press, 2013), 67.

26. Marcellus Blount, "Caged Birds: Race and Gender in the Sonnet," in *Engendering Men: The Question of Male Feminist Criticism*, ed. Joseph Boone and Michael Cadden (New York: Routledge, 2010), 237.

27. For a detailed biographical account of the life and legacy of Joseph Beam, see "In the Life of Joseph Beam" in Kevin Mumford, *Not Straight, Not White: Black Gay Men from the March on Washington to the AIDS Crisis* (Chapel Hill: University of North Carolina Press, 2016), 125–46.

28. Frank Parman, "*Brother to Brother* Review," *Gayly Oklahoman* (Oklahoma City), July 1, 1991, 13.

29. Hemphill also consulted Barbara Smith on editorial decisions, and despite her experience at Kitchen Table: Women of Color Press, many contributors to *Brother to Brother* complained about having a black lesbian perspective on the black gay experience.

30. Randy Boyd, "Ceremonies and Young Men: Interview with Essex Hemphill," *Frontiers*, July 3, 1992, http://randyboyd.blogspot.com/2008/08/interview-with-poet-essex -hemphill-1957.html.

31. Madison Moore, "Tina Theory: Notes on Fierceness," *Journal of Popular Music Studies* 24, no. 1 (2012): 72.

32. Kevin Quashie, *The Sovereignty of Quiet: Beyond Resistance in Black Culture* (New Brunswick, NJ: Rutgers University Press, 2012), 20.

33. Essex Hemphill, "When My Brother Fell," in *Ceremonies: Prose and Poetry* (Berkeley: Cleis Press, 2000), 31–32.

34. Hemphill, 32.

35. Beam's panel is red with a blue border. The inscription reads, "Joseph Fairchild Beam; Dec. 1954–Dec. 1988; Writer-Gay Activist; Philadelphia, PA."

36. Marita Sturken notes how many critics of the AIDS quilt argued that it did little to stop an "ongoing war" that produced more deaths than the war in Vietnam. This criticism squares firmly with the theme of war in Hemphill's poem and its criticism of the quilt. Marita Sturken, *Tangled Memories: The Vietnam War, the AIDS Epidemic, and the Politics of Remembering* (Berkeley: University of California Press, 1997), 173.

37. Boyd, "Ceremonies and Young Men."

38. Colin Robinson, "You Dared Us to Dream That We Are Worth Wanting Each Other," in *Sojourner: Black Gay Voices in the Age of AIDS*, ed. B.Michael Hunter (New York: Other Countries Press, 1993), 10; Assotto Saint, introduction to *The Road Before Us: 100 Gay Black Poets*, ed. Assotto Saint (New York: Galiens Press, 1991), xxi.

39. Cathy Caruth, introduction to *Trauma: Explorations in Memory*, ed. with introductions by Cathy Caruth (Baltimore: Johns Hopkins University Press, 1995), 6.

40. Cathy Caruth, *Unclaimed Experience: Trauma, Narrative, and History* (Baltimore: Johns Hopkins University Press, 1996), 4–5.

41. Hemphill, "When My Brother Fell," 33.

42. Sturken, *Tangled Memories*, 73.

43. Dorothy Beam, "Letter to Colin Robinson," March 11, 1989, Joseph Beam Papers, box 4, Correspondence Dorothy Beam folder, Schomburg Center for Research in Black Culture, New York Public Library.

44. Essex Hemphill, "For My Own Protection," in *Ceremonies*, 27; Beam, *In the Life*, 17–18.

45. Beam, *In the Life*, 18.

46. Sharon P. Holland, *Raising the Dead: Readings of Death and (Black) Subjectivity* (Durham, NC: Duke University Press, 2000), 26.

47. Essex Hemphill, "AIDS and the Responsibility of the Writer," plenary panel, Out-Write conference, San Francsico, 1990, http://www.frequency.com/video/outwrite-conference-1990-plenary-session/89978348 (web application is no longer available to the public).

48. Marlon Riggs writes, "Within the Black Gay community, for example, the Snap! contains a multiplicity of coded meanings. . . . The Snap! can be as emotionally and politically charged as a clenched fist." Marlon Riggs, "Black Macho Revisited: Reflections of a Snap! Queen," *Black American Literature Forum* 25, no. 2 (1991): 392. I read Hemphill's presentation as Snap! Queen performance to specify the forms of trauma that are "politically charged," but not necessarily able to be contained and disciplined for political use.

49. John Champagne, *Ethics of Marginality: A New Approach to Gay Studies* (Minneapolis: University of Minnesota Press, 1995), 59.

50. E. Patrick Johnson, "Quare Studies, or Almost Everything I Learned about Queer Studies I Learned from My Grandmother," *Text and Performance Quarterly* 21, no. 1 (2001): 7.

51. Hemphill, "AIDS and the Responsibility of the Writer."

52. For further discussion of "racial grief," see Anne Anlin Cheng, *The Melancholy of Race: Psychoanalysis, Assimilation and Hidden Grief* (New York: Oxford University Press, 2000).

53. Fred Moten, "Black Mo'nin'," in *Loss: The Politics of Mourning*, ed. David Eng and David Kanzanjian (Berkeley: University of California Press, 2002), 62.

54. Essex Hemphill, "Commitments," in *Ceremonies*, 50.

55. Hemphill, 50.

56. Robert F. Reid-Pharr, "At Home in America," in *Black Gay Man*, 63.

57. Fanon, *Black Skin, White Masks*, 10.

58. Fanon, 92.

59. Fanon, xii.

60. Fanon, 89.

61. Senator Daniel Patrick Moynihan's controversial report, *The Negro Family: The Case for National Action* (1965), popularly known as *The Moynihan Report*, argued that slavery and its legacy were central to the pathologies of the black family. Black feminist literary scholar Hortense Spillers criticizes *The Moynihan Report* for pathologizing the black family, particularly how it defines black pathology as symptomatic of the "black matriarchy." Spillers argues that the history of African captivity and enslavement and the New World symbolic order opened up captive black bodies for signification outside their "respective subject-positions of 'female' and 'male,'" and they "adhere to no symbolic integrity." She continues, "At a time when current critical discourses appear to compel us more and more decidedly toward gender 'undecidability,' it would appear reactionary, if not dumb, to insist on the integrity of female/male gender." Hortense Spillers, "Mama's Baby, Papa's Maybe: An American Grammar Book," *Diacritics* 17, no. 2 (1987): 66.

62. Robert F. Reid-Pharr argues that the "bad black mother," conjured up constantly in US sociological, political, and cultural inquiry, "creates a home in America. She turns us black." Reid-Pharr, "At Home in America," 68.

63. Amy Abugo Ongiri argues that black nationalists longed for a "masculine, whole subjectivity to compete with the physical and psychic threat of disintegration incited by acts of racist violence against the black body." Amy Abugo Ongiri, "We Are Family: Black Nationalism, Black Masculinity, and the Black Gay Cultural Imagination," *College Literature* 24, no. 1 (1997): 281.

64. Michelle Ann Stephens, *Skin Acts: Race, Psychoanalysis, and the Black Male Performer* (Durham, NC: Duke University Press, 2014), 2.

65. Joseph Beam, "Leaving the Shadows Behind," introduction to *In the Life: A Black Gay Anthology*, ed. Joseph Beam (Boston: Alyson Publications, 1986), 16.

66. Carolyn Dinshaw argues that contemporary readers and their queer ancestors can "touch across time," thereby "collapsing time through affective contact between marginalized people then and now" in order to "form communities across time." Carolyn Dinshaw, "Theorizing Queer Temporalities: A Roundtable Discussion," *GLQ* 13, nos. 2–3 (2007): 178.

CHAPTER THREE

1. Kevin McGruder, "To Be Heard in Print: Black Gay Writers in 1980s New York," *Obsidian III* 6, no. 1 (2005): 49–67.

2. McGruder, 52.

3. Cary Alan Johnson, interview by the author, 2014.

4. Sigmund Freud, "Mourning and Melancholia," in *The Standard Edition of the Complete Psychological Works of Sigmund Freud*, vol. 14, trans. and ed. James Strachey (London: Hogarth Press, 1953).

5. Sara Ahmed, *The Cultural Politics of Emotion* (New York: Routledge, 2004),156; Ann Cvetkovich, *An Archive of Feelings: Trauma, Sexuality, and Lesbian Public Cultures* (Durham, NC: Duke University Press, 2003); Douglas Crimp, *Melancholia and Moralism: Essays on AIDS and Queer Politics* (Boston: MIT Press, 2002); Michael Moon, "Memorial Rags: Emerson, Whitman, AIDS, and Mourning," in *Professions of Desire: Lesbian and Gay Studies in Literature* (New York: Modern Language of America, 1997); Jahan Rahmanazi, *Poetry of Mourning: The Modern Elegy from Hardy to Heaney* (Chicago:

University of Chicago Press, 1994); José Esteban Muñoz,"Photographies of Mourn-ing," in *Disidentifications: Queers of Color and the Performance of Politics* (Minneapolis: University of Minnesota Press, 1999).

6. Jonathan Flatley, *Affective Mapping: Melancholia and the Politics of Modernism* (Cam-bridge, MA: Harvard University Press, 2008), 2.

7. Dana Luciano, *Arranging Grief: Sacred Time and the Body in Nineteenth-Century America* (New York: New York University Press, 2007), 1–2.

8. Cary Alan Johnson, interview by the author, 2014.

9. G. Winston James, interview by the author, 2013.

10. Marvin K. White, interview by the author, 2013.

11. James, interview.

12. Allen Wright, interview by the author, 2013.

13. Scholars such as Douglas Crimp, Lauren Berlant, and Michael Warner have reconfig-ured promiscuity as a critical site of intimacy and prevention for gay men during the AIDS epidemic. Wright's critique of the established sites and modes of gay male inti-macy suggests that there are racial limits and qualifications to these scholars' positing of gay male promiscuity in this era as "a common language of self-cultivation, shared knowledge, and the exchange of inwardness." Lauren Berlant and Michael Warner, "Sex in Public," *Critical Inquiry* 24, no. 2 (1988): 561.

14. Donald W. Woods, "In the Upper Room," in *Other Countries: Black Gay Voices* (1988), 34.

15. Wright, interview.

16. White states in an interview, "Because it was a gay center, it allowed us to be far more open. . . . I can only imagine the first stop away from home, you take that deep breath; by the third stop, you know no one in your neighborhood goes that far down, so you take off your jacket. Two more stops down, you take off those pants and you have on your glitter shorts [*laughter*]. You just get closer and closer to the Village and transform. By the time people got to the workshops, they were ready. They had peeled a lot of stuff away." Marvin K. White, interview by the author, 2013.

17. White, interview.

18. "Letter to Ron Simmons," box 5, Black Gay Aesthetics folder, Ron Simmons Collec-tion, Schomburg Center for Research in Black Culture, New York Public Library.

19. GMAD and Men of All Colors Together, a group dedicated to ending racism in the gay community and celebrating queer interracial desire and diverse queer aesthetics, believed that renovating the room would "provide a tangible focus and visibility to the often unacknowledged role of people of color in LGBT struggles." "Letter to Ron Simmons."

20. Richard Iton argues, "There is currently a limited ability for blacks to discuss issues in arenas not accessible to others. Black life has, in many respects, become intensely public." This holds true also for Other Countries, whose meetings, though closed, were held in the public space of the community center. In this regard, the collective's desire for privacy, for a private blackness, is also a form of black/queer optimism. Richard Iton, *In Search of the Black Fantastic: Politics and Popular Culture in the Post–Civil Rights Era* (New York: Oxford University Press, 2008), 21.

21. Barbara Smith, "A Press of Our Own, Kitchen Table: Women of Color Press," *Frontiers: A Journal of Women Studies* 10, no. 3 (1989): 11.

22. Melissa Harris Perry discusses the limited notions of black manhood and the suspi-cion of women in the space of the barbershop, noting how narrow limits of mascu-linity often excluded black gay men from political participation. There is one rep-

resentation of a gay man in Liebow's *Tally's Corner*. Calvin is described as "a frail and ailing forty-year-old alcoholic and homosexual who looked after the children [Leroy's] in exchange for a place to live." Liebow describes the children's attachment to Calvin, more so than to their father Leroy, and that Calvin, "when he could summon the courage," often interceded on behalf of the children when Leroy dealt out punishment. Melissa Harris Perry, *Barbershop, Bibles, and BET: Everyday Talk and Black Political Thought* (Princeton, NJ: Princeton University Press, 2006), 1; Elliot Liebow, *Tally's Corner: A Study of Streetcorner Men* (Lanham, MD: Rowman and Littlefield, 1967), 55.

23. See Kevin Quashie, *The Sovereignty of Quiet: Beyond Resistance in Black Culture* (New Brunswick, NJ: Rutgers University Press, 2012), for a discussion of the centrality of resistance in black culture. For a discussion of black culture's investments in normative masculinity as the proper expression of political leadership, see Erica Edwards, *Charisma and the Fictions of Black Leadership* (Minneapolis: University of Minnesota Press, 2012).

24. This gesture can also problematically reinscribe femininity as "being" and not "doing," a conceit that comes dangerously close to disavowing women's activism, which influenced them greatly.

25. In *Golden Gulag*, Ruth Wilson Gilmore defines *racism* as "the state-sanctioned or extralegal production and exploitation of group-differentiated vulnerability to premature death." Ruth Wilson Gilmore, *Golden Gulag: Prisons, Surplus, Crisis, and Opposition in Globalizing California* (Berkeley: University of California Press, 2007), 5.

26. For an in-depth discussion of the politics of privacy and intimacy in black literature and culture, see Candice Jenkins, *Private Lives, Proper Relations: Regulating Black Intimacy* (Minneapolis: University of Minnesota Press, 2007), 7.

27. Daniel Garrett, "Other Countries: The Importance of Difference," in *Other Countries*, 19.

28. Garrett, 19.

29. "Chicago Resource Center Funding Proposal," 1, box 1, Proposal—Chicago Resource Center folder, Other Countries Papers, Schomburg Center for Research in Black Culture, New York Public Library.

30. "Chicago Resource Center Funding Proposal," 5.

31. "Chicago Resource Center Funding Proposal," 1.

32. Cary Alan Johnson, interview by the author, 2014.

33. Colin Robinson, "Sojourner: An Abandoned Manifest," in *Voices Rising: Celebrating 20 Years of Black Lesbian, Gay, Bisexual, and Transgender Writing*, ed. G. Winston James and Other Countries (Washington, DC: Redbone Press, 2007), 8.

34. Steve Langley, "Confection," in *Other Countries*, 43.

35. Allen Wright, interview by the author, 2013.

36. Wright, interview.

37. Jafari Sinclaire Allen, "For 'the Children' Dancing the Beloved Community," *Souls* 11, no. 3 (2009): 315.

38. Allen, 314.

39. "Behavioral Change Epilogue," 1991, box 1, Other Countries Papers, Schomburg Center for Research in Black Culture, New York Public Library.

40. For discussions of how the risk associated with HIV/AIDS has shifted gay men's sexual cultures and practices, see Douglas Crimp, "How to Have Promiscuity in an Epidemic," in *Policing Public Sex: Queer Politics and the Future of AIDS Activism*, ed. Dangerous Bedfellows (Ephen Glenn Colter, Wayne Hoffman, Eva Pendleton, Alison

Redic, and David Serlin) (Boston: South End Press, 1996); Simon Watney, *Policing Desire: Pornography, AIDS, and the Media* (London: Cassell, 1997). For a discussion of transgressive sexual cultures in the so-called post-AIDS moment, see Tim Dean, *Unlimited Intimacy: Reflections on the Subculture of Barebacking* (Chicago: University of Chicago Press, 2009).

41. Robinson, "Sojourner," 7.
42. Allen Wright, interview by the author, 2013.
43. "Behavioral Change Epilogue," 1991, box 1, Other Countries Papers, Schomburg Center for Research in Black Culture, New York Public Library.
44. ACT UP began the "Stop the Church" campaign to express its disagreement with Archbishop John Joseph O'Connor on the Roman Catholic Archdiocese of New York's stance against safe sex education in New York City public schools. In December 1989, forty-five hundred protestors gathered outside a mass at St. Patrick's Cathedral. A few activists entered the building and disrupted the mass; one protestor broke a communion wafer and threw it on the floor. One hundred and eleven protestors were arrested, and the wafer action was widely broadcast in the media. The "political funerals" were ACT UP's attempts to turn private grief into something public. It held public memorial services and dumped ashes and cadavers on the White House grounds and in front of state buildings.
45. B.Michael Hunter, "Allan Robinson, AIDS Activist," in *Sojourner: Black Gay Voices in the Age of AIDS*, ed. B.Michael Hunter (New York: Other Countries Press, 1993), 60.
46. Garrett, "Other Countries," 27.
47. Elsa Barkley Brown, "What Has Happened Here?: The Politics of Difference in Women's History and Feminist Politics," *Feminist Studies* 18, no. 2 (1992): 297.
48. Garrett, "Other Countries," 28.
49. Simon Dickel, *Black/Gay: The Harlem Renaissances, the Protest Era, and the Constructions of Black Gay Identity in the 1980s and 90s* (East Lansing: Michigan State University Press, 2012).
50. Robinson, "Sojourner," 7.
51. Though it might seem self-evident that these men would be writing about death, given that the AIDS epidemic is at its height at the time they are writing, this is also an aesthetic "choice" and political praxis. In *Black/Gay*, Simon Dickel notes that Joseph Beam's 1986 edited volume *In the Life: A Black Gay Anthology* (Boston: Alyson Publications, 1986) does not even mention AIDS or safer sex, or comment on the risks of sexually transmitted diseases. Essex Hemphill's 1991 edited collection, *Brother to Brother: New Writings by Black Gay Men* (Boston: Alyson Publications, 1991), includes one section on AIDS, out of a total of four. So thematizing an entire volume on AIDS, death, and mourning is aesthetically and politically significant. Dickel, *Black/Gay*, 29.
52. Quoted in Dickel, 9.
53. Quoted in Dickel, 10.
54. Quoted in Dickel, 10.
55. G. Winston James, interview by the author, 2013.
56. Akasha (Gloria T.) Hull, "Channeling the Ancestral Muse: Lucille Clifton and Delores Kendrick," in *Feminist Measure: Soundings in Poetry and Theory*, ed. Lynne Keller and Cristanne Miller (Ann Arbor: University of Michigan Press, 1994), 98.
57. Vazquez-Pacheco was one of the first self-identified Latinos in the Other Countries Collective. In an email, he stated that his intention in joining the group was "to broaden the discussions about 'blackness'": "Not all black people in the US identify

as African American despite the essentializing nature of US racial discourse." Robert Vazquez-Pacheco, permission email to the author, 2017.

58. Excerpted from Robert Vazquez-Pacheco, "Necropolis," in Hunter, *Sojourner*, 25.

59. Judith Herman argues that the will to deny trauma and the desire to tell the truth of trauma is its central dialectic. Judith Herman, *Trauma and Recovery: The Aftermath of Violence—from Domestic Abuse to Political Terror* (New York: Basic Books, 1992), 1.

60. "Allen Wright," box 1, folder 8, Other Countries Papers, Schomburg Center for Research in Black Culture, New York Public Library.

61. Marlon Riggs, "Letters to the Dead," in Hunter, *Sojourner*, 21.

62. My use of the term *gay voice* derives from A. B. Christa Schwartz's conceptualization of "gay voices" to map the literary performances of dissident sexualities in her study of homosexuality in Harlem Renaissance literature and culture. I extend Schwartz's term to think about the "gay voice" as an archive of black gay cultural memory that survives the bodies lost to the trauma of AIDS. A. B. Christa Schwartz, *Gay Voices of the Harlem Renaissance* (Bloomington: Indiana University Press, 2003).

63. Riggs, "Letters to the Dead," 23.

64. Queer of color scholars have demonstrated the importance of bodily performance to gay men negotiating intimate relations with family, community, and state forces. Martin Manalansan demonstrates how Filipino gay men in the diaspora perform shifting selves in the context of their situation as they negotiate their racial, class, gender, sexual, and national identities. Martin Manalansan, *Global Divas: Filipino Gay Men in the Diaspora* (Durham, NC: Duke University Press, 2003). Carlos Decena also demonstrates how Dominican immigrant men oftentimes do not verbally "come out," as this might rupture fragile familial and social bonds. But through their everyday performances, their identity is assumed. Carlos Decena, *Tacit Subjects: Belonging and Desire among Dominican Immigrant Gay Men* (Durham, NC: Duke University Press, 2011). Jeffrey Q. McCune discusses black men's performances of sexual discretion as "performance[s] always in motion." He continues, "It is only through engagement with actual bodies and texts that we can understand how subjects navigate racial and sexual lines." Jeffrey Q. McCune, *Sexual Discretion: Black Masculinity and the Politics of Passing* (Chicago: University of Chicago Press, 2014), 161.

65. E. Patrick Johnson, "Feeling the Spirit in the Dark: Expanding Notions of the Sacred in the African-American Gay Community," *Callaloo* 21, no. 1(1998): 406.

66. Marvin K. White, "Last Rights," in Hunter, *Sojourner*, 49–50.

67. For an in-depth discussion of how black queer people have transformed the prescribed "places" of black performance to open up a "space" for black queer performance, see Johnson, "Feeling the Spirit in the Dark."

68. Marvin K. White, interview by the author, 2013.

69. Robert F. Reid-Pharr, "A Child's Life," in *Black Gay Man: Essays* (New York: New York University Press, 2001), p. 177. See also the Gay, Lesbian, and Bisexual People of Color List, email listserv, accessed March 8, 2018, http://www.qrd.org/qrd/www/culture/black/essex/random.html.

70. Barbara Smith, "We Must Always Bury Our Dead Twice: A Tribute to James Baldwin," in *The Truth That Never Hurts: Writings on Race, Gender, and Freedom* (New Brunswick, NJ: Rutgers University Press, 2000), 79–80.

71. Douglas Crimp, "Mourning and Militancy," *October* 51 (1989): 9.

72. "Donald W. Woods, 34, AIDS Film Executive," *New York Times*. June 29, 1992.

73. Afro-Jamaican gay writer Thomas Glave published the O. Henry Award–winning

story "Final Inning," which fictionalizes the controversy surrounding Donald Woods's funeral. Glave's fictional account begins just after the legendary uprising by Assotto Saint. Thomas Glave, "Final Inning," *Kenyon Review* 18, nos. 3–4 (1996): 116–34.

74. Marvin K. White, interview by the author, 2013.

75. Allen Wright, interview by the author, 2013.

76. G. Winston James, interview by the author, 2013.

77. Colin Robinson, interview by the author, 2013.

78. For an in-depth discussion of the excision of queer genders and sexualities from black memory, see Matt Richardson, *The Queer Limits of Black Memory: Black Lesbian Literature and Irresolution* (Columbus: Ohio State University Press, 2013). See also Richardson, "No More Secrets, No More Lies: Black History and Compulsory Heterosexuality," *Journal of Women's History* 15, no. 3 (2003): 63–76. In contrast, Aliyyah Abdur-Rahman argues that from slavery to the contemporary moment, black American writers have used metaphors of sexual transgression to contest popular theories of identity, pathology, racial difference, and national belonging. However, Abdur-Rahman focuses primarily on forms of racial-sexual injury as modes of erotic transgression. Aliyyah Abdur-Rahman, *Against the Closet: Black Political Longing and the Erotics of Race* (Durham, NC: Duke University Press, 2012).

79. Though Saint's outburst at the funeral outraged Woods's biological family, it did attend the alternative service held by members of the black gay community. According to Robinson, Woods's father also apologized for suppressing aspects of Woods's life in the obituary and at the funeral.

80. Donald Woods's family sent Saint a thank-you card for giving Woods a plot (which Saint owned) in the Evergreen cemetery. "Card to Saint," box 4, Correspondence Long-McNeil folder, Assotto Saint Papers, Manuscript, Archives, and Rare Books Division, Schomburg Center for Research in Black Culture, New York Public Library; William G. Hawkeswood, *One of the Children: Gay Black Men in Harlem* (Berkeley: University of California Press, 1997), 191.

81. Robert F. Reid-Pharr, "Clean: Death and Desire in Samuel R. Delany's *Stars in My Pocket Like Grains of Sand*," *American Literature* 83, no. 2 (2011): 396; Rinaldo Walcott, "Queer Returns: Human Rights, the Anglo-Caribbean and Diaspora Politics," *Caribbean Review of Gender Studies* 3 (2009): 11–14; Dagmawi Woubshet, *The Calendar of Loss: Race, Sexuality, and Mourning in the Early Era of AIDS* (Baltimore: Johns Hopkins University Press, 2015), 22–24.

82. In *Feeling Backward*, Heather Love argues for dwelling on negative affect in the history of homosexuality to create a space in the present for those still relegated to the margins, unassimilable as homonormative subjects. In *If Memory Serves*, Christopher Castiglia and Christopher Reed also suggest that remembering the queer past might hold open a space for a more radical present. Heather Love, *Feeling Backward: Loss and the Politics of Queer History* (Cambridge, MA: Harvard University Press, 2009); Christopher Castiglia and Christopher Reed, *If Memory Serves: Gay Men, AIDS, and the Promise of the Queer Past* (Minneapolis: University of Minnesota Press, 2011).

83. See David Roman, "Not-about-AIDS," *GLQ* 6, no. 1 (2000): 1–28.

CHAPTER FOUR

The title of this chapter is a quotation from Dixon's diaries, and is meant to signal that uncertainty about the future does not preclude one's orientation toward it. Melvin Dixon, diary entry,

March 14, 1989, box 1, Journal Provincetown and New York June 6, 1988–September 26, 1989, Melvin Dixon Addition, Schomburg Center for Research in Black Culture, New York Public Library.

1. Melvin Dixon, diary entry, October 7, 1991, box 1, journal folder October 20, 1989–November 8, 1991, Melvin Dixon Addition, Schomburg Center for Research in Black Culture, New York Public Library.
2. Richard Horovitz was an executive director at the Panos Institute, a nonprofit organization that financed international information projects addressing environmental issues, and a program officer and representative of the Ford Foundation in Dakar, Senegal, where he helped finance international projects for AIDS patients. Owing to the nature of his work, Horovitz was often away from Dixon, and Dixon sorely missed him. Dixon visited Horovitz in Dakar for the month of December 1983, and again in 1985 as a Fulbright Professor at the University of Dakar. Once discussing his increasing discomfort talking to white people about politics, describing it as "a great waste of time and energy," Dixon described Richard as "so Afro-centric that he has greatly influenced my own thinking and experience." "Richard Horovitz, 44, Foundation Executive," *New York Times*, July 20, 1991, accessed March 8, 2018, https://www.nytimes.com/1991/07/20/obituaries/richard-horovitz-44-foundation-executive.html; Melvin Dixon, diary entry, June 26, 1981, box 1, journal folder February 23, 1977–May 11, 1984, Melvin Dixon Addition, Schomburg Center for Research in Black Culture, New York Public Library.
3. Kai Erikson, *A New Species of Trouble: The Human Experience of Modern Disasters* (New York: W. W. Norton, 1995), 229.
4. "On Being Poor Cousins of Modernity—Rinaldo Walcott," YouTube video, 1:57, Solo Flying: TVO, posted by TVO October 14, 2009, https://www.youtube.com/watch?v=2kcNmFgHiH8.
5. Melvin Dixon, diary entry, May 1, 1972, box 1, journal folder November 4, 1969–May 1, 1972, Melvin Dixon Addition, Schomburg Center for Research in Black Culture, New York Public Library.
6. M. Jacqui Alexander argues that the regulatory practices of heterosexualization register the continuities between various colonial formations. M. Jacqui Alexander, "Not Just Anybody Can Be a Citizen: The Politics of Law, Sexuality and Postcoloniality in Trinidad and Tobago and the Bahamas," *Feminist Review* 48 (1994): 5–23.
7. Ross Chambers, *Facing It: AIDS Diaries and the Death of the Author* (Ann Arbor: University of Michigan Press, 1998), 7.
8. Drawing from the work on black gay writer and scholar Samuel Delany, Ernesto Javier Martinez argues that storytelling has an epistemic value rather than just a representative one. Martinez argues for a realist paradigm that emphasizes how "narratives will organize and influence the social but never completely determine it." Ernesto Javier Martinez, *On Making Sense: Queer Race Narratives of Intelligibility* (Stanford, CA: Stanford University Press, 2012), 75–76.
9. Chambers, *Facing It*, 9.
10. Keguro Macharia, "Slicing the Hunger: Queering the Hunger in Melvin Dixon's *Change of Territory*," *Callaloo* 32, no. 4 (2009): 1263.
11. Melvin Dixon, *Ride Out the Wilderness: Geography and Identity in Afro-American Literature* (Urbana: University of Illinois Press, 1987), 2.
12. Dagmawi Woubshet, *The Calendar of Loss: Race, Sexuality, and Mourning in the Early Era of AIDS* (Baltimore: Johns Hopkins University Press, 2015), 44.

13. Quoted in Dixon's diary on Friday, July 3, 1979, journal folder February 23, 1977–May 11, 1984, box 1, Melvin Dixon Addition, Schomburg Center for Research in Black Culture, New York Public Library. Although various other presses rejected the novel in the late 1980s, it was eventually rewritten and accepted for publication in 1991 by Dutton Press, a division of Penguin Books. This work has rightly received more scholarly attention in black and queer literary studies than any of his other works. The novel still has not garnered nearly enough critical attention, however, and is currently out of print.

14. Melvin Dixon, diary entry, June 19, 1970, box 1, Employee of Urban League of Greater Hartford journal folder June 6, 1970–September 7, 1970, Melvin Dixon Addition, Schomburg Center for Research in Black Culture, New York Public Library.

15. Dixon, diary entry, June 23, 1970.

16. Dixon, diary entry, June 29, 1970.

17. Paul Gilroy, *The Black Atlantic: Modernity and Double Consciousness* (London: Verso, 1993), 19.

18. Akasha (Gloria T.) Hull argues that the conditions of black women's lives have not been compatible to diary keeping, and even the few women who have kept diaries "have been as hampered as their less fortunate sisters by subtler forms of prejudice." Hull's claims bring to the fore how racism, classism, sexism, and homophobia—often deemed matters of the public sphere—intersect to impact black (queer) women's ability to keep a diary, and how the labors of public resistance prevent them from engaging in the necessary task of making sense of experiences through life writing. Akasha (Gloria T.) Hull, *Give Us Each Day: The Diary of Alice Dunbar-Nelson* (New York: W. W. Norton, 1985), 13.

19. Articulating the ways in which space and place do in fact give black lives meaning, Katherine McKittrick argues that black people "struggle with discourses that erase and despatialize their sense of place," thereby rendering black women in particular, and black people more generally, as "ungeographic." Katherine McKittrick, *Demonic Grounds: Black Women and the Cartographies of Struggle* (Minneapolis: University of Minnesota Press, 2006), xxi.

20. Joanne Braxton, *Black Women Writing Autobiography: A Tradition within a Tradition* (Philadelphia: Temple University Press, 1989), 85.

21. Hull, *Give Us Each Day*, 13.

22. Melvin Dixon, diary entry, May 22, 1977, box 1, journal folder February 23, 1977–May 11, 1984, Melvin Dixon Addition, Schomburg Center for Research in Black Culture, New York Public Library.

23. Dixon, diary entry, December 12, 1973; February 10, 1974, journal folder December 1, 1974–February 16, 1977; March 19, 1985, box 1, Senegal and New York journal folder June 6, 1984–June 2, 1988, Melvin Dixon Addition, Schomburg Center for Research in Black Culture, New York Public Library.

24. Dixon, diary entry, "November 11, 1984, New York, Manhattan," box 1, Senegal and New York journal folder June 6, 1984–June 2, 1988, Melvin Dixon Addition, Schomburg Center for Research in Black Culture, New York Public Library.

25. Dixon, diary entry, "April 29, 1984, New York," box 1, journal folder February 23, 1977–May 11, 1984, Melvin Dixon Addition, Schomburg Center for Research in Black Culture, New York Public Library.

26. Dixon, diary entry, "December 5, 1973," box 1, journal folder July 22, 1973–May 2, 1974, Melvin Dixon Addition, Schomburg Center for Research in Black Culture, New York Public Library.

27. Charles Kaiser, *Gay Metropolis: The Landmark History of Gay Life* (New York: Grove Press, 2007), 284.

28. For examples of the links between race, nation, disease, and citizenship, see Nayan Shah, *Contagious Divides: Epidemics and Race in San Francisco's Chinatown* (Berkeley: University of California Press, 2001); Jim Downs, *Sick from Freedom: African-American Illness and Suffering during the Civil War and Reconstruction* (New York: Oxford University Press, 2015); Irene S. Vernon, *Killing Us Quietly: Native Americans and HIV/AIDS* (Lincoln: University of Nebraska Press, 2001); Andrew Jolivette, *Indian Blood: HIV and Colonial Trauma in San Francisco's Two-Spirit Community* (Seattle: University of Washington Press, 2016).

29. Richard Goldstein, "Go the Way Your Blood Beats: An Interview with James Baldwin," *Village Voice*, July 26, 1984, 14.

30. Melvin Dixon, diary entry, December 25, 1970, box 1, journal folder November 4, 1969–May 1, 1972, Melvin Dixon Addition, Schomburg Center for Research in Black Culture, New York Public Library.

31. Melvin Dixon, *Vanishing Rooms* (New York: Dutton, 1991), 99.

32. Dixon, diary entry, May 1, 1972.

33. Dixon, diary entry, November 6, 1973, box 1, journal folder July 22, 1973–May 2, 1974, Melvin Dixon Addition, Schomburg Center for Research in Black Culture, New York Public Library.

34. Lauren Berlant and Michael Warner, "Sex in Public," *Critical Inquiry* 24, no. 2 (1988): 561.

35. David Bergman, *The Violet Hour: The Violet Quill and the Making of Gay Culture* (New York: Columbia University Press), 133.

36. Charles Nero, "Toward a Black Gay Aesthetic" in *Brother to Brother: New Writings by Black Gay Men*, ed. Essex Hemphill (Boston: Alyson Publications, 1991), 229–52.

37. Keguro Macharia, "On Quitting," *New Inquiry*, May 3, 2013, https://thenewinquiry.com/on-quitting/.

38. Melvin Dixon, diary entry, February 3, 1974, box 1, journal folder July 22, 1973–May 2, 1974, Melvin Dixon Addition, Schomburg Center for Research in Black Culture, New York Public Library.

39. Phillip B. Harper, "The Evidence of Felt Intuition: Minority Experience, Everyday Life, and Critical Speculative Knowledge," *GLQ* 6, no. 4 (2000): 643.

40. Alex Weheliye, *Habeas Viscus: Racialized Assemblages, Biopolitics, and Black Feminist Theories of the Human* (Durham, NC: Duke University Press, 2014); Matt Brim, *James Baldwin and the Queer Imagination* (Ann Arbor: University of Michigan Press, 2014), 73–76.

41. Lauren Berlant defines "slow death" as "the physical wearing out of a population and the deterioration of people in that population that is very nearly the defining condition of their experience and historical existence. The general emphasis of the phrase is on the phenomenon of mass physical attenuation under global/national regimes of capitalist structural subordination and governmentality." Lauren Berlant, "Slow Death (Sovereignty, Obesity, Lateral Agency)," *Critical Inquiry* 33 (2007): 754.

42. Melvin Dixon, diary entry, December 9, 1971, box 1, journal folder October 28, 1971–July 20, 1973, Melvin Dixon Addition, Schomburg Center for Research in Black Culture, New York Public Library.

43. Harper, "The Evidence of Felt Intuition," 652.

44. Dixon, diary entry, February 13, 1979, box 1, journal folder February 23, 1977–

May 11, 1984, Melvin Dixon Addition, Schomburg Center for Research in Black Culture, New York Public Library.

45. Dixon, diary entry, February 16, 1979.

46. Dixon, diary entry, April 23, 1970, box 1, Employee of Urban League of Greater Hartford journal folder June 6–September 7, 1970, Melvin Dixon Addition, Schomburg Center for Research in Black Culture, New York Public Library.

47. Dixon, diary entry, July 26, 1985, box 1, Senegal and New York journal folder June 6, 1984–June 2, 1988, Melvin Dixon Addition, Schomburg Center for Research in Black Culture, New York Public Library.

48. Sarah Jane Cervenak defines "wandering" as "a rare moment of privacy for someone whose experience in the world is never free from the trespassive enactments of others." Sarah Jane Cervenak, *Wandering: Philosophical Performances of Racial and Sexual Freedom* (Durham, NC: Duke University Press, 2014), 2.

49. Dixon, diary entry, August 8, 1976, box 1, journal folder December 1, 1974–February 16, 1977, Melvin Dixon Addition, Schomburg Center for Black Culture, New York Public Library.

50. Dixon, diary entry, June 10, 1971, box 1, Europe journal folder June 5–27, 1971, Melvin Dixon Addition, Schomburg Center for Research in Black Culture, New York Public Library.

51. Dixon, diary entry, December 18, 1974, box 1, journal folder December 1, 1974–February 16, 1977, Melvin Dixon Addition, Schomburg Center for Research in Black Culture, New York Public Library.

52. Dixon, diary entry, June 28, 1971, box 1, Europe journal folder June 5–27, 1971, Melvin Dixon Addition, Schomburg Center for Research in Black Culture, New York Public Library.

53. Dixon, diary entry, October 24, 1974, box 1, journal folder December 1, 1974–February 16, 1977, Melvin Dixon Addition, Schomburg Center for Black Culture, New York Public Library.

54. Dixon, diary entry, January 26, 1978, box 1, journal folder February 23, 1977–May 11, 1984, Melvin Dixon Addition, Schomburg Center for Research in Black Culture, New York Public Library.

55. Dwight McBride, "Straight Black Studies: On African American Studies, James Baldwin, and Black Queer Studies," in *Black Queer Studies: An Anthology*, ed. Mae G. Henderson and E. Patrick Johnson (Durham, NC: Duke University Press, 2005), 68–89.

56. Phillip Brian Harper, "Interview with Melvin Dixon," *Gay Community News* vols. 33–34, March 22–April 4, 1992, box 1, folder 1, Melvin Dixon Papers, Schomburg Center for Research in Black Culture, New York Public Library.

57. Dixon, diary entry, January 24, 1990, box 1, journal folder October 20, 1989–November 8, 1991, Melvin Dixon Addition, Schomburg Center for Research in Black Culture, New York Public Library.

58. Dixon, diary entry, July 15, 1986, box 1, Senegal and New York journal folder June 6, 1984–June 2, 1988, Melvin Dixon Addition, Schomburg Center for Research in Black Culture, New York Public Library.

59. Toni Morrison's rejection of Dixon's novel on the basis that sexuality was "who the characters are" could be read as homophobic given her widely remarked-on representation of homosexuality as an impossibility for male slaves in *Beloved*.

60. Dixon stated that BWMT "was interested in fighting racism, but it became clear to me that if an interracial relationship is built upon racist assumptions, then the partners

in that relationship may not be inclined to work on civil advancement, because that relationship depends on racial discrimination. But they didn't seem to want to take up that issue—it was a little too rough. For example, it's all right if the black man loves opera, and loves classical music, and has abandoned everything that represents his own sense of culture. But don't let him bring up any of these more 'ethnic' concerns. You know, I was going to write a book on interracial relationships, but it fizzled. I've talked to a lot of people about this and I may go back to that project someday." Quoted in Christopher Bard Cole, "Other Voices, Other Rooms," *Christopher Street* 14, no. 1 (1991): 24–25.

61. Cole, "Other Voices, Other Rooms," 25.

62. Melvin Dixon, diary entry, January 26, 1978, box 1, journal folder February 23, 1977–May 11, 1984, Melvin Dixon Addition, Schomburg Center for Research in Black Culture, New York Public Library.

63. Dixon, diary entry, May 1, 1972, box 1, journal folder November 4, 1969–May 1, 1972, Melvin Dixon Addition, Schomburg Center for Research in Black Culture, New York Public Library.

64. Dixon, diary entry, December 18, 1974, box 1, journal folder December 1, 1974–February 16, 1977, Melvin Dixon Addition, Schomburg Center for Research in Black Culture, New York Public Library.

65. Daniel Patrick Moynihan, *The Negro Family: The Case for National Action* (Washington, DC: Office of Policy Planning and Research, United States Department of Labor, 1965).

66. Dixon, diary entry, October 1, 1972, box 1, journal folder October 28, 1971–July 20, 1973, Melvin Dixon Addition, Schomburg Center for Research in Black Culture, New York Public Library.

67. Dixon, diary entry, December 1, 1984, box 1, Senegal and New York journal folder June 6, 1984–June 2, 1988, Melvin Dixon Addition, Schomburg Center for Research in Black Culture, New York Public Library.

68. Paula Treichler, "AIDS, Homophobia, and Biomedical Discourse: An Epidemic of Signification," *October 43* (1987): 65–66.

69. Hansberry's heavy smoking surely contributed to her death from pancreatic cancer, but the fact that black women and men are more likely to die of cancer than any other ethnic group, according to the Centers for Disease Control and Prevention, raises questions about how antiblackness (and sexism and homophobia) negatively impacts health. In 2013, the CDC reported that incidence rates and death rates for cancer were highest in black men (518.6/100,000), while black women ranked highest for cancer death rates (158.4/100,000) and came second only to white women for the highest incidence rate (393.6/100,000). Centers for Disease Control and Prevention, "Cancer Facts for Demographic Groups: Racial and Ethnic Variations," accessed March 8, 2018, https://www.cdc.gov/cancer/dcpc/data/ethnic.htm.

70. James Baldwin, "Sweet Lorraine," in *The Price of the Ticket: Collected Nonfiction, 1948–1985* (New York: St. Martin's/Marek, 1985), 443–47.

71. For an in-depth discussion of the anti-Haitian, and by extension antiblack, US scientific discourses that figured Haitian immigrants as carriers of AIDS and the cause of the epidemic in the United States, see Paul Farmer, *AIDS and Accusation: Haiti and the Geography of Blame* (Berkeley: University of California Press, 2006), 1–4, 208–12. For a discussion of the dispossession and violent containment of Haitians during the early era of AIDS, see A. Naomi Paik, "Testifying to Rightlessness: Haitian Refugees Speaking from Guantánamo," *Social Text* 23, no. 3 (2010): 39–65.

72. Essex Hemphill, "Now We Think," in *Ceremonies: Prose and Poetry* (Berkeley: Cleis Press, 2000), 155.

73. Lauren Berlant, "Thinking about Feeling Historical," *Emotion, Space, and Society* 1 (2008): 5.

74. Karla F. C. Holloway, *Passed On: African American Mourning Stories; A Memorial* (Durham, NC: Duke University Press, 2003), 2.

75. Melvin Dixon, diary entry, March 5, 1987, box 1, Senegal and New York journal folder June 6, 1984–June 2, 1988, Melvin Dixon Addition, Schomburg Center for Research in Black Culture, New York Public Library.

76. Darieck Scott, *Extravagant Abjection: Blackness, Sexuality, and the African American Literary Imagination* (New York: New York University Press, 2010), 28.

77. Rinaldo Walcott, "Somewhere Out There: The New Black Queer Theory," in *FORECAAST: Blackness and Sexualities*, ed. Michelle Wright and Antje Schumann (Berlin: Lit Verlag, 2007), 30.

78. Dixon, diary entry, July 17, 1986, box 1, Senegal and New York journal folder June 6, 1984–June 2, 1988, Melvin Dixon Addition, Schomburg Center for Research in Black Culture, New York Public Library.

79. Jaime Harker, "'Look Baby, I Know You': Gay Fiction and the Cold War Era," *American Literature* 22, no. 1 (2010): 194–96.

80. Arthur Flannigan Saint-Aubin, "'Black Gay Male' Discourse: Reading Race and Sexuality between the Lines," *Journal of the History of Sexuality* 3, no. 3 (1993): 468–90. Essex Hemphill wrote a letter to the journal protesting Saint-Aubin's article. Martin Duberman describes Hemphill's response this way: "When the prestigious *Journal of the History of Sexuality*—which at the time leaned heavily in the direction of LGBT content—published an essay by a black gay man that Essex found 'ridiculous, pedestrian,' he used the occasion as a means to make a larger point: namely, that the journal did not have a single black gay male on either its editorial or advisory boards. In this letter of protest to the editor, Essex forestalled one familiar response by writing, 'please don't tell me there are no Black gay and lesbian scholars or scholars of color available to work with you all.' He offered his help in recommending 'a number of very capable and brilliant scholars to you.'" Martin Duberman, *Hold Tight Gently: Michael Callen, Essex Hemphill, and the Battlefield of AIDS* (New York: New Press, 2014), 261.

81. Chambers, *Facing It*, 6–7.

82. Chambers, 7.

83. Melvin Dixon, diary entry, "September 11, 1987, Manhattan," box 1, Senegal and New York journal folder June 6, 1984–June 2, 1988, Melvin Dixon Addition, Schomburg Center for Black Culture, New York Public Library.

84. Essex Hemphill, introduction to Hemphill, *Brother to Brother*, xxvii.

EPILOGUE

1. Joseph Beam, "Caring for Each Other" (editorial), *Black/Out* 1, no. 1 (1986): 9.

2. Beam, 9.

3. Daniel Garrett, "Beam's Photograph, Note and Poem," box 3, folder 2, Assotto Saint Papers, Schomburg Center for Research in Black Culture, New York Public Library.

4. Garrett.

5. Christina Sharpe, *In the Wake: On Blackness and Being* (Durham, NC: Duke University Press, 2016), 117.

6. Sharpe, 123.

7. Harvey Young, *Embodying Black Experience: Stillness, Critical Memory, and the Black Body* (Ann Arbor: University of Michigan Press, 2010), 4.

8. Garrett, "Beam's Photograph, Note and Poem," box 3, folder 2, Assotto Saint Papers, Schomburg Center for Research in Black Culture, New York Public Library.

9. Garrett.

10. Young, *Embodying Black Experience*, 4.

11. Garrett, "Beam's Photograph, Note and Poem," box 3, folder 2, Assotto Saint Papers, Schomburg Center for Research in Black Culture, New York Public Library.

12. Garrett.

13. Krista Thompson, *Shine: The Visual Economy of Light in African Diasporic Aesthetic Practices* (Durham, NC: Duke University Press, 2015), 14.

14. Garrett, "Beam's Photograph, Note and Poem," box 3, folder 2, Assotto Saint Papers, Schomburg Center for Research in Black Culture, New York Public Library.

15. For a discussion of the racialized and gendered visual and rhetorical logics that naturalize the equating of blackness with sexual duplicity, see C. Riley Snorton, *Nobody Is Supposed to Know: Black Sexuality on the Down Low* (Minneapolis: University of Minnesota, 2014).

16. Garrett, "Beam's Photograph, Note and Poem," box 3, folder 2, Assotto Saint Papers, Schomburg Center for Research in Black Culture, New York Public Library.

17. Garrett.

18. Garrett.

19. For an excellent account of how contemporary artists have innovatively engaged the discourses of modern black nationalism, see GerShun Avilez, *Radical Aesthetics and Modern Black Nationalism* (Urbana: University of Illinois Press, 2016).

20. Garrett, "Beam's Photograph, Note and Poem," box 3, folder 2, Assotto Saint Papers, Schomburg Center for Research in Black Culture, New York Public Library.

21. Beam, "Brother to Brother," 242.

22. Garrett, "Beam's Photograph, Note and Poem," box 3, folder 2, Assotto Saint Papers, Schomburg Center for Research in Black Culture, New York Public Library.

23. Thompson, *Shine*, 14. Kimberly Juanita Brown further defines *afterimage* as "the figurative register of what gets left over when the eye no longer has the image before it." Kimberly Juanita Brown, *The Repeating Body: Slavery's Visual Resonance in the Contemporary* (Durham, NC: Duke University Press, 2015), 13.

24. Ashon Crawley uses "otherwise possibilities" to describe the means of "announc[ing] the fact of infinite alternatives to what is." Ashon Crawley, *Blackpentecostal Breath: The Aesthetics of Possibility* (New York: Fordham University Press, 2016), 2.

INDEX

Page numbers in italics refer to illustrations.